His Holiness
the
Dalai Lama

His Holiness
the
Dalai Lama

THE ORAL BIOGRAPHY

Deborah Hart Strober
Gerald S. Strober

WILEY

John Wiley & Sons, Inc.

Copyright © 2005 by Deborah Hart Strober and Gerald S. Strober. All rights reserved

Published by John Wiley & Sons, Inc., Hoboken, New Jersey
Published simultaneously in Canada

Photos courtesy of the following (numerals refer to page numbers): AP Photo (119, 120 bottom); Richard Blum (127); Clinton Presidential Library (122 bottom); Lama Surya Das (121 bottom); Roberto Dutesco (iii, 128); Father Laurence Freeman (125 [bottom photo by Siddioi Ray]); Dr. Blu and Rabbi Irving Greenberg (122 top); Dr. Piet Hut, photo by Eiko Ikegami (124 bottom); International Campaign for Tibet, photo by Nancy Jo Johnson (126 top); Annette and Representative Tom Lantos (121 top, 126 bottom); Professor Jonathan Mirsky (124 top); *Pittsburgh Post-Gazette*, photo by V. W. H. Campbell Jr. (123); Khediroob Thondup (120 top).

Design and composition by Navta Associates, Inc.

For general information about our other products and services, please contact our Customer Care Department within the United States at (800) 762-2974, outside the United States at (317) 572-3993 or fax (317) 572-4002.

Wiley also publishes its books in a variety of electronic formats. Some content that appears in print may not be available in electronic books. For more information about Wiley products, visit our web site at www.wiley.com.

Library of Congress Cataloging-in-Publication Data:

Bstan-'dzin-rgya-mtsho, Dalai Lama XIV, 1935–
   His Holiness the Dalai Lama : the oral biography / Deborah Hart Strober,
Gerald S. Strober.
       p.   cm.
   Includes bibliographical references and index.
   ISBN-13 978-0-471-68001-7 (cloth : alk. paper)
   ISBN-10 0-471-68001-X (cloth : alk. paper)
 1. Bstan-'dzin-rgya-mtsho, Dalai Lama XIV, 1935–   2. Dalai lamas—Biography.
3. Tibet (China)—History. I. Strober, Deborah H. (Deborah Hart), date
II. Strober, Gerald S. III. Title.
   BQ7935.B777A3 2005
   294.3'923'092—dc22   2004025913

To our grandchildren, with our deep love, appreciation,
and hope for a better future

Eyal Jonathan Benjamin
Ran Michael Benjamin
Kai Wesley Philip Sterling
Marley Grace Sterling

CONTENTS

PART IV

CONFRONTING CHALLENGES
AND UNCERTAINTIES

PART V

LOOKING AHEAD

Illustrations follow page 118

PREFACE

In 2003, having written oral histories of three of the major American presidents of the latter half of the twentieth century—Kennedy, Nixon, and Reagan—as well as having chronicled the life and reign of the eminently newsworthy Queen Elizabeth II, we were confronted with the considerable challenge of selecting as our next subject a personality whose life, actions, and impact on the world would warrant extensive examination and documentation.

Uppermost in our consideration in this politically volatile and celebrity-driven era was to identify an individual of living memory whose impact would endure far beyond his or her lifetime—one who would likely prove to be truly unique in this universe of spiritual and temporal leaders. Following many months in our process of research, discussion, and elimination, we chose as our subject the Fourteenth Dalai Lama, the latest incarnation in the nearly seven-hundred-year-old Tibetan institution that has riveted the attention of the Western world; kept alive the hope of millions of Tibetans, both within their own nation and in the diaspora; and perplexed and stymied its main adversary, the People's Republic of China.

In compiling *His Holiness the Dalai Lama: The Oral Biography*, we have been truly blessed to have been able to relive through the recollections of our interviewees the experiences of a most courageous people and their uniquely endowed leader.

ACKNOWLEDGMENTS

His Holiness the Dalai Lama: The Oral Biography could not have come to fruition without the participation of our interviewees. They included members of the Tibetan community, Western supporters, and even a representative of Free Tibet's formidable adversary, the People's Republic of China. Each of these individuals responded in a timely manner to our interview request, offering opinions on a variety of issues. And many of our interviewees shared with us their personal, often humorous, recollections of the fourteenth Dalai Lama.

We would like to express particular appreciation to officials of the Tibetan community in the United States. Nawang Rabgyal, Rinchen Dharlo, and Annie Warner, in New York, were especially helpful as our project got under way. Lodi Gyari, the Dalai Lama's representative in Washington, offered wise counsel, and his associate, Lesley Friedell, always fulfilled our requests with courtesy and efficiency. In Toronto, Canada, we were greatly assisted in covering the April 2004 Kalachakra for World Peace by Rigzin Dolkar and Estelle Halbach, the event's media director and media officer, respectively.

We are indebted to our dear friends Bonnie Cutler and Mark Heutlinger, who introduced us to Christine and Eric Valentine. Eric in turn, put us in touch with Stan Wakefield, who responded with enthusiasm and most welcome encouragement when shown our proposal for *His Holiness the Dalai Lama: The Oral Biography*. Stan presented our proposal to John Wiley & Sons, where it was taken on by Hana Lane, an editor of exceeding compassion and wisdom. We also appreciate the efforts of editorial assistant Naomi Rothwell, as well as senior production editor Devra K. Nelson. And how could we have completed our manuscript without Vincent Joseph, who very patiently brought our computer software into the twenty-first century.

In any author's life, the encouragement of friends is like manna from heaven. We are truly fortunate in having had the interest and support not only of Bonnie and Mark, but of Joan and Charles Bialo; Ruth Gruber; Evelyn and Raphael Rothstein; Marcia and Rabbi A. James Rudin; Barbara Seaman; Florence and Harry Taubenfeld; Sarah and Ze'ev Shiff; Elaine and Martin Zuckerbrod; and Sheila and Herbert Zweibon.

And how could we have made it through these many months without the devotion of our family? We want to express our deep appreciation to our siblings and their equally supportive mates: Judith and Dr. Mortimer Civan; Mindy and Myron Strober; Joseph Hochstein; and Ruth Hockstein.

Through our children, we are privileged to know and to count among our close friends Dorrit and Meir Nocham, parents of Jeremy's wife, Gabi; Daphne and Hummarde Sterling, parents of Lori's husband, Bryan; Gene Meyers, father of Robin's friend, Michelle; and Gene's wife, Jan Book.

Lastly, we want to pay tribute to our beloved, always supportive children and their partners: Jeremy Benjamin and Gabi, the parents of Eyal Jonathan and Ran Michael; Lori and Bryan Sterling, the parents of Kai Wesley Philip and Marley Grace; Jonathan Strober; and Robin Strober and Michelle Meyers.

CHRONOLOGY OF THE FOURTEENTH DALAI LAMA

JULY 6, 1935—Lhamo Dhondrub, the fifth child, and fourth son, of a farming family, is born in the village of Taktser, in northeastern Tibet

1937—Recognized as the reincarnation of the Thirteenth Dalai Lama

FEBRUARY 22, 1940—Enthroned in Lhasa as the Fourteenth Dalai Lama

1949–1950—Chinese troops invade Tibet and remain as an occupying force

NOVEMBER 17, 1950—Assumes full power as head of state and government at the age of fifteen

1954—Meets in Beijing with Chinese Communist leaders Mao Tse-tung, Chou En-lai, and Deng Xiaoping

EARLY MARCH 1959—Passes final examination for the Geshe Lharampa [Doctor of Buddhist Philosophy] degree

MARCH 10, 1959—Major popular uprising against the Chinese occupation begins in Lhasa

MARCH 17, 1959—Escapes from Lhasa wearing civilian clothes, accompanied by family members and key aides

MARCH 31, 1959—Crosses the Indian border and is granted political asylum

1960—Moves to permanent headquarters in Dharamsala, a former British hill station in Northern India

1960s—Establishes the Tibetan Government-in-Exile, oversees the resettlement of the tens of thousands of Tibetans who have escaped to India, and establishes monasteries

1963—Government-in-Exile adopts constitution based on Buddhist principles and the Universal Declaration of Human Rights

1973—Dalai Lama makes first visit to the United Kingdom and European nations. By 2004 he will have visited forty-six countries—some of them more than once—and will meet with heads of state, prime ministers, clergy of many faiths, and scientists as well as hold teaching sessions and public lectures

1979—Makes first visit to the United States

1987—Articulates Five Point Peace Plan as first step toward determining the future status of Tibet

1989—Receives the Nobel Peace Prize

1990 TO THE PRESENT—Writes best-selling books, meets with world leaders to plead Tibet's cause, advocates a Middle Way approach for solving the issue of Tibet, relinquishes some governmental responsibilities, and is firmly established as one of the world's most admired people

THE INTERVIEWEES

Arjia Rinpoché is the incarnation of Lumbum Gye, the father of Tsong Khapa, the founder of the Gelupa sect of Buddhism. The only high Tibetan lama of Mongolian descent, Arjia Rinpoché is the former abbot of the Kumbum Monastery. He is the founder of the Tibetan Center for Compassion and Wisdom, located in California. He was interviewed on July 27, 2004, by telephone.

Dr. Alexander Berzin, an American-born convert to Buddhism, is a founding member of the Translation Bureau of the Library of Tibetan Works. He lived in India for twenty-nine years, where he translated for and worked with the Dalai Lama on several books. He lives in Berlin, Germany, where he teaches and lectures. He was interviewed on July 6, 2004, by telephone.

Dr. Frank B. Bessac arrived in Beijing, China, on a Fulbright scholarship in 1947. He entered Tibet on April 29, 1950, and was received by the Dalai Lama in Lhasa. On his return to the United States, he held academic positions and is currently an emeritus professor in the University of Montana's department of anthropology. He was interviewed on February 25, 2004, by telephone.

Richard Blum, who first met the Dalai Lama in 1972, later served as an adviser to presidents Jimmy Carter and Bill Clinton on Tibetan issues. With his wife, Senator Diane Feinstein [D-CA], then mayor of San Francisco, Mr. Blum lobbied the Carter administration to allow His Holiness to visit the United States. Mr. Blum serves as president of the American Himalayan Foundation. He was interviewed on September 3, 2004, by telephone.

Dr. Abelardo Brenes is a professor in peace education at the University for Peace and a professor of psychology and researcher at the University of Costa Rica's Institute of Psychological Research. He first met the Dalai Lama in 1987, when he arranged for him to participate in a seminar in Costa Rica on the Buddhist approach to peace. He was interviewed by telephone on October 8, 2004.

Pema Chhinjor was one of the Tibetan freedom fighters who in 1959 prevented the Chinese Communists from capturing the Dalai Lama as he fled into exile. A founding member of the Tibetan Youth Congress, Pema Chhinjor served as minister of security in the Tibetan Government-in-Exile. He was interviewed on August 26, 2004, by telephone.

Ven. Thubten Chodron, a Jewish convert to Buddhism and an ordained nun, lived for some years in the Tibetan community in exile in India, where she studied and interacted with the Dalai Lama. She was an observer at the Jewish/Buddhist dialogue in Dharamsala in October 1990. She was interviewed on August 12, 2004, by telephone.

Dr. Howard Cutler, an American psychiatrist, first met the Dalai Lama when he received a grant to study Tibetan medicine in Dharamsala. He is the coauthor, with the Dalai Lama, of the best-selling books, *The Art of Happiness: A Handbook for Living* and *The Art of Happiness at Work*. He was interviewed on August 28, 2004, in New York City.

Professor Paul Davies, a professor of natural philosophy at the Australian Centre for Astrobiology at Macquarie University in Sydney, Australia, is an author and winner, in 1995, of the Templeton Prize. He first met and interacted with the Dalai Lama during a scientific dialogue held in London. He was interviewed on July 26, 2004, by telephone.

Rinchen Dharlo, born in Nyanang, Tibet, escaped with his family to India in 1959. Beginning his service to the Tibetan Government-in-Exile in 1972, he was the director of the Office of Tibet and His Holiness's representative in Nepal from 1978 to 1987; a board member of various business enterprises and the Snow Lion Foundation; assisted in the establishment of Tibetan schools in Nepal; and was representative of His Holiness the Dalai Lama to the Americas from 1987 to 1997, heading the Office of Tibet in New York City. He currently serves as president of The Tibet Fund. He was interviewed on July 9, 2004, in New York City.

Paula J. Dobriansky, undersecretary of state for global affairs in the administration of President George W. Bush, serves as the special coordinator for Tibetan issues. She first met the Dalai Lama more than twenty years ago, during one of his visits to the United States, and interacts with him in her current position. She was interviewed on October 15, 2004, by telephone.

Tsunma Jampa Dolkar, née Sue Macy, an American convert to Buddhism, is an ordained nun. She has attended the Dalai Lama's teachings both in the United States and in India, and met His Holiness at his quarters in Dharamsala several days before her ordination. She was interviewed on April 26, 2004, in Toronto, Canada, during the Kalachakra for World Peace.

Adam Engle, the cofounder, chairman, and CEO of the Mind and Life

Institute, located in Boulder, Colorado, of which the Dalai Lama is the honorary chairman, first met His Holiness in April 1986. Since that time, His Holiness has participated in many Mind and Life conferences. He was interviewed on August 6, 2004, by telephone.

Robert Ford, CBE, first met the Dalai Lama while a radio officer to the British Mission in Tibet, where he served from 1945 to 1947. An employee of the Tibetan government as its first radio operator from 1947 to 1950, Mr. Ford was imprisoned by the People's Republic of China from 1950 to 1955. He was interviewed on July 28, 2004, by telephone.

Father Laurence Freeman, a monk of the Monastery of Christ the King, London, United Kingdom, first met the Dalai Lama in the late 1970s. An author and lecturer, Father Freeman, now the director of the World Community for Christian Meditation, has participated in recent years with His Holiness in interreligious dialogue. He was interviewed on April 15, 2004, in New York City.

Patrick French, a noted writer, was a young boy living in Britain when he first met the Dalai Lama there. Following an investigative trip to Tibet in 1999, Mr. French chronicled his experiences and observations in *Tibet, Tibet*. He was interviewed on March 29, 2004, in London, the United Kingdom.

Sister Mary Margaret Funk, OSB, executive director of the Monastic Interreligious Dialogue Board, first met the Dalai Lama in 1995. She served as coordinator of the Gethsemani Encounter, which took place in 1996, and has interacted with him on several occasions since then, including a visit to Dharamsala in the 1990s to report on her visit to Tibet. She was interviewed on July 23, 2004, by telephone.

Gelek Rinpoché, born into a wealthy family in Tibet and an incarnate lama, earned his Geshe Lharampa degree from the Drepung Monastery. A former monk, he escaped from Tibet as a teenager and was chosen by the Dalai Lama to work in Dharamsala as an educator, as well as to go to the United States for advanced studies. He is the founder of the Jewel Heart Organization for the Preservation of Tibetan Buddhist Culture. He was interviewed in New York City on August 13, 2004.

Tenzin Gephel, born in Dharamsala to parents who had escaped from Tibet, is an ordained monk of the Namgyal Monastery in India, the personal monastery of the Dalai Lama. In 1992, the Namgyal Monastery Institute of Buddhist Studies was established in Ithaca, New York, as the institution's North American seat and its sole branch in the West. He was interviewed on April 26, 2004, in Toronto, Canada, during the Kalachakra for World Peace.

Richard Gere, the actor, social activist, philanthropist, practicing

Buddhist, and close friend of the Dalai Lama, first met His Holiness in 1981, in Dharamsala. He is president of The Gere Foundation and serves as chairman of the board of The International Campaign for Tibet. He was interviewed on October 7, 2004, by telephone.

Dr. Blu Greenberg is an author, lecturer, and the founding president of the Jewish Orthodox Feminist Alliance (JOFA). She was a participant, with her husband, Rabbi Irving "Yitz" Greenberg, in Jewish-Buddhist dialogue with the Dalai Lama in Washington, New Jersey, in 1988, and in Dharamsala, India, in 1990. She was interviewed on July 7, 2004, in Riverdale, New York.

Rabbi Irving "Yitz" Greenberg is president of the Jewish Life Network and the founding president of the National Jewish Center for Learning and Leadership (CLAL). He was a participant, with his wife, Dr. Blu Greenberg, in Jewish-Buddhist dialogue with the Dalai Lama, in Washington, New Jersey, in 1988, and in Dharamsala, India, in 1990. He was interviewed on July 7, 2004, in Riverdale, New York.

Geshe Tsultim Gyaltsen, born in Tibet, began his monastic training at the age of seven and escaped to India as a teenager. Holder of the Lharampa Geshe Degree, the highest degree in Tibetan Buddhist studies, he is an author and the founder and spiritual director of the Thubten Dhargye Ling ["Land of Flourishing Dharma"] Center, so named by the Dalai Lama, and located in Long Beach, California. He was interviewed on September 21, 2004, by telephone.

Heinrich Harrer, a mountain climber and a member of the Austrian Olympic Team in 1936, was invited to participate in the Nanga Parbat Expedition, in India, in 1939. On the outbreak of World War II, he was interned by the British in a camp near Bombay. Escaping in 1944, he made his way to Tibet, arriving in Lhasa in 1946. Received by the young Dalai Lama's family, he became a confidante and unofficial tutor to His Holiness. Leaving Tibet following the Chinese invasion, he wrote of his experiences there in *Seven Years in Tibet*. He now lives in Lichtenstein, where he has played host to the Dalai Lama. He was interviewed on July 22, 2004, by telephone.

Dr. Jeffrey Hopkins, an author and translator, first met the Dalai Lama in 1972 while on a Fulbright scholarship in India. After serving as His Holiness's chief English language interpreter for ten years, Dr. Hopkins continued to interpret for the Dalai Lama on occasion. He is now a professor of religious studies at the University of Virginia. He was interviewed on July 14, 2004, by telephone.

Dr. Piet Hut, an astrophysicist and professor of interdisciplinary studies at the Institute for Advanced Study in Princeton, New Jersey, first met the Dalai Lama in 1997, during a scientific dialogue held in Dharamsala. Dr. Hut was interviewed on September 17, 2004, in New York City.

Ven. Bhikshuni Tenzin Kacho, an American Buddhist nun, was ordained by the Dalai Lama in 1985, in Dharamsala. A resident teacher at the Center for the Study of Buddhism and Tibetan Culture in Colorado Springs, Colorado, she also serves as the Buddhist chaplain at the United States Air Force Academy. She was interviewed on August 2, 2004, by telephone.

Lama Lobsang Thamcho Nyima, the eighth incarnation of the Nyentse Lama, the spiritual and temporal head of the Nyentse lineage, began his monastic education at the age of seven in Amdo. He escaped from Tibet in 1993 at the age of seventeen. He first met the Dalai Lama in 1997, in Dharamsala. A teacher, he is the founder of the Menhang/Buddhist Medical Center in Manali, India. He was interviewed on August 17, 2004, by telephone.

Lama Surya Das, né Jeffrey Miller, an American Jewish convert to Buddhism, first met the Dalai Lama in 1972. The author of *Awakening the Buddha Within*, he is a meditation teacher, scholar, and the founder of the Western Buddhist Teachers Network. He has organized meetings for the Dalai Lama in both California and Dharamsala and served as an assistant to His Holiness in France in the 1980s. He was interviewed on August 4, 2004, by telephone.

Ven. Lama Thubten Zopa Rinpoché, the incarnation of Lawudo Lama, first met the Dalai Lama in Dharamsala as a young lama, after having studied for six months in Delhi. Now the spiritual director of the Foundation for the Preservation of the Mahayana Tradition, he has visited Tibet three times, in 1986, 1987, and 2002. He was interviewed on August 3, 2004, by telephone.

Dr. Thubten Jinpa Langri, who grew up in the exile community, was first known to the Dalai Lama as a Buddhist scholar in various monastic universities. In 1985, while visiting Dharamsala to attend teachings by His Holiness, he filled in as interpreter on the first day. He serves as His Holiness's English-language interpreter to this day. He was interviewed on September 13, 2004, by telephone.

Annette Lantos, who first met the Dalai Lama in 1987, is the executive director of the Congressional Human Rights Caucus. She and her husband, Rep. Tom Lantos [D-CA], are close friends of His Holiness. She was interviewed on September 20, 2004, by telephone.

Representative Tom Lantos [D-CA], a member of the U.S. House of Representatives since 1981, and now the ranking Democratic member of the House International Relations Committee, is the founder and cochair of the Congressional Human Rights Caucus. He was interviewed on September 20, 2004, by telephone.

Mickey Lemle, a documentary filmmaker who in 1993 made *Compassion in Exile: The Story of the Fourteenth Dalai Lama*, has known His Holiness since 1985. He now serves as chairman of The Tibet Fund. He was interviewed on August 15, 2004, in New York City.

Professor Jonathan Mirsky, an authority on China, was a visiting professor at Dartmouth and the East Asian editor of *The Times of London*. He is a frequent contributor to the *New York Review of Books*. He has been a close observer and friend of the Dalai Lama for nearly a quarter of a century. He was interviewed on August 10, 2004, by telephone.

Dr. Chaim Peri, director of the Yemin Orde Wingate Youth Village, in Israel, first met the Dalai Lama during a visit to Brandeis University in 1998, and again in Jerusalem in 2002. He is the cocreator of the Israel-Tibet Institute at Yemen Orde Wingate. He was interviewed on July 1, 2004, in Tel Aviv, Israel.

Sir Malcolm Rifkind, KCMG, PC, QC, then the foreign minister of the United Kingdom, met with the Dalai Lama during the latter's visit to London in 1996. In deference to the view of Foreign Office officials that their meeting could have a negative impact on Sino-British negotiations regarding Hong Kong, the Dalai Lama was received by Sir Malcolm at his official residence rather than at his ministry. He was interviewed on May 31, 2004, by telephone.

Rabbi A. James Rudin, then the American Jewish Committee's director of Interreligious Affairs, participated with the Dalai Lama in an interreligious dialogue held in Greensburg, Pennsylvania, on November 11, 1999. Rabbi Rudin is a columnist for *Religion News Service*. He was interviewed on June 21, 2004, in New York City.

Yossi Sarid, in 1994 the leader of Israel's Meretz Party and minister of environment in the Labor government, received the Dalai Lama. In 1999, Mr. Sarid, by that time minister of education, and then speaker of the Knesset, Avraham Burg, welcomed His Holiness in Jerusalem. He was interviewed on September 28, 2004, by telephone.

Orville Schell, dean of the University of California at Berkeley's School of Journalism, an expert on U.S.–China relations and the author of *Virtual Tibet*, first met the Dalai Lama in 1994. He was interviewed on August 13, 2004, by telephone.

Tsering Shakya, born in Lhasa in 1959 of Nepalese ancestry, was expelled with his parents by the Chinese to Nepal in 1967. Mr. Shakya first came into the Dalai Lama's presence as a young refugee child in India. In 1972, he received a scholarship to study in Britain. Now an author and fellow in Tibetan Studies at London University, he interviewed the Dalai Lama while writing his book, *The Dragon in the Land of Snows*.

He was interviewed on March, 30, 2004, in London, United Kingdom.

Dr. Ronald B. Sobel, now emeritus, was the senior rabbi of Congregation Temple Emanu-El of the City of New York when in 1998 he welcomed the Dalai Lama there on the occasion of the latter's address to the International Campaign for Tibet's annual Light of Truth Award ceremony. He was interviewed on June 24, 2004, in New York City.

Geshe Lhundup Sopa, holder with highest honors of the *geshe* degree from Sera Monastery, served as debating partner to the Dalai Lama in Tibet during His Holiness's own examination for the geshe degree. Formerly a professor in the University of Wisconsin's Department of South Asian Studies, he is the founder of the Evam Buddhist Monastery and Deer Park Buddhist Center, located in Oregon, Wisconsin, where the Dalai Lama offered the Kalachakra Initiation in 1981. He was interviewed on August 2, 2004, by telephone.

Rt. Rev. William E. Swing, the Episcopal bishop of California since 1980, is the president and founding trustee of the United Religions Initiative. In the latter capacity, he was received by the Dalai Lama in 1996 in Dharamsala, with Mrs. Swing. The Swings have also met with His Holiness in Jerusalem. He was interviewed on August 16, 2004, by telephone.

Dr. Tenzin Tethong is the nephew of T. C. Tethong. He served as the representative of His Holiness in the Office of Tibet in New York City from 1973 to 1986; as special representative of His Holiness the Dalai Lama in Washington, D.C.; as head of the International Campaign for Tibet from 1987 to 1990; and as a cabinet member in the Tibetan Government-in-Exile, Dharamsala, from 1990 to 1995. A resident of California since 1995, he is an activist in Tibetan human rights groups, including The Committee of 100 for Tibet and the Dalai Lama Foundation, a foundation for peace and ethics. He teaches courses on Tibet at Stanford University. He was interviewed on July 20 and 21, 2004, by telephone.

T. C. [Tsewang Choegyal] Tethong is the uncle of Dr. Tenzin Tethong. In the early years of exile, he served as an aide in the Private Office of the Dalai Lama and as director of Tibetan settlements in Karnataka State, South India. More recently, from 1997 to 2001, he was minister of information and international relations in the Tibetan Government-in-Exile. He was interviewed on August 11 and 15, 2004, by telephone.

Lowell Thomas Jr. is the son of the world traveler, broadcaster, and writer Lowell Thomas Sr. A world traveler and explorer in his own right, he in 1949 joined his father as only the seventh and eighth Americans, respectively, to be permitted to travel to Tibet and to be received by the Dalai Lama in Lhasa. He chronicled that expedition in a book, *Out of This World*. He was interviewed on June 9, 2004, by telephone.

Professor Robert A. F. Thurman, a former Buddhist monk, the first Westerner to become one, was ordained by the Dalai Lama in 1965. A close associate and ardent supporter of His Holiness and the Tibetan cause since that time, Professor Thurman is the Jey Tsong Khapa professor of Indo-Tibetan Studies at Columbia University; the author of *Inner Resolution and Infinite Life* and other books; and the cofounder and president of Tibet House in New York City. He was interviewed on September 29, 2004, in New York City.

Justin Trudeau, an educator and a son of the late Pierre Elliott Trudeau [1919–2000], who served as prime minister of Canada twice, from 1968 to 1979 and from 1980 to 1984, is active in the foundation bearing his father's name. The prime minister had been very welcoming of Tibetan immigrants and had enjoyed a long and close relationship with the Dalai Lama. Mr. Trudeau was interviewed on June 2, 2004, by telephone.

Norbu Tsering, born in India to parents who had fled Tibet in 1959, met the Dalai Lama several times during his childhood. Now a member of the Tibetan exile community of Canada, Mr. Tsering is president of the Canadian Tibetan Association of Ontario, the official host organization of the Dalai Lama's visit to Toronto in the spring of 2004. He was interviewed on July 7, 2004, by telephone.

Ven. Nicholas Vreeland, a Christian convert to Buddhism, first met His Holiness in 1979. A holder of the geshe degree from the Rato Dratsang Monastery in India, he was ordained as a monk by the Dalai Lama. He is the director of the Tibet Center, located in New York City. He was interviewed on September 3, 2004, in New York City.

Sun Wade is the spokesman and press counselor of the Embassy of the People's Republic of China in Washington, D.C. He was interviewed on April 15, 2004, by telephone.

Annie Warner is the former coordinator of culture and communications at the Office of Tibet, located in New York City. Ms. Warner was in His Holiness's entourage during the 2004 Toronto Kalachakra for World Peace. She was interviewed on August 26, 2004, by telephone.

Harry Wu, a Chinese-born former prisoner in the Laogai, the gulag of the People's Republic of China, now lives in the Washington, D.C., area with his wife and young son. A human rights activist, he is the executive director of the Laogai Research Foundation. Mr. Wu was deeply moved when the Dalai Lama told him, "You know, Harry, we are brothers." He has written of his experiences in *Bitter Winds: A Memoir of My Years in China's Gulag*; *Laogai: The Chinese Gulag*; and *Trouble Maker: The Story of Chinese Dissident Harry Wu*. He was interviewed on June 15, 2004, in Washington, D.C.

PART I

Simple Monk,
World Leader

Chapter One

THE *PUBLIC* DALAI LAMA: HIS APPEAL TO THE MASSES

Justin Trudeau, educator, son of the late Pierre Elliott Trudeau [1919–2000, prime minister of Canada, 1968–1979; 1980–1984] I have done a lot of reading on him, trying to understand him. The one thing that keeps coming back is how people are physically affected by his presence. And to be quite honest, I had sort of dismissed that a little bit—I figured it was something that people would get overly worked up about or were particularly religious—and when he walked over to me and greeted me [just before Mr. Trudeau introduced the Dalai Lama at an appearance at the SkyDome in Toronto, Canada, in April 2004], his presence was like a physical blow, like a wave that actually hit me, and it absolutely amazed me. He exudes this joy and this strength and this simplicity that absolutely *floored* me. I had been given a scarf to hand to him, for him to put on me, and he took the scarf that I had been given, put it aside, and took out one of his scarves, which I think was of better quality—and certainly more beautiful—and he had me bend over and he put it around my neck. He sort of smiled and nodded and said a couple of words of thanks and greeting. And then he pulled me in toward him and pressed his temple against mine and just held me for a moment. I have rarely felt as welcomed and comfortable with someone as I did in that moment of connecting with him. I was on the verge, and slightly over the verge, of tears for the entire experience. I thanked him and walked down

3

off the stage and back to my seat and for the first fifteen minutes of his talk, I was basically in a daze, which was wonderful, so it was a very, very powerful, moving experience.

Professor Robert [A. F.] Thurman, former Buddhist monk, ordained by the Dalai Lama in 1965; Jey Tsong Khapa professor of Indo-Tibetan Buddhist Studies, Columbia University; author of *Inner Resolution, Infinite Life*, and other books; cofounder and president, Tibet House, New York City   There is such a thing as the charisma of office, then there is the charisma of person. In the case of the Dalai Lama, there is definitely the charisma of person. My wife and I were once asked by an Indian gentleman, "Have you ever seen the Dalai Lama perform a miracle or do something magical?" I had seen a few funny things happen around the Dalai Lama, but I thought it wasn't a good idea to talk about them. But my wife said, "Oh yes, I've seen *plenty* of miracles. You know that the Dalai Lama is a very busy person and while I've seen him in many different settings, I have never seen it happen that he was with somebody and didn't give the person his total attention and total focus." The Indian gentleman was disappointed, but my wife insisted that the Dalai Lama's response to people is miraculous. When people walk into his field, they feel a different kind of space for themselves. Normally, when we meet each other, we reach out to the person *over there* and communicate. With the Dalai Lama, there isn't this person who is *over there*. He is *over here*, with *us*.

Richard Gere, actor; social activist; philanthropist; president, The Gere Foundation; chairman of the board, International Campaign for Tibet   I first met him in 1981, in Dharamsala. I had been a Zen Buddhist for some time before I went there, but I had a strong impulse to meet the Dalai Lama, although I had not read much of his material. And we had a mutual friend, John Avedon. John was just finishing up a book he was writing, called *In Exile from the Land of Snows*. I really had not known—as almost no one on the planet knew—what had happened to the Tibetans. It had been a very guarded secret for some reason. John arranged for me to go to Dharamsala and I stayed with His Holiness's younger brother, Ngari Rinpoché.

They were very skillful with me. They said, "His Holiness will be able to see you but it will probably be ten days to two weeks before he has the time. In the meantime, while you're waiting, we want to show you the community. So they spent ten days to two weeks showing me everything about the Tibetan community in exile, and it was quite an extraordinary education. Of course, by the end of that, I was pretty much a card-carrying Tibetan. And then, when I met His Holiness, Ngari Rinpoché was there. He was educated in an English school in Darjeeling, so his English is impeccable, and he was kind of the interpreter when it was required.

I came there with my girlfriend at the time. He was very gracious and quite striking in his appearance—quite handsome and formidable as a person—and he had the kind of aura that a powerful public person has. At the same time, he was utterly simple and direct. In many ways, he reminded me of my father in his directness, in his simplicity.

Do People Admire Him More for His Spiritual Search, His Political Symbolism, or His Great Celebrity?

Sir Malcolm Rifkind, KCMG, PC, QC, former foreign minister, United Kingdom It's a combination of all these factors. After Nelson Mandela he's probably the nearest thing to a global icon there is. If you think of Mandela, if you think of the Pope, and if you think of the Dalai Lama, there are not many others today who have that global reputation based, essentially, on their personality and their values, and the fact that they combine these personal qualities with an unswerving political set of objectives. So he's not just a spiritual leader and he's not just a politician; it's the combination that makes him remarkable and makes me compare him with the other two people whom I've mentioned.

Dr. Ronald B. Sobel, Senior Rabbi, Congregation Temple Emanu-El of the City of New York; host of the Dalai Lama's appearance there in 1998 I suppose if I were a political figure, it would be his political struggle that would be on the forefront of my consciousness—although it's on my consciousness, it's not on the forefront of my consciousness. But even while saying that, history has thrust this Dalai Lama into a position where political leadership and world statesmanship are not divorced from his religious role, and it was his overwhelming humanity that impressed me. Now, obviously, we have different theological affirmations; our world views are hardly the same; the cultures are significantly disparate. But there are similar factors that we sense: his exile and his people's diaspora, the Jewish people's exile and diaspora, even though it's been a hundred years since my maternal and paternal grandparents came to America, fleeing a world of pogrom and persecution and horror. And what I see in the Dalai Lama are qualities that I would wish always to see in myself but, alas, do not. So, in that sense he becomes also an exemplar for me, by giving values toward which I, personally, should strive to attain.

Reasons for His Popularity in the West

Sir Malcolm Rifkind   It's a combination of things, but it also reflects an awareness of the total disparity of power between China and Tibet—China a billion people, Tibet a handful of people; China incredibly powerful, Tibet effectively no power at all in the conventional sense; China a great empire well-known around the world, Tibet still relatively unknown. So there's a romantic element to it, there is the David-and-Goliath relationship, and there is also awareness that in the last twenty years it has been demonstrated that even the impossible can happen. People are saying it *looks* impossible; it probably *is* impossible; but after what we've seen just in the last twenty years in other parts of Asia and in other parts of Europe, you can't say it's impossible.

Tsering Shakya, born in Lhasa in 1959 of Nepalese ancestry; expelled with his family to Nepal by the Chinese; author; fellow in Tibetan studies, London University   Historically, the fascination with the Dalai Lama was always there; the institution of the Dalai Lama was there. There has always been support by Western travelers, and a lot of books and religious figures have created this fascination, so the institution of the Dalai Lama has always been mysterious and something unique. At the same time, the present Dalai Lama has created this type of personality and stature just out of his own work and his own engagement with the world and the West. So part of the institution of the Dalai Lama is historical, and there has been this fascination, but mainly today's standing really has to do with his own engagement with the world and how he has managed to be so successful—to engage and encounter and relate to the modern world. The Dalai Lama in some ways is really fantastic at understanding about psychological and social conditions of the postindustrial society. That's why he is able to relate so well to Western society; he can relate to these conditions and have the answers and the solutions to the problems you have.

Patrick French, visitor to Tibet in 1999; author, *Tibet, Tibet*   It's hard to say what it is that makes the Dalai Lama such a globally popular figure.

It's not really because people are directly following Tibetan Buddhism; it's not really because they're interested in the politics of Tibet. It's that there is something about him, personally, that seems to catch people's imagination, the fact that he has some kind of personal presence. And I think it's very much linked to the fact that he appears to represent the transmission of some ancient spiritual lineage that he's discovered in this extraordinary way, through supposedly recognizing objects that belonged to his predecessor, and that he attained this position of considerable political and religious power at a very young age. Then he had the experience of trying to cohabit with the Chinese communists, fleeing across the Himalayan Mountains into exile. It's a very glamorous story. And I also think that people feel that, somehow, by being around him or by listening to him, that they are going to get some kind of secret and maybe that will help them to live their lives in a happy way.

I've often noticed when I've been with him that people come to him who need help of some kind. Normally, people who have emotional, psychological, personal, or health problems come to the Dalai Lama because they think he's going to reveal a secret, or he's going to heal them in some way. And he's extremely patient and compassionate in how he deals with people like that. He will interrupt what he's doing to give his full attention to somebody who says, "I've just been diagnosed with cancer," or "I have some major upset in my life." I've even noticed that when people know you've had some interaction with the Dalai Lama, they want a little bit of that: "What was he like? What did it feel like, being around him?" They want some of the magic that he appears to give off. In the end, it's not something that's definable; it's more than a religious thing.

Lama Surya Das, né Jeffrey Miller, American convert to Buddhism; author, *Awakening the Buddha Within*; meditation teacher; scholar; founder, Western Buddhist Teachers Network; assistant to the Dalai Lama in France The Dalai Lama was very, very impressive. I never expected that much from somebody in his position. I would never have sought out the Dalai Lama of Buddhism or the Pope: growing up in the fifties and sixties and being somewhat disillusioned with such people, I didn't expect that much from statesmen and leaders. But he was everything and *more*. I felt such a profound personal connection with him. He was really interested in me; when he was with me, it was the most important thing he had to do in the world, which is quite a marvelous feeling. Even if it's just one moment, he's really *there*, although he definitely has other important things to do.

Father Laurence Freeman, monk of the Monastery of Christ the King, London, United Kingdom; author; lecturer; director, World Community for Christian Meditation Some are born to greatness; some have greatness thrust upon them. He does keep a certain distance. Sometimes he responds to questions when it's best not to respond to them, and then the media jump on that. There have been some unpleasant, negative articles about him, but on the whole the media haven't turned on him as they tend to turn on people they idolize at some point. He had to handle that very delicate situation and at the same time be the father of his people and the symbol of their integrity, their unity, and their culture. Tibetan history is full of conflicts. Even now, the Tibetan monastic world has its conflicts and rivalries, and he's carrying an enormous burden as the symbol of unity. So I think very few people would have been able, in terms of character or temperament, to carry that off, and he has done it in a most amazing, mysterious way. At the same time—maybe this is the answer as to why—he has kept his own identity as an individual.

Lama Surya Das I asked my own personal teacher, Tulku Pema Wangyal Rinpoché, who is one of the leading teachers in France, "How is it that some of our lamas, who are known to be the greatest of lamas—the Dalai Lama himself goes to the teachings—don't seem to have so much outreach, know so much, and touch people so widely?" And he said, "The Dalai Lama's quality is sort of turned inside out to the world because of his role and position in the world, and some of the other Tibetan sages don't have that role or position, so their qualities are more luminous within for those who can see." I thought that was very interesting, that even the Dalai Lama's teachers, who, he would probably say, are even more enlightened than he is, still don't have that kind of charisma or outreach or skillful means to touch all modern people, to speak to people of the different religions the way he does.

Harry Wu, Shanghai-born former prisoner in the Laogai, the gulag of the People's Republic of China; human rights activist; executive director, The Laogai Research Foundation; author of *Bitter Winds: A Memoir of My Years in China's Gulag*; *Laogai: The Chinese Gulag*; and *Trouble Maker: The Story of Chinese Dissident Harry Wu* When I met the Dalai Lama for the first time, he touched my hand and he said to me, "You know, Harry, we are brothers." The Dalai Lama is a very special character. You cannot ask John Paul, the Pope, "What do you think about sex?" or, "Do you ever think about being with a woman?" The Dalai

Lama will answer these questions. You can ask any question. He's always calm, he's always smiling. There was only one time when I was with him that he almost cried, when he was talking about the Tibetan people. All other times, he is always smiling. There is a phrase in Tibet: "As the rains fall into the ocean, there is no decrease or increase," because you're the *ocean*; you're not a lake, you're not a river, you're not a pond, you're not a reservoir; you're the *ocean*, no matter how heavy the rain.

Sister Mary Margaret Funk, OSB, executive director, Monastic Inter-religious Dialogue Board; coordinator, Gethsemani Encounter, 1996 He considers himself first and foremost a monk. I sat through his Kalachakra Initiation Rite in Bloomington, Indiana, in 2001, and I realized that in their tradition, it's a very privileged life to be a monk or a nun, especially a monk. And he's a bodhisattva, which means that he turned down being just in nirvana and came to this realm to help other sentient beings. And he sees monkhood as kind of like sainthood in this realm, so he's raised up all of us to think highly of being a monk or a nun. It is his identity: he has no other persona; he always wears the robes. His favorite topic is "The Lifestyle of a Monk or Nun and Prayer," and he sees our role as teaching everyone to live a life that would reduce suffering in this realm and raise up everybody else.

However, he believes in democracy and he believes in separation of church and state and secularization. And that is what appeals to him about the American experiment. At our Gethsemani Encounter dialogue in 'ninety-six, he just was right at home; he lived the life right with us. One time, he went up to one of the Christian nuns and said, "Am I being too casual?"

Dr. Chaim Peri, director, Yemin Orde Wingate Youth Village, Israel; cocreator, Israel-Tibet Institute As the result of a visit of prominent Tibetan educators to our village [Yemin Orde Wingate Youth Village, in Israel], I met the Dalai Lama for the first time at Brandeis University [near Boston, Massachusetts] in 1998. I went to Dharamsala, where I met his sister, Jetsun Pema, whom I envision as the Henrietta Szold [1860–1945, American Zionist, founder of the women's organization, Hadassah] of the Tibetan people, and I had a meeting with their education officers, including the minister of education, Mr. [Rinchen] Choegal, and we devised a program by which they would send children to Israel. I had in mind that this would be a big part of our program from now and forever. And we really brought these children. We brought twelve kids and two educators for a three-month program here, as a pilot. Then the intifada started and this was the last one.

But one of these kids, Ngawang Loser, was stubborn enough to tell me, "I want to be a living bridge between these two nations and fulfill your dream." He's now at the Hebrew University, studying philosophy. His Hebrew is already impeccable; he has humility; he has a sense of mission. So we created an anchor here, not just an ambassador, but an anchor—a child who in his formative years has absorbed Israel. The Dalai Lama's office now contributes two hundred dollars every month toward his board in Jerusalem, while we pay the tuition. This small connection must be advanced; we have to work with it, to continue it. And I'm working on long-range plans with this young man. The second time I saw the Dalai Lama was in Jerusalem, at the King David Hotel, and he expressed his satisfaction with the fact that Tibetan youngsters are coming to Israel. Holding my hand very strongly, he said, "Give strength to our children." I felt his strength pouring into me in many ways and that has continued ever since.

Yossi Sarid, former leader, Meretz Party; minister of environment; minister of education, Israel [During their second meeting, in Jerusalem, in 1999] the Dalai Lama asked for a broadening of the program where youngsters from Tibet come to Israel. Since he is very familiar with the Jewish experience of being in exile and surviving, he probably finds this very interesting and encouraging as to how his people exist, struggle, and [will] win at last. Needless to say, I was very cooperative and later on, we made sure that more Tibetan students were able to come to our country. I met with these students on several occasions. I hope more Tibetan students will come—and not necessarily just those in exile. If it would be possible for students living in Tibet to come to Israel, they would be most welcome.

Is It Surprising That the Dalai Lama Has Attained Such World Renown?

Richard Blum, president, American Himalayan Foundation; adviser to presidents Jimmy Carter and Bill Clinton on Tibetan issues; husband of Senator Diane Feinstein [D-CA] When I first knew him, I never imagined that the Dalai Lama would have the esteem of the Western world that he enjoys today. Every two years we have an AHF event which is addressed by His Holiness. The tickets, priced at two hundred dollars apiece, sell out even before notices of the event ever go out. I recall having gone to one of his teachings near San Jose. This was not user-friendly stuff. He spoke in Tibetan, with some translation. In the past, the dharma kids would come to these events but today, people attend from all walks of life and the not-inexpensive tickets for the lectures sell out. So the question is: what is there about His Holiness that has such a universal appeal? He has written that you can be a religious person and not be a very *good* person. You can have no interest in religion and be a fine person. What's important is that you are spiritual—that you care more about other people than yourself. As far as I am concerned, that's the best possible message a religious leader can ever give to anybody in the world. His religion is about kindness and compassion. He has really stuck to what he is supposed to be as the Dalai Lama.

Heinrich Harrer, mountain climber and member of the Austrian Olympic Team, 1936; invitee on the Nanga Parbat Expedition, Kashmir, India, 1939; internee of the British near Bombay on the outbreak of World War II; escapee from internment camp and arrival in Tibet, 1944; arrival in Lhasa, 1946; author of *Seven Years in Tibet* There was a Gallup poll here and he got 39 percent; he's the number-one person—the second was the Pope, with 18.5 percent of the vote, the third and fourth were two Africans, and the fifth was the Western scientist, [Stephen] Hawking. That shows the popularity of His Holiness. He gives every year one or two Kalachakras and ten thousand people—so many people are coming, admirers of his Holiness. He visited me also twice in my home; he came to Lichtenstein. I succeeded in convincing the Lichtenstein government to have three stamps made for the Tibetans. So when he came here, he stayed with the duke in his castle. That was a very wonderful thing of the government of Lichtenstein to issue these three stamps. The Chinese government protested.

Robert Ford, CBE, radio officer to the British Mission in Tibet, 1945–1947; employee of the Tibetan government as its first radio operator, 1947–1950; prisoner of the People's Republic of China, 1950–1955 When we first met—in 1945—the world was a different place and he was a little boy. I don't know what would have happened if the Chinese had not invaded. It's quite possible that His Holiness would not have achieved the world status that he has—he might have been a recluse in Lhasa. He doesn't court publicity, in a sense, and he doesn't go out of his way to seek all this: this comes, as he often says, from his position as being the Dalai Lama, not for him, personally, but for his teaching, for his views on world affairs and what life is about.

Tsering Shakya   I'm not surprised that the Dalai Lama has become such a world celebrity. There is, obviously, this fascination of people with the Dalai Lama, created a long time ago, from the late nineteenth century, by travelers who came to Tibet. So, coupling that image and what the Dalai Lama has been able to do, it is likely that he would have become such a figure. [The reason] he has gained stature is that he really hasn't abandoned his responsibility; he hasn't said: I live in the modern world; this whole thing with the Dalai Lama is nonsense and I'll just live in California. He has stayed very much traditional in his belief system. So that adds to his weight of authority. Another thing is that he has never abandoned his community. He has said, "My responsibility first is to my community, to the Tibetan people." He says, "The future of the Dalai Lama is with his followers, what they decide, what they feel; if they feel the need for a Dalai Lama, they will create one, whether I want it or not."

The Dalai Lama's Impact on People

Patrick French   I suppose the spark was meeting the Dalai Lama when I was a child. That's probably true of quite a lot of people—the reason that they become involved in the Free Tibet Movement is because they're interested in the figure of the Dalai Lama. It was one of the things that encouraged me to actually want to go to Tibet; it made me read about the history of Tibetan culture and religion. But then I got to know Tibetans who were living in exile.

At that time he was a completely alien figure as I had grown up in England in the 1970s and the eighties. So to see somebody who looked so different, who was dressed in these exotic robes and platform flip-flops, surrounded by an entourage of other Buddhist monks, he seemed extraordinary to me—really kind of glamorous and exotic.

But then I also realized, almost straight away, that he had this intense personal charisma. He has this ability to make not only each person whom he is speaking to, but each person he is with, feel, somehow, that there is an electric current going through them. And that's something that I've noticed again and again, this way that he can have an effect on people. And not only on people who have an existing religious or political or cultural interest in him. I remember once seeing him in one of the big

London hotels and there was a really hard-bitten camera crew, really cynical in that way that people who spend too much time attending press conferences can be. And I remember walking out with these guys; they had never been in the presence of anybody like *that*.

T. C. [Tsewang Choegyal] Tethong, uncle of Dr. Tenzin Tethong; aide, Private Office of the Dalai Lama; director, Tibetan Settlements, Karnataka State, South India; minister of information and international relations, Tibetan Government in Exile, 1997–2001   Back in 1959, a reporter for the *New York Times* who had a camera slung around his neck came for an interview with His Holiness. When he went in to the office, His Holiness noticed the camera and immediately identified its make. When the interview ended, the reporter began to take some pictures but he was fumbling around and almost dropped the camera. I have often seen how people get emotional in His Holiness's presence. Even for me, as one who has been very close to His Holiness, every morning, when I would report to him, I would feel his aura all the time.

Mickey Lemle, documentary filmmaker, *Compassion in Exile: the Story of the 14th Dalai Lama* [1993]; chairman, The Tibet Fund   I was invited to a small, private reception for His Holiness [in Davos, Switzerland]. We were introduced and shook hands and he looked at me and I looked at him. There was a palpable sense of presence about him. Usually, when I meet a powerful person, I have the sense that he or she is looking at me, thinking: how can I use this person to enhance my power? With the Dalai Lama, I had the sincere feeling that he was looking at me, thinking: who *is* this person and how can I help him? Once he said to me, "My religion is kindness." And that is what you feel from him—a sense of kindness.

Annette Lantos, executive director, Congressional Human Rights Caucus; founder and chair, International Free Wallenberg Committee   He has no worldly power, whatsoever; he has no armies he commands; no politburo; no secret police. But we see the tremendous impact that the Dalai Lama has in just appearing as a simple man and having people recognize that he embodies answers to the problems of the world.

Ven. Nicholas Vreeland, director, Tibet Center, New York City; holder of Geshe degree from Rato Dratsang Monastery, India   I first met His Holiness in 1979, just as the monsoon was arriving in Dharamsala. I had requested an audience in order to photograph His Holiness for a book. After a few weeks, I was granted the audience and was instructed to set up my equipment quickly so as not to take up too much of His Holiness's time. I decided that the best place to take the photograph was in his office, with him seated behind his desk. There was a window behind the desk, so the way to take the photo would be for His Holiness to turn away from his desk at an angle to the window and the desk and face the camera. His Holiness had a swivel chair, which would make it easier for him to turn toward the camera. As I was getting my light reading done, I realized it would be a very slow exposure—there wasn't much light; the skies were already very cloudy. His Holiness was going to have to hold the pose for a full minute, which is a very long time.

Suddenly, I heard this very deep voice giving instructions. And, as he approached, I also heard the far more subdued voices of his entourage. So my first impression was one of force, of authority, of strength. And there was a quality of down-to-earthiness about His Holiness's tone. And though I didn't know what he was saying, there was a matter-of-factness about the exchange. Suddenly, His Holiness was in the room and when he saw me, he laughed, in a way to make me feel welcome. I then offered him a white scarf and explained to him that I was in India taking photographs of the great lamas of Tibet who had come into exile. His Holiness sat down and I said to him that it would be necessary for him not to move for about a minute. But after forty-five seconds, he began to swivel in his chair. As a result, we went through many sheets of film. His entourage began to become anxious. Suddenly, after several attempts, His Holiness burst into roaring laughter and I did also. That took all the tension out of the situation. It was obvious that we were not going to be able to photograph him while he was seated in the swivel chair. I then asked His Holiness if he would stand against the greenish wall of his office—there was a nice, soft light on the left side of his face. I took the photo and it was wonderful. As I packed up my gear, I asked His Holiness what I might do in gratitude for being able to photograph the great lamas. He replied that I should study. And that's what I did.

Lama Lobsang Thamcho Nyima, the Eighth Incarnation of the Nyentse Lama, the spiritual and temporal head of the Nyentse lineage; escaped from Tibet in 1993 at the age of seventeen; teacher; founder, Menhang/Buddhist Medical Center, Manali, India I met His Holiness in 1997 in Dharamsala. I received the full ordination as a monk. His Holiness advised me to be a good monk and to observe

Buddhism. I had deep feelings and I told him that I would really try to follow his advice. Two years earlier, I had seen him from a distance of thirty meters when he visited South India. That gave me a great feeling; it was very emotional for me to see his face.

Adam Engle, cofounder, chairman, and CEO, Mind and Life Institute, Boulder, Colorado, of which the Dalai Lama is the honorary chairman The first time I was in his presence was in London in the early 1980s. I remember going to a talk he was giving in the Royal Albert Hall. The program that was passed out before he actually arrived said, at the bottom, "My religion is very simple; my religion is kindness." That really kind of blew me away. I listened to the talk and then took a teaching for the next few days. It was incredibly impressive. At first I didn't really understand the teaching consciously, but I noticed there were some very significant internal shifts in the way that I thought about things over the succeeding year.

Tsering Shakya   I met him when I was doing my book. I was trying to tell him, "I want to write history because there is a need for Tibetans to be looking at their own history, not just for the sake of trying to have propaganda material, but simply to understand in the fastest possible way what really happened in history." He was very supportive of that idea. He often encourages Tibetans to write their stories; he tells people who have come from Tibet recently, "You all have stories to tell and you have to tell your story. We have to tell the world about our future."

It was very difficult to respond because as a Tibetan you are so reverential that it is not an interview like any other. I personally felt it was really a complicated situation; I could not contradict him so, in a way, the interview was very tense for me, and there were many questions I wanted to ask but in his presence just couldn't ask. For a Tibetan raised in the Tibetan community, it becomes really totally impossible to interview him in a normal way.

Pema Chhinjor, Tibetan freedom fighter; founding member, Tibetan Youth Congress; former minister of security, Tibetan Government-in-Exile   After I had visited Tibet in 1992, I had a personal audience with His Holiness to report to him on my trip. I felt very emotional in his presence, so much so that I found it difficult to express my views on what I had seen in Tibet. Tears kept rolling down from my eyes. This is natural for every Tibetan because we have so much faith in him. He is always present at the bottom of our hearts.

The more I see him, the more emotional I become. I had an audience with him when he was in Southern California in early 2004. I couldn't say *anything*; I was just weeping and weeping. While there are in the world famous politicians and great religious leaders, there is no one like the Dalai Lama. He never thinks of himself; all of the time he thinks not only of Tibetans but of all sentient beings.

Annie Warner, former coordinator of culture and communications, Office of Tibet, New York City   In my experience, I have not seen anyone not have an emotional reaction on meeting him for the first time. People will have a sort of look of bewilderment in their eyes or will break into tears or will tearfully fall into a full prostration. Everyone seems to have a profound reaction at meeting him or being in his presence.

Dr. Piet Hut, astrophysicist; professor of Interdisciplinary Studies, Institute for Advanced Study, Princeton, New Jersey   At the end of the meeting [a scientific dialogue held in Dharamsala in 1997], we were invited by the principal of a school—its students are either orphans or have parents who do not reside in Dharamsala—to visit an exhibition of science projects. Some of the children had made posters, some contraptions. While we, a group of Western scientists, were interesting to the children, they were far more interested in the fact that we had just spent five days with the Dalai Lama. To these children, we didn't come to school with the aura of being scientists, but with the aura of having talked with *the Dalai Lama*. On one poster, a student had drawn a very detailed picture of a rocket and on the rocket were not the words "USA" or "China" or "Russia," but, in Tibetan, the word "Tibet." I found this very touching— there was the hope that Tibet would one day be its own nation and join the major nations launching a rocket.

Adam Engle   The first time I ever met him personally was in April 1986, when I had a one-hour audience with him in Dharamsala. The sense of presence, humility, genuineness, friendliness, caring, and compassion was overwhelming. I was quite nervous prior to the appointment; I felt that I was meeting with a great Being. At that point, he was not as well-known as he is now. He had not yet won the Nobel Prize. So it wasn't so much a "fame" thing as just being with a great person.

Orville Schell, dean, School of Journalism, University of California, Berkeley; author, *Virtual Tibet*; expert on U.S.–China relations   I first met him about ten years ago [in 1994] at a quasi-public event. My first impression was that this is a one-of-a-kind human being who instills awe and respect. You don't quite know how to categorize him. Ironically, I think that this is exactly the reaction that he struggles so hard against. He is constantly trying to get people to treat him as an ordinary mortal. They have a need to treat him as something unusually exceptional, so there is this unusual pas de deux that goes on when people meet him for the first time. I was painfully aware of that.

Dr. Howard Cutler, M.D., psychiatrist; coauthor, with the Dalai Lama, of the best-selling books *The Art of Happiness: A Handbook for Living* and *The Art of Happiness at Work* In my last year in medical school at the University of Arizona, I received a grant to study Tibetan medicine for a three-month period in Dharamsala. I lived in a government guesthouse where I got to know His Holiness's brother, Lobsang Samten. During my time there, it was suggested that I meet His Holiness. I really had no agenda but I was curious to meet him. I had been to Tibet and I thought he might be interested in the photographs I took there.

As I sat in a waiting room, I began to get nervous; I could feel my heart beating and I was perspiring. I was thinking: this is a world spiritual leader—the political leader of his people—he is *the Dalai Lama*. I didn't know what to expect—I imagined he would be this awe-inspiring, formal type of person. But when I went in to meet him, he came over and shook my hand and was very warm. Within about five minutes, we were sitting down and talking—one human being to another—and I forget that he was *the Dalai Lama*.

He has a good understanding about people; he can be challenged at times; he can have incredibly complex intellectual discussions. But underneath it you feel: here is a man who means well. And people respond to that. It's not that he's talking to you because of your title or your position or wealth. He has this way of communicating where he is the same with everybody. I have noticed over the years that he treats the waiter in the restaurant with the same respect and friendliness as he might a president or prime minister.

Tenzin Gephel, Tibetan monk, Namgyal Monastery Institute of Buddhist Studies, Ithaca, New York, North American seat of the personal monastery of His Holiness the Dalai Lama His Holiness is always saying he's one of the monks—we have 175 monks and he says he's one of these monks, so we always think that we have a very special connection. Our monks have more opportunity to see him, to hear him, because the very nature of our monastery is to make preparations for the Dalai Lama's public activities. Every day, four of our monks have to go to the Dalai Lama's palace to make special ritual prayers, in the evening. And when we have ritual ceremonies on a monthly basis, the Dalai Lama will come to participate in the ceremony.

Dr. Ronald B. Sobel   I had never met the Dalai Lama before April 30, 1998, although I had been in his presence on two other occasions. The first was about twenty years ago [1984] at the annual convention of the Central Conference of American Rabbis [CCAR], the organization that represents Reform liberal rabbis in the United States and Canada. There were five or six hundred rabbis in a large auditorium. I was sitting way in the back. The moment he walked into that space I could sense the humility that absolutely enveloped him and came forth from him. It is so, so rare that you sense a genuine humility and when it is experienced, one is overwhelmed, so although I could barely understand a word he said, I remained over-whelmed. But little did I know that what I experienced in that large room so many years before would be magnified when I met him one-on-one.

Professor Jonathan Mirsky, authority on China; retired East Asian editor, *The Times of London*; author; frequent contributor, the *New York Review of Books*   When Tibetans meet important people, they often will give that person a white scarf, and then the more important person gives the less important person back an even better scarf. I had several of these scarves often, at various points. [On one occasion] I brought with me the scarf of the soccer team here that I support, called Tottenham Hotspur, a white scarf that says "Tottenham" on it. I held out this scarf—it was very long, about five feet long—and he said, "Oh, what is that?" and I said, "It's the scarf of the football [soccer] team I support, Your Holiness." Of course he gave me a scarf and then he said, "Oh, can I play for them?" And I said, "Well, you know, Your Holiness, your English is very good but it's not perfect. Did you say 'play' or 'pray'"? And he said, "Well maybe I could *pray* for them." And I said, "They need all the prayers they can get because they're very near the bottom of the league." So he said, "I will pray for them." And that year, suddenly, the team's fortune turned around: they went right up to the top and won the league.

Dr. Thubten Jinpa Langri, Buddhist scholar; English-language interpreter to the Dalai Lama since 1984   I grew up in the exile community in India, so His Holiness has always been a large presence, even when I didn't see him *physically*—his photos were in the schools, we recited prayers for his long life, and everyone was aware of his presence from a very early age.

T. C. Tethong   In India in 1959, we were traveling in a motorcade of five or six cars and when we stopped in a remote village to rest, all the villagers came and flocked around him. In Bombay, he went to a reception at a Buddhist temple in the middle of the day. He went in and prayed for about forty-five minutes and when he came out, the whole courtyard was filled with people. When he went to get into his car, people rushed up to greet him. This happens wherever he goes. He takes it in his stride.

Professor Abelardo Brenes PhD, professor in peace education, University for Peace; professor of psychology and researcher, Institute for Psychological Research, University of Costa Rica   In 1987, I obtained the support of the University for Peace, the government of Costa Rica, and President Oscar Arias, personally, to invite His Holiness to come to Costa Rica to share with us the Buddhist approach to peace. It was going to be just a small seminar, but it took on a life of its own and evolved into a very large international conference on the true meaning of peace. It was the first time that the Dalai Lama, as a head of state, was invited by a Latin American government. It was also the first time that an interfaith ceremony was held at the National Basilica. I was tremendously impressed by His Holiness, who sensed a strong bond between Tibet and Costa Rica. Costa Rica was inspirational to him in terms of what he thought Tibet could be someday.

Rinchen Dharlo, director, Office of Tibet and His Holiness the Dalai Lama's representative in Nepal, 1978–1987; representative of His Holiness the Dalai Lama to the Americas, 1987–1997; president, The Tibet Fund   He's aware of how much impact he makes on other people. Yet this doesn't make him proud; he always thinks of himself as a simple Buddhist monk. When he visited Costa Rica there was a huge interfaith service and it was held in a church. He was walking in the center and on his right side he had President Arias and on his left side he had the Archbishop of San Jose. People just reached over from both sides to touch the Dalai Lama because they love him. Costa Rica is a Catholic country and there's no connection between the Dalai Lama and the Christians in Costa Rica and yet—it was spontaneous—people wanted to touch him so much. He had that power. And I've also seen him in Venezuela—he went to give a talk at the university and after he finished giving the talk, he just walked out and there were students outside and some of them managed to shake hands with him. And those who shook hands with him were sharing it with others. That surprised me. I think it's because of his love and compassion—his unconditional love.

Dr. Tenzin Tethong, nephew of T. C. [Tsewang Choegyal] Tethong; Representative of His Holiness, Office of Tibet in New York, 1973–1986; Special Representative of His Holiness the Dalai Lama in Washington, D.C., and head of the International Campaign for Tibet, 1987–1990; member, cabinet of the Tibetan government in exile, Dharamsala, 1990–1995; activist in Tibetan human rights groups, including The Committee of 100 for Tibet and the Dalai Lama Foundation, a foundation for peace and ethics; teacher of courses on Tibet, Stanford University He's quite aware of the positive effect he has on people. But at the same time, he's aware that it doesn't necessarily affect everyone—there's an aspect that, maybe, applies in almost all realms of his activities or his life—it could be a very Tibetan Buddhist kind of characteristic—that he's developed or acquired, that you accept all the realities of what's out there, which means that you do your best on all accounts, and you can be quite sure that the reaction, or the results, should be according to the good effort you put in, but that not necessarily everything will turn out the way you want. There will always be a disappointment or something that didn't work out. He's always conscious of that, so whenever he's dealing with people, he knows that if he says the right thing, does the right thing, it will have a positive result. But he is almost always aware that every now and then, or in many cases, the result won't be as one hoped for.

Tsering Shakya Dalai Lamas are made aware very early that they are different. And once you are brought up in that situation, either of two things happens: you collapse, you break down, you just can't cope with it; or you engage with it and you develop. And Dalai Lamas have been able to do that; they engage and accept this authority and are able to function. Psychologically, I cannot explain why some leaders can function and cope with it and why some cannot.

With this Dalai Lama, it goes back to very early socialization. From the very young age of five, he has been socialized in a totally different situation where he was introduced to grandeur, the charismatic quality of leadership, that because of the aura surrounding him, you are made to feel special. You have known from a very young age that you are different from everybody else, including your brothers and your sisters. You are that *Presence*. So that naturally emerges out of how you have been raised. However, in trying to socialize like that, trying to be so often with the people—a prince can never be an ordinary person; he knows from the moment he is born that he is different—you exude confidence and charismatic authority.

Dr. Piet Hut   If you compare the Dalai Lama and the Pope, the Pope achieves *his* position at a relatively old age, after a lifetime of moving through the ranks in a competitive process. The Pope gets chosen at age sixty or more; the Dalai Lama received tenure at age three. And if you get tenure at that age, you know that you don't have to spend your energy in competing; you are already at the top. This means that you can spend all of your time on fulfilling your responsibilities and trying to make the world a better place without any threat to your position. With all due respect to democracy, if the Dalai Lama had been chosen by election or had come up through the ranks, he would never have had the wall of stability around him that has enabled him to branch out in all directions.

Orville Schell   How do you approach him as an ordinary human being? My view may be somewhat idiosyncratic. The problem in interacting with him is that it's never *him*; it's always the other person who is thrown into some state—either very ritualistic or very reverential, somewhat like the "deer in the headlights" syndrome. The irony is that he is so human and unpretentious, but people in his presence, unless they know him, tend to become starstruck, ecclesiastically. It must be very difficult for him because he is struggling with a barrier that is thrown up between him and other people that is hard to transcend, despite his Herculean efforts.

Annette Lantos   He is the same now as he was then [in 1987]—full of smiles and good-will and love. He is a very accessible person; he establishes relations with *everybody*. He shakes your hand and bows and when he looks at you, you have the feeling that he can see into the depths of your soul. After you speak to him you have the feeling that you have known him all your life. The sense of love and peace that emanates from him is something that one rarely encounters on this earth.

Given the Fourteenth Dalai Lama's Achievements, Will His
Successor Be Able to Have a Positive Impact upon People?

Dr. Howard Cutler   A new Dalai Lama would not go through the crucible that so affected His Holiness. People are not going to listen to a
young kid the way they listen to *this* Dalai Lama.

Dr. Tenzin Tethong   I don't think he's setting up a benchmark to make
it difficult for the next Dalai Lama. My sense is I don't think he's thinking
that way at all; he is simply doing what he can do under the circumstances
he's facing and he's also taking advantage of every occasion to do something good for the Tibetan people, or for the enlightenment of everyone.
He's making his own personal contribution to better understanding
between people.

His interest is in interreligious dialogue, in trying to have substantial
discussion between science and spirituality. Also, in a strange way, he's trying to say that even scientists should not be closed-minded. Usually we
take it the other way around—scientists as being inquiring and open-
minded and others being less open-minded—but in the present context,
he's also challenging scientists who are very rigid in being totally material-
ist, to say that they should be more open to what the human mind is capable of beyond just the physical aspects of body and mind.

Did the Dalai Lama Define His Role, or
Did the Institution Define the Man?

Dr. Alexander Berzin, convert to Buddhism; author; teacher; lecturer;
founding member, Translation Bureau of the Library of Tibetan
Works   His Holiness takes his position very, very seriously, as the one
person who all the Tibetans look up to and who really shoulders the
responsibility for trying to help the Tibetan situation and the Tibetan
people. Now, cause and effect—which one comes first—did he say, "Okay,
I'll do it," or is this something that he felt naturally and then took the
role? You can't really say that with His Holiness because he's taken
this role since he was four years old. How much he really realized the
responsibility that he has certainly came as a young teenager, when he had
to deal with the Chinese. So I think it's a more organic, natural thing with
His Holiness.

Lama Surya Das   He is who he is supposed to be—the multidimensional Buddha of love and compassion in human form. He is definitely a human being, and a Buddhist would never claim he's anything else. We are all equal, but some are more equal than others. He's also extremely well trained; he's been a monk for fifty-five to sixty years. That is an incredible background, the best that the whole country could offer in the country that specialized in this. Also, he's had to step up in many ways. He's been challenged: he's been thrust into world events at such an early age; he's had to bear down with all his capacities and develop all his potential. I think he's the real deal.

Dr. Ronald B. Sobel   There are great, great talents in the world who are never fulfilled because the circumstances don't allow for it, or don't encourage it. So it was a happy circumstance that those who were responsible for designating the Fourteenth Dalai Lama chose this little infant. Would it have been different if it had been someone else? I don't know. Would the history of the United States have been different if John Kennedy did not have to go to Texas that November to mend political fences within the Democratic Party of the state of Texas? The *what ifs*. But what can be answered, I think, very definitively, is, given the history of the second half of the twentieth century, it was divinely fortuitous that the Fourteenth Dalai Lama is who he is.

Sir Malcolm Rifkind   There are two things. First of all, he became a global figure in the 1950s, and that was the beginning of the world communication revolution. What we have seen in the last fifty years is that people who might otherwise have been hardly known outside their country, or their own people, can through television, through newspapers, through other media, become global icons.

Because the Dalai Lama was chosen as a very, very small child to be the new Dalai Lama, then in a sense he is in the same position as the son of a reigning king or a reigning emperor—in other words, he's been brought up since childhood to positions of authority and leadership. And, therefore, if that happens by good fortune to combine with natural qualities, you get a very powerful consequence. Probably as far back as he can recollect, he knew he had a position of leadership for his people. That puts him in the same position as any king or emperor in the world today, or at any other time. Sometimes people just don't have the personal qualities to use these to their best advantage. But sometimes they do. And when they do, then the results can be quite remarkable.

Patrick French   When the Dalai Lama was young, there were a hundred and one different rituals around him, different regulations about how people could behave when they were in his presence—people, for example, weren't allowed to leave the room by turning their back on him, so they'd have to crouch and shuffle in reverse—and the Dalai Lama tried to stop that. But there is something so deeply instilled within Tibetans that they can never fully accept that. So no Tibetan can have an equal relationship with the Dalai Lama. What's interesting is that he tends to be quite different around Tibetans than he is around Westerners, so the laughing, fun Dalai Lama, roaring with laughter with his very distinctive laugh, that's something you don't see very much when he's around Tibetans. It's almost like he knows that he can have a certain effect on Westerners, and so he plays up to that a bit. I think he likes the informality of Westerners; you could ask him direct questions that a Tibetan would never ask and he enjoys that. But it's only one, perhaps relatively superficial, aspect of him. It's hard to know whether it's coming from him or whether it's coming from the people around him.

Harry Wu   We have a very old, traditional question: Does the history make the hero or does the hero make the history? My view is both. The historical opportunity is offered to many people. If you don't have the character, you don't have the capacity, sorry, you've missed it. But, the other way, if there's no historical opportunity, even if you have such a huge character, or personality, you cannot do it. In your life, in my life, all the time there are all kinds of opportunities. But you have to make a choice, make a decision: which one is important? His Holiness the Dalai Lama is very special. I sometimes say: "This damn guy is damn wonderful!"

The Dalai Lama's Quickness of Mind

Mickey Lemle   When I pitched the idea of making a movie about him, he listened and then said, "Do you think this is a worthwhile undertaking?" I replied, "Your Holiness, if I didn't think so, I wouldn't spend my time doing it." And he said to me, "That's a very American way of looking at it." It wasn't until I had spent years with Tibetan Buddhists that I realized that to them, the most important aspect of any act that you take is: "What is your motivation?" I was with the Dalai Lama once and he remarked, "If you are going to go on a peace march and have anger in your heart, stay home." So what he was really asking me was what my motivation was in wanting to make the movie. I missed it completely.

Richard Gere   We very quickly got through the greetings and I offered a *katak*, and quite quickly he started to speak in Tibetan with Ngari Rinpoché. He'd been asking questions about me in Tibetan, then started speaking in English to me, and he said, "I understand from my brother that you are an actor." I said, "Yes, that's true." He thought for a second and said, "Well, would you mind telling me something? When you do this acting and you're laughing or crying, or whatever your emotions may be, is that *real*?" I kind of fell back on an "actorish" response to that and I said, "Well, of course, when they're as real as possible, the performance is more effective." And he said, "So they're *real*." And I said, "Well, I *think* so."

Then he looked me very deeply in the eye and just started laughing hysterically. The simplicity of that encounter has stayed very clearly with me for several reasons. One was his ability to very quickly hit to the core of who I was. He used my profession and the focus of who I was at that time, an actor, to teach a spiritual lesson that was quite subtle, that, in fact, emotions are not real. Even though I was conjuring up emotions, I had a belief in them and, like we do in everyday life, we have a myriad of emotions and we tend to believe they're real and definitive and come from their own side. But, in fact, they're just a magician's trick, just like an actor does in conjuring up an emotion.

He was able, by asking his brother two simple questions about me, to cut to the gist of how he could discuss something with me that was meaningful and *have* it be meaningful. So this encounter, although it appeared quite simple in the way we were conversing with each other, in fact cut to the quick to a very genuine spiritual issue for all of us.

Father Laurence Freeman   When he agreed to do the [Good Heart] seminar I was delighted, and then we needed to talk about how he was going to approach it—it was a three-day event at which he was the sole speaker—so I went to see him. I had this idea that rather than him just speaking on his usual themes that we would give him more of a challenge and ask him to comment on the Gospels. He looked a little surprised at that approach; he said, "Well I don't know much about the Gospels; I don't know anything about the Gospels, really." So I said, "Well, I would help you to contextualize them and you would just comment on them as a religious feature." And so he said, "Okay!" That captured his capacity for quickness of mind and his intuition, his very clear mind and his good judgment. It was quite a risky thing to agree to and do. It wasn't impetuous, but it was spontaneous—spontaneity with wisdom, which is a rare gift—and that's a definite part of his character.

Mickey Lemle   I was with him some years ago when he received an honorary degree from Columbia University. In his address after the investiture, he said, "I really *like* these honorary degrees because I receive them but didn't have to work for them." He never misses a chance for a dharma teaching, so he looked around at this august group of academics and said, "When I come to Western institutions of higher learning, I am concerned because a trained mind without a trained heart is dangerous, and the issue is: where in our educational systems is *compassion* taught?"

Richard Gere   We still have a running argument about my photographs. I have a photographic book. The first time he saw my photographs, they were in a museum in Houston. It was my first museum show, and I was quite proud of them. The photographs I like that I've taken tend to be a bit expressionistic—they're not straightforward, in-focus, portrait kinds of shots; they're a bit soft-focus sometimes and they blur out, they grain up quite a bit—not straightforward photographs in any sense of the word.

His Holiness saw them and politely pulled me to the side—there's press all around—and he said, "These are very poor quality." Of course I was terribly shocked by that because I was so proud of them. But, for whatever reason, that wasn't his idea of a photograph, and for the last fifteen years, his comment about the poor quality of my photographs has come up *continually*. He *never* lets me off the hook.

His Interests

Annie Warner   He has a keen interest in the Discovery Channel. At Harvard in 2003 he was asked to name his favorite television show and replied that he liked watching animals in their natural habitats.

Rinchen Dharlo   He likes to watch *National Geographic*—the animals, the different species. And he reads magazines about arms and ammunition, different types of planes. When we fly, he immediately knows how many engines the type of plane that he is flying in has; he knows almost all the details, the number of seats and everything. When he was young, he read a lot of magazines on different subjects. And his memory—once he reads, it stays there—he's like a computer.

I really don't think he's tried to learn computers. He's getting older; his interest in mechanics and engineering was when he was young. Sometimes he tries to do that. I remember in 'eighty-eight he was staying in a hotel and the air conditioner did not work properly. He wanted the room to be cold. I entered and I tried to open the air-conditioning and he said, "Don't do it. If there was something wrong I would have already fixed it; I've already done what you have done. You'd better call the mechanic." If there's a problem, he will try to fix it himself. Ten years ago, he still used to repair watches, clocks. But these days I don't think he does that. And he loves gardening very much. He's very well-rounded.

T. C. Tethong   When His Holiness returns to Dharamsala from a trip abroad, the cabinet must receive him. We would go up to his residence before he arrived to await the motorcade. One day, as I waited in the residence, I saw His Holiness's study room and on his desk were some Tibetan books that were open to specific pages. On the side of the desk were some gardening tools, and underneath I saw plant food and fertilizer.

Professor Robert Thurman   Some years ago, I was with the Dalai Lama in Costa Rica. We went out to the countryside and he was wearing this kind of goofy, floppy hat and he found a plant that was the same as one he had in Dharamsala. A photo was taken of him holding a leaf of the plant and looking very pleased. He said to me, "Next life I'm going to be a naturalist."

Richard Gere   Henry Luce [III] asked him at a lunch that I had put together, "What do you do for *fun?*"—I was kind of shocked that he asked him something like that—and His Holiness said, "Well, you know, I have my garden and birds and my animals" and he left it at that. It was a truthful answer; he likes puttering in his garden and taking care of his birds and the dogs. But I remember once seeing a picture of him in a horse carriage in Lapland, going across the tundra, laughing hysterically. I asked him about it later and he said, "I was having *such fun!*" I had never heard him say that before.

Orville Schell   He likes to putter with his clocks. He meditates; he has an inner group of people with whom he can be frank. Yet his life is limited in many ways. He doesn't have a wife and children; he has given that up for something else—something he takes very seriously and has kept true to.

Cutting-Edge Science

Dr. Thubten Jinpa Langri   Initially, his interest in science grew out of a natural curiosity and as someone who had access to mechanical objects that had belonged to the Thirteenth Dalai Lama. Also, his educational training was monastic in nature and included a good deal of debate. That is quite conducive to a scientific mode of thinking and analysis. His Holiness's interest took a deeper turn when the tremendous influence of science and technology dawned upon him, particularly the modern world's understanding of the nature of reality. And from his earliest trips to Europe and America, he was able to establish personal friendships with some major figures in the scientific world.

Adam Engle   I had heard a rumor in 1983 that he was interested in meeting scientists, and I thought this was an extraordinary rumor. If it was true, I thought I might actually get to meet him. After a year, I made contact with Tenzin Choegyal, his youngest brother, at a teaching mission the Dalai Lama was giving in Los Angeles in the fall of 1984, and through his intervention, I got the authorization to go forward to set up a meeting. When we met, I wanted to see whether he was still interested in meeting with scientists, what his motivation was, and how I could fulfill his wishes and goals.

Professor Paul Davies, professor of natural philosophy, Australian Centre for Astrobiology, Macquarie University, Sydney, Australia; author; winner, Templeton Prize, 1995   My first meeting [with the Dalai Lama] was at a conference organized by the company IBM; they ran annual conferences for their executives for a bit of relaxation and refreshment. These were weekend conferences that contained a somewhat eclectic mix of speakers, and they liked to have overarching themes of a challenging nature. On that particular occasion, the theme was "The Nature of Time," and the Dalai Lama and I gave back-to-back lectures: I spoke about "Time in Science" and he spoke about "Time in Eastern Philosophy." This was a rather unusual conjuncture because I spoke in the manner of a science popularizer, using an overhead projector, a lot of humor, and a few equations and diagrams. He spoke in Tibetan, which was, of course, translated, and his delivery was measured and very dignified, so we made a somewhat peculiar couple. At the conclusion of this double address, there was a recess. We went outside and the Dalai Lama took my hand—I remember this very well—and one or two of his devotees came out, prostrated themselves in front of us, and offered him flowers. This, of course, for a humble scientist was a rather bizarre experience. And then, after a few moments of that, we ended up sitting side by side at a table of the sort that authors sit behind to sign books and we took questions from various members of the audience, and then it was a more conventional arrangement.

It was very courageous of the Dalai Lama to come to a conference of this sort, which is primarily a scientific one, and to basically present his ideas to an audience that probably, although open-minded, would have been fairly hard-headed science-and-technical people from the computing industry.

My impression was that this was a man who was continually doing a balancing act between two somewhat conflicting roles. On the one hand, he is clearly an extremely nice individual who has diverse interests and, you imagine, would like to get closely involved in a number of things. But on the other hand, he represents his country, or what's left of it, or a particular political movement, and so he's always looking over his shoulder to be politically correct. And that's a very uneasy combination of roles to undertake. My impression was also that, in some ways, he rather resembles Prince Charles, who has to do a similar sort of thing. He's got diverse interests and would probably like to spend much more time in a lab or something, talking to scientists, but the dictates of his office mean that he has to balance that against lots of other things.

Adam Engle   He has a multifaceted interest in science. On a personal level, he is extremely interested in the workings of the mind and the nature of reality. He has always been interested in gadgets. In a way, he has a scientific mind; he wants to know how things work, so it is theoretical but it is also practical.

He has said that if science has disproved something that is inconsistent with Buddhism, then Buddhism has to change. He is very aware of the fact that in today's world, if Buddhism is taking positions that are unscientific, it loses credibility and relevance. So in his role as a spiritual leader, he is very interested in keeping Buddhism updated according to what science has proven and understands. He is not threatened by science *at all*.

One of his passionate initiatives is in the field of what he calls "secular ethics; ethics for the new millennium." He believes that it is great for people who have some kind of religious training to follow that training, but there are billions of people on the face of the earth who are not interested in standard religions. What can be provided for them, to help them to get through their lives in a happier, healthier, more peaceful, and successful way? He feels that Buddhism might have developed tools and techniques to help people to improve their lives. What he has done is to challenge science to take these techniques and test them in Western labs, and then, if they are proven to be effective in some significant way, to find ways to teach them in a secular environment, outside of Buddhism.

Dr. Piet Hut   To my knowledge, the other participants in the dialogue did not have a background in Tibetan Buddhism. My impression was that they went to Dharamsala with the idea of having an interesting cultural experience. They wanted to share *their* knowledge and were curious about what they would hear from the other side. As the discussions developed, they were quite surprised to find somebody who was so much on an equal level as an intellectual, in the way of debating, arguing, and discussing. They had expected to find somebody who was more focused on cultural and religious issues.

Mickey Lemle   His twenty-three-year course of study that eventuated in his receiving the equivalent of a Doctor of Philosophy degree included history, science, language, poetry, and astronomy. He is a great believer in science and is fascinated by it. He understands all of the cutting-edge brain research. I once attended a Mind and Body meeting where a couple of the participants tried to simplify their language, speaking to him as if he were a fifth grader. This was a miscalculation on their part.

Professor Robert Thurman   I am bothered that in some documentaries and books the Dalai Lama has been portrayed as a person who is a very cute and quaint figure, a *super saint*. Actually, he is a tremendous intellectual. His dialogues with scientists have been helpful in this respect, although if you study those dialogues, he is listening more to the Westerners than they are to him. It is like they are giving him Physics 101 and psychology lessons and telling him all the neat things they are doing in their labs and he is going: gee, aah.

The scientists assume that they are the great intellectuals but they don't understand what the Tibetan intellect and the ancient Indian philosophical, scientific, and psychological intellect is like. It is my work, and my students' work, to make it clear to people that in the Indo-Tibetan sphere you have twenty Freuds, ten Wittgensteins, and Buddha himself is a kind of mega Plato or Socrates—that you are talking to intellectual peers here; you are not just talking to some natives who were conquered and, therefore, were inferior. They were conquered because they were superior.

Dr. Jeffrey Hopkins, author; translator and former chief English language interpreter to the Fourteenth Dalai Lama; professor of religious studies, University of Virginia My impression is that it's something that he went out on, on his own. There's no question about it. I think it comes from a quest for truth and an application of Buddhist doctrines of compassion, and via the truth, his interest in astronomy and his total lack of interest in Tibetan astrology, which is a break with tradition. It was quite a shock to people, but here were these astronomers, telling us things about the universe that were different than what was said in Buddhist texts, and he wanted to pursue what was being said because it was done on the basis of experimental observation. And so his interest in the truth means he doesn't just want to mouth an old tradition, but he also is very wise about not giving up old traditions that have not been shown definitively to be wrong. So I think that in part explains some of his interest in science.

On the other side, he has seen that Tibetan culture, particularly with regard to medicine and deeper states of mind function, has something to offer international science. So his interest then leads to dialogue. Then, in terms of compassion, this has compelled him to notice, to register, to appreciate that other religions and systems speak of many of the same goals that Buddhism does and have very positive results for people who practice them. Thus, he has sought to set aside an overemphasis on differences in philosophies for the sake of recognizing similarities of effect on the personality. And I know that he has worked very hard to work up a message based on Buddhist principles that appeals, as he says, not just to Buddhists or people who believe in religion, but to all people. And if one knows Buddhism, one can see how these principles come from Buddhism but are not tied to it. This has become his message to the world, and the world has responded very, very favorably.

Professor Paul Davies [re the Dalai Lama's interest in astronomy] On the first occasion a lot of my discussion about the nature of time was on the subject of the origin of time, the Big Bang, the theory of relativity. He did, in his address that came after mine, address the issue of the Big Bang cosmology and he gave a way of trying to incorporate that into his existing thinking about the nature of the universe. In Buddhism, traditionally the universe is cyclic and eternal, and this seems to be decisively opposed to the Judeo-Christian-Islamic traditions of a linear time, with an origin at some particular moment and the universe coming into existence because of a creation event. The scientific worldview, which took that onboard, basically proceeds from that assumption—that time is linear and that the universe evolved in a directional manner.

These two things seem to be in direct conflict with Eastern thought, generally, and Buddhism seems to be the opposite from the monotheistic, Western, and scientific tradition. Therefore, you'd think it would be interesting to probe those differences in a discussion with the Dalai Lama. I felt he was trying to reach a compromise by showing us that maybe Eastern thought could accommodate something like the Big Bang, being as the scientific evidence is so strongly in favor of it. But it was never possible to go beyond his rather superficial remarks on that.

At the end of the day, it's going to be observations that will balance. And so the difficulty for a spiritual leader like the Dalai Lama is that he has to uphold a certain spiritual and philosophical tradition, and he's not really free to just change his mind if the latest evidence shows that he got it wrong the first time around, whereas scientists have to do that. They have to say, "I've considered all the evidence and I favor Theory X." Then along comes a new observation, and he has to say, "Well, I guess X is no longer tenable so I'll throw my weight behind Y." But religious traditions can't do that quite so easily, and that makes the path of science and religion perilous from the religious side; it doesn't affect scientists because they can fiddle around. But some people, like the Pope, have to consider very, very carefully before they decide to take a position on a certain scientific issue in case the wind changes. Then they've got to do a U-turn, and that doesn't look very good for a religious leader.

Does He Consider That He Is Still Learning?

Mickey Lemle   After I had spent some time interviewing him for my film, I asked His Holiness, "Who around you can tell you when you've made a mistake?" He replied, "Everybody. I don't like hearing it, but how else am I going to grow?"

Rinchen Dharlo   He is a very good student; he is such a great scholar. His name, "Ocean of Wisdom," is so fitting for him. He's sixty-nine years old and has studied for sixty-four years—every day he studied, and he still studies, and he still receives teachings from different Buddhist traditions. He receives oral transmissions and reads textbooks every day, not only from Buddhist traditions but also learns from other religious traditions. Whenever he meets someone, he tries to learn. I've seen him, like in 'ninety-four, when he spent five days in Gethsemani, Thomas Merton's [1915–1968, American-Christian religious figure and author] monastery in Kentucky, and every day he met priests from that monastery as well as other Christian leaders who were attending the conference. After coming back from that monastery, I saw him speaking to other people, asking them to try to learn from the Christian traditions. He always asks the Tibetan people to learn from Christian traditions like charity and social service, and he admires the Christian ministries and the way Christian brothers and sisters meet. He was so impressed and has already started bringing some changes within the Tibetan monasteries.

Father Laurence Freeman   He does have limited knowledge of Christian theology. I think he's picked up a lot; I don't think he has studied it in a coordinated way. He said to me at the end of the seminar that he had learned more about Christianity through that experience than he had since his meeting with Thomas Merton back in the sixties. He had a few very powerful meetings with Merton during Merton's visit, which Merton describes, and that again gave him some new insights. The Christians were struck by his sense of reverence and the depth of his insight into them; the Buddhists, many of them Western Buddhists, were surprised to see that respect, and also to see the depth of meaning in texts that had been very familiar to them, probably in their childhood, that they hadn't explored before.

   I think he liked the risk of it too. As we walked out—I was showing him to the stage for the first time—I suddenly realized what a kind of a "knife edge" he was. I think he enjoyed that challenge, the intellectual and the personal. And his curiosity was genuinely aroused about the meanings of questions that came up through the Gospels. He would sometimes turn to me as I was sitting next to him on the stage. In the beginning, the early texts we chose were very obvious: Jesus' teaching on non-violence. As we went further through the seminar, we ended up at the Resurrection, and he had some very insightful things to say about the Resurrection. He said, "This is a unique feature of Christianity"; he recognized that it wasn't rebirth, it wasn't reincarnation. And he said, "Tell me about the Resurrection." It's a difficult concept for most Christians to express also, so I don't know how much he conceptualized it, but I think his insight is very deep and clear.

And he loves to compare; he seeks out contrasting ideas. There are times when in subsequent occasions I've been in dialogue with him and you feel this sort of common search for truth going on; you're looking at the wisdom contained in two different texts, or two different approaches, such as Resurrection and rebirth. He keeps probing and questioning, and then, when you've reached the limit of that particular foray into the truth, the common ground, he makes a joke, or he laughs—humor then takes you into the next stage of the conversation.

Orville Schell   His Holiness is basically a curious and very open man. How he got to be that way is hard to say. Perhaps his experiences with someone like Heinrich Harrer did have a profound effect. But, actually, he had no other place to go. He could either have become an isolated religious recluse, or he could have chosen to confront the world; ever since he was a little boy, he was interested in the world. Then, when he was thrust out into the world, he embraced it. That speaks of some very unusual qualities. The Dalai Lama has truly changed without compromising or betraying his original principles. Yet he has allowed himself to be influenced by the outside world.

Professor Robert Thurman   Once Carl Sagan asked him what he would do if an airtight experiment disproved reincarnation. The Dalai Lama thought for a moment and said, "Well, I would cease to believe in it!"

Mickey Lemle   I attended a conference in Davos, Switzerland, where a woman asked every speaker, "What do you think is going to happen in the world fifty years from now?" After His Holiness addressed the audience, this lady asked him what *he* thought was going to happen in the world fifty years from now. He was silent for a few moments and then said, "Madame, I don't have any idea. I don't know what kind of tea I will have with my dinner tonight, so how am I supposed to know what is going to happen in the world fifty years from now?" and he just *laughed*. I thought to myself: when was the last time I heard a political or religious leader acknowledge that he didn't know something?

Chapter Two

GLIMPSES OF THE *PRIVATE* DALAI LAMA: HIS CHARACTER AND PERSONALITY

The line between the public and private behavior of the Dalai Lama is often blurred as he fulfills his dual responsibility as both spiritual and temporal leader of the Tibetan people. There are many occasions, however, when His Holiness has the opportunity to share private moments with those with whom he interacts in his very public role. Many of these exchanges are punctuated by his quick wit and irreverent, sometimes seemingly childlike sense of humor.

Rt. Rev. William E. Swing, Episcopal Bishop of California, 1980–; president and founding trustee, United Religions Initiative   We went to the Palace of the Armenian Patriarch, where we all had our picture taken. The Dalai Lama was just silly; he would poke a finger in your rib while the photo was being taken.

Dr. Thubten Jinpa Langri   He has this deeply childlike quality to him. He is quite spontaneous and very unpredictable: he will be thinking about something and, all of a sudden, he will break into laughter. He has an amazing sense of humor. There is a combination of the ability to focus very intently along with a lightheartedness. That is a real gift.

Mickey Lemle   What is remarkable is how funny he is; he is almost surprising in his humor. He laughs a lot. There is something about the tension between the darkness of what is happening in Tibet and the lightness of his being, and it is not frivolous—he gets it all—but he doesn't let it weigh him down. So there is a lightness and, at the same time, a profundity. When he was at the Fleet Center in Boston, in September 2003, he told the audience, "I am just a simple human being. If you came here to see the Dalai Lama expecting to have a spiritual experience, you are going to be disappointed. Those people who have come for a healing are going to be disappointed. I don't know about healers. If they really work, how come they can't do something about my knee?"

Professor Jonathan Mirsky   Before I was married, I took a girlfriend of mine and her two children to see him when he was here in London on one of his trips. I introduced them to him, and he said to the two children, who were paralyzed by meeting him, "Oooh, your father is a very great man." And I said, "Your Holiness, their father is indeed a very great man but he's not *here*." And he said, "Oooh, well," pointing at me, "he, too, is a very great man!"

He was at Yale to get an honorary degree and he was going to stay in Jonathan Edwards College, so the master of that college asked me if I would like to come down—I was a visiting professor at Dartmouth then— so I went down there and the day before the Dalai Lama arrived, or maybe on the telephone, the master said to me, "We'd like to give him a present, something special. What does he like?" I said, "Well, the Dalai Lama's hobby is fixing watches, so you might give him a very good set of jeweler's tools." He said, "That's a very good idea; there's a very high-class jeweler here in New Haven; we'll get him to make up some tools and then we'd like to give him a more Yalelike present." I said, "Give him a Yale scarf; he'd like that; he likes scarves." So the Dalai Lama arrives— Richard Gere was there then too. Then there was this ceremony. The Dalai Lama came out and he was wearing the Yale scarf around his neck. I was sitting in the audience, in the first or second row, and when he saw me, he did a little dance—kind of a boogie, kind of a hula with his hips— and he held the scarf in both hands, out as far as he could hold it. There was a journalist sitting next to me and he said, "What's that?" and I said, "Oh, it's a kind of ritual dance that he does with that scarf." And I saw that the next day in the paper; it said that " . . . when the Dalai Lama came off the stage, he saluted the audience by doing a Tibetan ritual dance with a scarf." Actually, he was just being playful.

Father Laurence Freeman   In Florence, we went to the Palazzo Vecchio where he was given the Citizenship of the City. All the buglers and trumpeters were in their costumes, and as we got out of the car, he walked up and started fooling around with the hat of one of the trumpeters. That was spontaneous. He's relaxed about that; he doesn't put on pretense. I arranged a meeting for him with the cardinal of Florence—they spent about fifteen minutes together. I knew the cardinal was a very open, very sympathetic character. We had the meeting in my room in the monastery in Florence. It took a few moments before the conversation got going, and the Dalai Lama was kind of waiting, and then he gave a big yawn and the cardinal was amused.

It's very genuine; he relaxes in that way, but I don't think he loses control. It's not like some people in public positions of responsibility where they have to go through a lot of ceremonies, and when it's all over they sort of . . . [Father Freeman making a sighing noise] because they've really been playing a role and so there's a release. But from what I know of him, that is what he does. The discipline that he has is primarily in his own spiritual practice—he prays four hours every morning; he doesn't do things in the evening; he will never go to a dinner, or give a talk late at night, after six or seven o'clock—so he carries his monastery with him in that sense: he's a monk, like an abbot on a big scale; he carries a lot of responsibilities, a lot of confidences, and a lot of projection.

Professor Jonathan Mirsky   I got beaten up in Tiananmen Square in 1989 and I was supposed to see him here in London, but I was so beaten up that I couldn't go to see him. His secretary came round to me with a letter from him and described to me what the Dalai Lama felt. He said, "His Holiness is very sorry he can't see you, he's very sorry that you were beaten up and, in particular, he said he thinks it was very unfair." Then the secretary patted himself on top of his head—I don't have a lot of hair on top of my head and the Dalai Lama certainly doesn't—"And he said it was particularly unfair in your case because, like him, you are undefended *on top.*" He meets you where you are. I was joking with him once in the back of a car and we were pinching and poking each other. He turned to his secretary, then pointed at me and said, "Sometimes very spiritual; sometimes very silly."

His Insights

Mickey Lemle   At Central Park [in 2003] he told the crowd that he had recently been at a peace rally where small white birds had been released into the air. "That is not how you get peace," he said. "You get peace by transforming the individual human heart. Letting these birds go is just an empty gesture. All it does is to agitate them."

Annette Lantos   If I have ever seen a leader I could trust implicitly, it would be the Dalai Lama. I can understand why people have complete trust in him. He is a *presence*—a man who symbolizes that which is the best in all of us. There is the power of his innocence, purity, and lack of ego. He has awakened to the truth in himself—something we are seeking for *ourselves*. He has a lack of guile; given his background, his humility is amazing. This takes a highly evolved, very old soul.

His Modesty

Rabbi Irving "Yitz" Greenberg, president, Jewish Life Network; founding president, National Jewish Center for Learning and Leadership (CLAL); participant in Jewish-Buddhist dialogue with His Holiness the Dalai Lama, Washington, New Jersey, 1988, and Dharamsala, India, 1990   Others do look up to him, and I'm sure back in Tibet the worship was pretty close to what we would call "My God." For the most part [in dialogue with a Jewish group in Dharamsala], they did not speak in his presence; they basically deferred to him and certainly treated him as a being of a very special order and kind. What is most impressive is that he didn't get to believe his own impressiveness; he was totally unspoiled—human, as he was in this case and in other cases, with respect and sensitivity.

Rinchen Dharlo   He always looks at other people as human beings. He says, "It's always easier for me to communicate when I think of myself as a human being and think of the other person as a human being—not as an American, not as a Tibetan, not as a scholar, not as a politician. So when you meet some other person, always speak as a human being." And that makes him comfortable. With the previous Dalai Lamas, because of all those formalities sometimes, even though they wanted to walk down and be with other people, there were certain procedures.

Annie Warner   He is so humble and down-to-earth that if someone comes in doing the full prostration or is crying or wailing, he always says, "Oh no, no. Please stop," and he puts his arm around the person and tries to make them realize that he doesn't demand being put on a pedestal. He tries to bring the person to *his* level and converse as friends and make them feel at ease. He always tries to reach out to people.

Dr. Ronald B. Sobel   Everyone who was coming to hear His Holiness [at Temple Emanu-El in 1998] used the Fifth Avenue doors to the temple, and that's where all the security apparatus was going on. In order to enhance the security, it was arranged by the police authorities that His Holiness would arrive on Sixty-sixth Street and enter through our religious school building. It was, of course, protocol for me then as the temple's senior rabbi to be waiting at the entrance for his car and the other members of the entourage and I was in my assigned place. The car drove up, out he stepped, and I stepped forward to greet him. Before I could even extend my hand in greeting, he bowed to me. I was not quite taken *aback*, but all of that humility that I had felt sitting in the back of the room I was now experiencing one-on-one. I welcomed him; he indicated how pleased he was to meet me and to be in this great Jewish house of worship that he'd heard so much about, and we were about to go through the door when I made the gesture indicating that he should precede me. He indicated, no, that he wanted me to go before he would enter, and I kept insisting that I follow him. He grabbed my arm and I was startled: this spiritual figure had a grip that was so strong. He didn't hurt me, but he grabbed my arm and made it very clear at that moment that I didn't have a *choice* and I was going in before him; he was in *absolute* command. We were standing on the street and I wasn't about to argue, so I walked in half a step ahead of him.

We gathered in what is called the Rabbi's Robing Room. There were several other luminaries present in that room, and it was a fascinating forty-five minutes of waiting. There, Richard Gere, this great actor, was sitting on the floor—the Rabbi's Robing Room isn't all that large a space and the room was kind of crowded; there weren't enough chairs—and this great, world-famous actor is sitting cross-legged on the floor, at the feet of His Holiness the Dalai Lama. The conversation was about some events that had taken place earlier that day here in New York, and whoever came into the room—even if it was the photographer—the way in which the Dalai Lama greeted and responded, the genuineness of that soul and the purity of that heart, was absolutely extraordinary.

Adam Engle   According to Tibetan Buddhist tradition, he is the reincarnation of previous Dalai Lamas. If you believe that, there is an ongoing thread that could be responsible for this incredible genuineness and humility. But putting that aside, we do know that he is an incredibly bright and gifted human being. Think about it. Before he was discovered, he was an infant in Eastern Tibet, a place that is about as remote as any place on the planet. Then look at the fact that as an infant who had certain capabilities, he consciously chose when he grew up to train his mind according to the Buddhist tradition and to sidestep all of the sex games, all of the power games, and all of the money games that we are brought up to revere, and to train his mind. At each decisive point in his life, the guideline he used is: what benefits the most beings? If you do that diligently for more than sixty years, you get to be who *he* is.

Professor Jonathan Mirsky   I have interviewed him many times. In about 1981 or 1982, I interviewed him in the Dean's Residence at Westminster Cathedral [a Catholic house of worship in London]. He hadn't been in England much and he had a very attentive entourage that wanted him to be treated in an extremely deferential way. He wasn't like that. I had with me from *The Observer* a very famous woman photographer, Jane Bown, and she wanted the Dalai Lama to turn his head in a certain way. She put her hand on his head, which, according to Tibetan custom, is absolutely forbidden. The entourage all went rigid, but he just waved them away and said, "No, Let Mrs. Bown do her work" so I thought he was modest and straightforward.

He has always been the same, and we always hug each other when we see each other, which I believe to be rather unusual. The last time I saw him, not only did we hug each other but he pinched my nose. And his secretary said, "Well, I know it's unusual that His Holiness hugs people—he doesn't do that very often—but I have never seen him *ever* pinch anyone's nose!" He did it because we like each other and he was being cute.

Dr. Howard Cutler   He came to New York after our book, *The Art of Happiness*, had been on the best-seller list for about six months. He was not aware of this, and I thought I'd better brief him in case it was mentioned to him by someone in the media. His immediate response was, "Has the book been helpful to people?" I answered, "Yes," and he asked, "In what way?" His only concern about the book was whether it had engendered any criticism from people of other faiths who thought he was proselytizing Buddhism because that was not his intention in writing the book. Then in 2003, after our book, *The Art of Happiness at Work*, was published and made the *New York Times* best-seller list, he was again in New York. As we were riding in an elevator, I told him about the listing and he looked at me and said, "That's good, right?"

Rabbi A. James Rudin, then director, Interreligious Affairs, American Jewish Committee; participant in dialogue with the Dalai Lama, November 11, 1999 He went into this big thing when I met him in the green room [before an interfaith dialogue held in Greensburg, Pennsylvania]. It was not like "Some of my best friends are Jews," but he was so glad to meet a rabbi. He was glad I was there and it was genuine. When we said good-bye, he was very warm and said that he hoped we would meet again. I was a little warmer to him at the good-bye than I was at the beginning. Not that I wasn't going to like the guy, but based on my work with the cults, I'm always dubious. I wouldn't call *him* a destructive cult leader— not at all—and his message was not about him as much as it was about what I would call simple ethics. I'd like to meet him again.

Tsunma Jampa Dolkar, née Sue Macy, Buddhist nun ordained December 19, 2002 I went to a talk by him, which was at Brandeis University. It was in a gymnasium and there were a lot of people—it was just a few months after I had met my teacher—and I remember the way he looked out at everybody: he goes, "Oh, everybody is showing me their teeth," meaning that everybody was giving him big smiles. I was sitting way in the back, but I was thinking: Wow! He's looking just at *me*! And everybody is like "Wow!" He has this kind of presence that really makes him very accessible in terms of the Buddhist teachings and being able to connect. It's impossible to be in his presence, even in a huge gymnasium, without knowing that he's a true spiritual being. It was really great.

Father Laurence Freeman I first met him in 1979, when I was a junior monk in Montreal. I had gone to Montreal with [the late] John Main [OSB, founder, World Community for Christian Meditation], my teacher, and we had started a small Benedictine community of monks and lay people dedicated to teaching Christian meditation. John Main was invited by the archbishop to welcome the Dalai Lama at an interfaith service that was being organized at the cathedral. In the build-up to the event, he had persuaded the authorities to put a period of meditation into the service. Of course, the cathedral was filled and the Dalai Lama was very warmly received, and there were speeches and prayers and singing.

Then there was a twenty-minute period of meditation, and the Dalai
Lama remarked afterward that this was the first time he had ever medi-
tated in a Christian context. I remember John Main saying to him, "Your
Holiness, we'd be very flattered if you would like to come and visit us in
our little community here in Montreal before you leave." One of the Dalai
Lama's staff was beside him and he rushed in, of course, to protect him
and said, "You know, that will be impossible." The Dalai Lama looked at
him and said, "It *will* be possible." So he came the following Sunday to join
us for our midday meditation, which was in a small house, and stayed for
lunch. The real occasion was for him and John Main to speak, so after
lunch they spent some time in conversation. The Dalai Lama and he
formed a rapport, a deep sense of recognition. And the Dalai Lama was
fascinated to meet a Christian monk who was teaching meditation along
with the Christian tradition, so they talked about that and about the
importance of meditation as a way not only of interreligious understanding, but a way of spiritual renewal for the world. He left and John Main
died a couple of years after that. Then there was no direct contact until
quite a few years later. I wrote to the Dalai Lama and reminded him that
this meeting had taken place, and I said that we had started an annual
seminar in John Main's memory and we would be honored if he led it. So
he replied immediately, to my surprise, and said that he remembered the
meeting very warmly and that he would very much like to do the seminar.
That became the next major event we did together. That was in 1994; it
was called "The Good Heart Seminar" and it was held in London.

Rinchen Dharlo   He is so unpretentious, so informal. There was a big
luncheon of world businessmen in 'eighty-nine, in New York, and he was
giving the keynote speech at that gathering. He happened to speak as the
soup was served. He was very much engaged in speaking, and somehow
his robe slipped from his shoulder and it dipped into the soup. He saw that
one part of his robe was in the soup and he picked it up and said, "Oh, how
silly! My robe just fell into my soup."

Compassion

Mickey Lemle   I first met him at a conference in Davos, Switzerland, in
1984. The venue was a ballroom in a major hotel, with about eight hundred people present in three sections of tiered seating. The wall behind
the speaker's platform was made entirely of glass and looked out upon the

Alps. There was an ageing hippie couple there who had a five-year-old child, and their concept of child care was to leave him outside to watch the Alps. The child watched them for about five minutes and noticed that they weren't moving, so he got bored and started banging on the glass door, mouthing, "Let me in! Let me in!" I was trying to focus on what the Dalai Lama was saying but was distracted by this small child. At this point, the kid's mother got up from the third section, walked directly in front of the Dalai Lama, opened the door, and the kid jumped into her arms. As she made her way back toward her seat, she again walked directly in front of the Dalai Lama. At this point, I had lost any hope for a spiritual experience. As the hippie walked by the Dalai Lama, he looked at the kid, grinned and waved, and held the kid's eye until the mother and the kid arrived back at her seat. All the time the kid was looking wide-eyed at the Dalai Lama, and I thought: *that* is compassion. I don't really remember much of what he said in his talk, but I will never forget his act of compassion to a five-year-old child who was feeling lonely.

Dr. Blu Greenberg, author; lecturer; founding president, Jewish Orthodox Feminist Alliance (JOFA); participant in Jewish-Buddhist dialogue with His Holiness the Dalai Lama, Washington, New Jersey, 1988, and Dharamsala, India, 1990   When we walked in [to the Jewish group's first encounter with the Dalai Lama at the Dharamsala dialogue], the last one to enter the room was Jonathan Ober-Man. Jonathan had been afflicted with polio when he was a child and he wore these metal braces. We were all seated and then Jonathan walked in. The Dalai Lama, once he saw Jonathan, looked for a second—he didn't know that he was going to come in with this disability—and then he jumped out of his seat to help Jonathan to his seat. It was so touching, and I thought, This is not somebody who sees himself as God on a throne; this is somebody who was raised by his mother and father to be a fine, well-mannered, considerate human being.

Mickey Lemle   He would always try to greet the refugees who escaped from Tibet. For these people, this is the highest moment of their lives. In the early 1990s, we were filming one such audience. All of a sudden, two young nuns came before him, and he asked them where they were from. They named a nunnery near Lhasa. Then he asked where they were staying and they said, "Nowhere," because they didn't have a place to stay. He said, "Don't worry. You will be taken care of." He then asked an assistant to make sure that the nuns had a place to stay. So his compassion is not for show.

With All the Violence in the World, Is He Frustrated
Because He Wishes for Love and Compassion?

Orville Schell   I have examined the way in which the Dalai Lama has deported himself in relation to China, his adversaries, and his potential enemies—the way he has dealt with his people's hardships of life and exile and the way that these hardships have, and haven't, influenced his attitudes and policies, the way he has been able to adhere to his spiritual principles and make those principles incarnate in the real world, which he has been forced to deal with.

Rinchen Dharlo   When there's a problem, he is always saying, "Look at your problem from different angles and then your problem won't depress you"—that's the kind of advice he always gives. I've seen him with people who tell him, "I'm sick, I'm affected with HIV," and he always gives them such good advice. Very often he tells them to think in a positive way, like, "If there's a cure, why not try to get the treatment? And if there's no cure, simply worrying is not going to help." He does it in a positive way, "and whatever years remain, do something good for humanity; don't think of yourself alone." And I've seen many young Tibetans completely changed. He always says, "Try to help other human beings. And if you are not in a position to help others, at least refrain from harming others." I've seen so many who say, "I don't harm them. I can't be helpful with others, but I don't harm them." I've seen many Tibetans who, when they go to the toilet and see an insect floating in the water, don't flush it. They just get something and save it—put it in the garden outside.

Father Laurence Freeman   We held a large seminar in Belfast, Northern Ireland, with him as the key figure. John Main sent a number of representatives, including Mary McAleese, the president of Ireland. His Holiness was speaking about peace as a way of unity and interreligious dialogue as a contribution to healing the wounds of division. He had public sessions as part of the seminar but he also had a parallel program; he met with young people, victims of violence, religious leaders, and political leaders. And what was remarkable was how warmly he was received, actually, by both sides—Protestants and Catholics. There were a few exceptions, but he was overwhelmingly well received. He had a rather dramatic ceremony at what they call the "Peace Wall"—it's actually a wall of fear that divides the Protestants and Catholics—and he walked through that; there was a Catholic priest from the area and a Protestant clergyman from the other side. He went through the wall and then held the hands of the two clergymen. He was very humble. He said to people, "I really don't understand what all this fighting is about—why Protestants and Catholics—I don't see that there is such a difference." Politically, it was a very complex situation; historically, he didn't have background knowledge of it. But his personal directness and truthfulness won people over and enabled people from different sides to look at each other differently through him. That was very evident when he came to the meeting with victims of violence.

Is the Dalai Lama Aware of His Great Celebrity?

Orville Schell   He is *painfully* aware of his celebrity.

Rinchen Dharlo   He should be but he doesn't care. He's so informal; he always says, "Even in my dreams, I feel I'm just a Buddhist monk; I don't dream that I'm the Dalai Lama. I'm a Buddhist monk." That's the way he looks at himself. Always, if he happens to meet another religious person, be it another Buddhist monk or a Christian father or brother or a rabbi, he will go down to greet them; you won't find that with other famous religious people. There's a great humbleness there. There was a gathering of Nobel laureates at the University of Virginia, where Jeffrey Hopkins teaches, and I saw him in a photo opportunity with some of the Nobel laureates who were sitting on chairs. Others were standing, and he was among those who were standing—right behind Archbishop [Desmond] Tutu—and when I met Jeffrey, I said, "Jeffrey, why didn't you ask His Holiness to sit? Among those Nobel laureates he is someone who should be sitting on a chair, not standing behind." And he said, "What can I do? He chose, himself, to stand." There was a chair and they wanted him to sit in the center and he said, "No. Ask Archbishop Tutu, he's older; *he* should sit here." And then they let him [the Archbishop] sit there and then he said, "*I'll* stand here."

Rt. Rev. William Swing   Even if he did not understand his celebrity, which I am sure he does, the people around him certainly do. They are forever yelling audibles at the line of scrimmage, changing the game plan. This is because he is *big*, and these few people from Tibet have to make those Hollywood kinds of decisions. The people around the Dalai Lama

are deeply spiritual, not public relations types working for a client. These
are people who have grown up in the Buddhist faith and carry out
their ministry by planning for, and protecting, the Dalai Lama. In terms
of how he integrates celebrity status into his life, I don't think he sweats
a lot of things. He relaxes and goes along with the decisions made by his
associates.

Lama Surya Das   He has learned more and more what his celebrity
means. We discussed that with him at one of the Western Buddhist
teacher's conferences. We put a panel together dealing with populariza-
tion, diluting the dharma, and commercialism. And I myself pointed out to
him that he was one of the most popularizing forces for Buddhism in the
West. In fact, his face is on billboards and in ads. He replied that while
this was not one of his favorite forms of Buddhist activity, whenever people make a connection or see the teacher's face or hear the word "dharma,"
that could be a positive and auspicious connection. Of course, preserving
the authentic principles and practices is the most important thing. He
doesn't really think of his celebrity as we do. His Holiness sees charisma
and celebrity as attracting and magnetizing and making things happen, not
as personal celebrity. He would say it is a matter of karma and prayers from
the past and interconnectivity that this would happen, not that it's because
he is a remarkable person or different from other people. Someone like His
Holiness knows that he is the same as everyone else. But other people
don't know that they are the same as him. That's a big difference. He can
see the Buddha-ness in them better than they can see it in themselves, in
most cases.

Dr. Howard Cutler   While he *is* aware of his celebrity, it is an aspect of
his life that he has purposely tried to disregard. Humility is one of the
important values for an ordained monk. As I have talked to him and asked
him how he sees himself, I understand that his personal identity is not as
the Dalai Lama but as a simple Buddhist monk. Over the years, he has
engaged in much spiritual practice, specifically to avoid the traps of thinking about how much impact he has on others, or how famous he is, or how
he's changing the world. He told me that a reporter once asked him: "What
would you like your legacy to be?" His Holiness dismissed the question,
saying that he didn't think about that. When the reporter pressed him, he
got angry since he did not consider it an appropriate question, because it
was not right for him to think about legacy.

The Dalai Lama's Awareness of the Celebrity of Others

Rabbi A. James Rudin   The interaction between the Dalai Lama and Mr. Rogers [during an interfaith dialogue in Greensburg, Pennsylvania] was very warm. They had a lot to talk about. The Dalai Lama may not have known who he was—maybe somebody from Seton Hill said, "This is a big PBS children's program and he's a gentle man"—and so he may have had some idea of who he was, but not like most kids who grew up with Mr. Rogers, like my daughters. What they wanted—and what they got—were autographs not from the Dalai Lama, but from Fred Rogers.

Annie Warner   He is aware that his friend, Richard Gere, is in movies and is well-known. I think he gets a little bit of a kick out of that. With Gere and Uma Thurman, people with whom he has long-standing relationships, he understands their celebrity status. At certain times, he may not know the celebrity who is going to introduce him, so we brief him concerning the person's background—which films or what the person has done. On the plane from Vancouver to Ottawa, he didn't watch the film even though his friend, Uma Thurman, was in it.

Professor Jonathan Mirsky   The Dalai Lama likes famous people. Some people criticize him for this—they say that he's a fucker for celebrity. He likes Richard Gere, he likes Steven Segall, and he is unfailingly polite and cheerful to everybody. Gere is one of his great admirers. Gere was in Strasbourg and he, the Dalai Lama, and I were going to go across this big amphitheater in the Palais des Nations to have lunch. The Dalai Lama, arguably the most famous person in the world, Gere, a famous actor, and I, a nobody, were walking across this huge space, and all of a sudden a hell of a lot of doors flew open all around this big amphitheater and all of the secretaries and other people who worked for all the countries in the European Community came out. It was a warm day, so all of them came out in their short skirts and their thin blouses. This sound rose up among them, this high female screaming sound, and they began to run toward us—I remember seeing their bare knees as they ran in our direction—and as these hundreds of young women ran in our direction, Gere undid the top button of his shirt and pulled down his tie, and all of a sudden he was hit by a couple of hundred of these women who were pulling his clothes off. Nobody paid any attention to the Dalai Lama, who was standing on the edge of all this with me, and as this amazing scene is going on, he points at Gere and chuckles and says, "Oooh, very famous."

Patrick French   It probably surprises and amuses him. But to the Dalai Lama, whether he's pictured in *Hello* magazine standing next to Goldie Hawn or Richard Gere would not interest him either way. I've even heard stories from people from within his entourage who have talked about the occasions when the Dalai Lama has met very big-name Hollywood figures, had these intense conversations with them for three minutes, which are photographed and beamed round the world, and afterward he's said, "Who was that guy?" I don't think he's very interested in the celebrity culture. It's very unusual in the twenty-first century not to be. On the other hand, he does accept part of it. But I think that he feels that any publicity for the Tibetan cause is somehow going to be helpful. I don't think he's right about that, but that's what the people around him feel. It's also important to remember that after he came into exile in 'fifty-nine, from then until the late eighties, nobody was particularly interested in the Tibetan cause; it wasn't something that was promoted widely; you didn't have books and TV programs and movies about it. Then there was the period in the early nineties when suddenly Tibet was getting major exposure and there were idiotic public relations stunts that were being used; C-grade celebrities were attaching themselves to the Tibetan cause. People around him thought: this is all good because it's helping to make people learn more about what's happening in Tibet. They took the view that all publicity is good publicity, which is something that I don't believe is true.

The Dalai Lama's Emotional Life: Can He Have Friends?

Patrick French   It's probably easier for a monarch to have friends than it is for the Dalai Lama.

Professor Robert Thurman   Some of the people who work for him are his friends. He also has a very wide circle of people he thinks of as old friends. There is a kind of "honored category" you get into—I count myself and my family in that category—where you have a hard time seeing him because you're such an old friend that you know he is too busy with people and needs more time to himself. Instead of chatting with him for an hour, you discuss the main points of mutual interest and then you leave him alone.

Orville Schell   In a certain sense, although he is a very warmhearted and open man, loneliness is implicit in his position. One has to remember that he is celibate, so that kind of intimacy and closeness to other human beings is denied him. That's a burden on friendship. The paradox is that it is very difficult for him to have very close friendships because of the mitigating circumstances of his religious position and celebrity.

Father Laurence Freeman   He's Tibetan—he's Asian—so friends are friends, but the Western idea of friendship is different from that of the Asian; the whole concept of the individual is much more highly intensified in Western culture. He's told me that he feels very privileged and very lucky—privileged in the sense that he's surrounded and supported by people who are so concerned and so caring toward him; he appreciates that, he doesn't take it for granted.

There are obviously those with whom he can share confidences and be a bit more relaxed on a personal level. But he's not isolated by power or by celebrity, so he feels protected emotionally, in a way, I suppose, although there is also a very powerful solitude to him. That's partly because of his position, but less because of his public position and more because of his monastic, interior life. But his solitude is not loneliness, and that's why when he comes into a huge room of people he has this ability, naturally, spontaneously, and genuinely, to make everybody feel connected with him. It's not that he's playing the crowd, but it's actually the depth of his own solitude that gives him the ability to connect personally with people. And he's extremely detached emotionally. I think people seeing him so relaxed are not always appreciative of that; Westerners sometimes are not so detached emotionally. But he is very warm, very compassionate, very caring, *very* detached.

Professor Jonathan Mirsky   He gave a talk to members of the House of Lords and some other parliamentarians. He came in and greeted people with his usual clasped hands. And then he saw a friend of his in the room [with Professor Mirsky] and he pointed at us and said, "Oooh, very good friends here." Then he gave a short spiritual talk after which all these MPs were trying to shake his hand, and he just walked right through all these people, right up to the two of us, first to the other fellow and then to me, and that's when he gave me the hug and the nose-pinch. So I think that he is also, in addition to all the things that he is, a very friendly being. He likes affection and he likes his friends and he's a loyal friend. And I'm nobody. The only thing about me that is of any importance to him is that he knows I've always been on his side about the Chinese. And I think he knows that I know a certain amount about the Chinese, so in our conversations, he's always said, "What do you think the Chinese are likely to do?" But I'm by no means the only person of whom he would ask such a question. We genuinely like each other.

Dr. Frank B. Bessac, Fulbright scholar studying in China; entered Tibet on April 29, 1950   We've communicated by air mail and then by talking with his elder brother [Thubten Jigma Norbu], who sometimes lived in our house. My ideas about how I felt about Tibet and the Dalai Lama were readily transmitted when his older brother lived with us for a while at Berkeley and then around the corner in the early fifties, when I was at the University of California. He was a Buddhist monk at that time and had a lot of responsibilities, but while he was in the United States he was getting an education in the Western world.

Heinrich Harrer   He came to visit me in Lichtenstein and then at the Harrer Museum in my birthplace in Carinthia—he was there twice. And in the meantime, just recently, he came again to Lichtenstein and stayed with me—I didn't invite many other people. I made, of course, the food he is served in Dharamsala. I had visited there several times, so I know exactly what he likes to eat. In Austria there's a very famous beef with a little fat on the edge and the Tibetans love to eat fat. If the sheep had fat only the thickness of a finger, it was very cheap meat that they bought, but if it had two fingers' width, then it was much more in demand and cost much more. And the fat that was three fingers thick was the most expensive. When they dried the meat we had it in winter to eat. But it was not dried in an oven; it was air-dried. It was very popular. He also likes sweets.

We talked about old times. We were very easygoing, and I usually was able to tell him some jokes in the Tibetan language—he said, "Let's talk Tibetan because nobody else can understand us." But recently, he is surrounded by so many people. As a matter of fact, I've withdrawn now a little bit because he's in such big demand from all over the world, so I don't want to interfere. But in the autumn of last year [2003] he was again here to see me. He came to my eightieth birthday also [in 1999]—by chance, we have the same birthday, the sixth of July—and so I asked him one day whether that was fate or kismet. And he said, "Brother, we're all together in that we have the same day our birthdays."

Is It Difficult for the Dalai Lama to Maintain His Position as Spiritual Leader in Exile?

Lama Surya Das   Of course. His Holiness might emphasize the opportunity for it, but first, you have to state the problem: it's a boon for the rest of the world, but it's a big tragedy for Tibet and the Tibetan people and

Buddhism in Tibet, and also for the environment on the Roof of the World, which is going to have long-lasting implications. There are a lot of problems with the loss of the culture and the language that Tibetan Buddhism is imbedded in, and loss of the old training centers and routines, so that the new generation of *tulkus*, monks, lamas, nuns, and geshes can get the traditional training, which is a lot more than a few years of college and a few years of graduate school—it's a twenty-thirty-forty-year monastic, philosophical, yogic, tantric, and retreat training that these great old lamas from Tibet went through. It's impossible for anyone to replicate that today, so that's a big loss.

Orville Schell It must be incredibly difficult. What keeps him going involves his sense of purpose and spiritual discipline. He doesn't fulfill his responsibilities just for himself or Tibet; there is some other field of gravity operating within him. There is no more difficult job in the world—even including being a head of state; there are all these people who want you, who want to be reverent and worshipful. It is extremely difficult for him to have a relationship that is equal and truthful.

Dr. Howard Cutler He has told me that sometimes it's hard—that leading the Tibetan government in exile is not something he really enjoys doing. Yet he understands that this is part of his role as the Dalai Lama. He would rather be studying or meditating than going to government meetings.

Dr. Jeffrey Hopkins Being in exile certainly presents problems. However, I think he has had more influence. You see, he is a lama from a particular sect—from the Gelupa sect. To the left hand side of the monastery was the Ganden Potam, the "Joyous Palace," [the residence of the Dalai Lama and the headquarters of the Tibetan government before the construction of the Potala] the name of which is given to the government that eventually moved out of there. And a lot of the old government was directed toward support of this huge Gelupa hierarchy and monasteries.

This Dalai Lama, however, despite the fact that his primary education, being his main education, was from the Gelupa perspective and using those textbooks—and about which he has that tremendous facility of knowledge—he has become nonsectarian. He has sincerely, and with a lot of effort, studied the major systems of Tibetan Buddhism—asked the lamas from the traditions to come in and teach him—and he has opposed sectarianism within Gelupa to the consternation of many Gelupas. It would have been very easy for him to go with the predominant group. Or one might think it would be nice in exile for everybody to work together—that it would be easy to go with the dominant group. He didn't go with the dominant group; he instead has become a friend to all orders of Tibetan Buddhism and he considers that everything that he does in his office is totally nonsectarian. In fact, you can see that—it's not something he just wishes. And then, in his own practice, he has incorporated teachings from all of the sects. This is unusual and has given him more influence with other sects than most dalai lamas would have.

Geshe Lhundrup Sopa, holder, with highest honors, Geshe degree, Sera Monastery; debating partner to the Dalai Lama; former professor, Department of South Asian Studies, University of Wisconsin; founder, Evam Buddhist Monastery and Deer Park Buddhist Center Of course, when he was in the Potala he was a great help to the Tibetan people. But, actually, my own feeling is that when he is in exile, he is independent. Many of the free countries can thus support him in his struggle for the liberation of the Tibetan people. In exile he has added to his spiritual leadership and he has been able to advance Tibetan culture. He has opened up this culture unlike any previous Dalai Lama. This Dalai Lama is known everywhere in the whole world. His message goes everywhere. So, therefore, I think that in some way exile has been most beneficial.

Tenzin Gephel   We have to first understand the Dalai Lama; we believe in Tibet that he is one with Buddha; he is a manifestation of Buddha's conversion. And with the understanding of his quality as well as the knowledge of him—how powerful his conversion is—when we understand him, our devotion and faith or trust in him is increasing. On the basis of that very firm spiritual connection—the teacher-and-student connection—then we have to try our best to follow his teaching, his advice.

Dr. Tenzin Tethong   I don't think he necessarily assumed this is a greater responsibility or burden, because from a young age he was aware that as the Dalai Lama he was meant to have both a very key spiritual and political role. I should point out that most dalai lamas were expected to be both spiritual and political when they were in office, or when they grew to adulthood, although quite a few did not play both roles that intensely. But a few, like the previous Dalai Lama, the Thirteenth Dalai Lama, was quite active both spiritually and politically, and in fact, in the Thirteenth Dalai Lama's case, a little more active politically, maybe.

In this case [the Fourteenth Dalai Lama's], not only did His Holiness feel, or understand, that he was both political and spiritual, he also did take on both responsibilities rather seriously. And in addition to that, he proved to be actually quite good, or effective, in both roles. Unfortunately, the overwhelming circumstances of the Chinese invasion turned the period when he was a young man into a total disaster. He had to become a refugee but he nevertheless proved even after his exile began that he could be very effective as both a political and spiritual leader. This is a unique feature of the Fourteenth Dalai Lama, who is playing these two almost contradictory roles with considerable intensity and success.

Patrick French   What's extraordinary is that Tibet has historically been diverse; you've had people speaking different dialects that are not mutually intelligible; you've had people following the four main schools of Tibetan Buddhism. Now you've got all that, plus you've got a community of over a hundred thousand people in exile. And yet somehow he managed to span that. Okay, there have been cases of controversy when some sections of the Tibetan community have gone against him, but he basically has the ability that somebody like [Nelson] Mandela had, of somehow being able to encompass everything and everybody, probably at the cost of some kind of moral compromise—if you're trying to be all things to all people, then you create some kind of ambiguity. But it is absolutely extraordinary how he has managed to pull that together, and also he has gone on having a very close working knowledge and understanding of what is happening inside Tibet. So the globe-trotting Dalai Lama—the Dalai Lama who makes a large audience laugh—that, in a way, is all secondary to the fact that here's this deeply religious figure who keeps a very close eye on what's happening inside Tibet. I believe that the public Dalai Lama is a very secondary figure; he remains a very Tibetan figure; he is not particularly interested in the world of Hollywood or in the whole Western enthusiasm for what he's about. Okay, he'll go and give the public lectures, and books will be produced in his name. But for him personally that's not really of any great importance. Some of his contemporaries were very taken by the 1960s, and by the fact that there were a lot of hippies coming to Dharamsala and presenting monks with bottles of acid. He was never interested in any of that.

Dr. Ronald B. Sobel   The crowd finally gathered [on April 30, 1998, at Temple Emanu-El in New York City], the security people did what they had to do, and we were advised that we could begin. We walked out from the Robing Room onto the Bima, the altar, and the Dalai Lama stopped in the middle of that space—that altar—and looked around the soaring ceiling, then turned to me and said, "*This* is a place of holiness; I am privileged to be here." We proceeded to our seats. By blessed coincidence, April 30, 1998, was Yom Ha'atzmaut, Israel's independence day, and it was, by blessed coincidence, the fiftieth anniversary of the founding of the modern State of Israel. In my welcoming words, I made note of the fact that it was modern Israel's—the Third Jewish Commonwealth's—fiftieth anniversary on that day, and I expressed the hope that one day in the not-too-distant future, His Holiness and the people of His Holiness would be able to celebrate their renewed independence. Then I asked the rhetorical question, "How in the meantime, Your Holiness, do you and your people survive?" And because it was a rhetorical question, I answered, "You survive as the Jewish people survived for nineteen centuries. It is possible for a government to disappear, but it is impossible for a people and a culture and a dream to disappear as long as the people refuse to disappear, and that ultimate victory is not the dependence upon armies or navies or air forces, as important as those things are in a real world, but those things mean nothing if the dreams are not held to."

When the Dalai Lama ascended to the pulpit to respond, he said that it has been the experience of the Jewish people that has been a modality for him and his people to emulate in their struggle for survival. And he made it clear that there's no other parallel of which he knows that so accurately reflects his experience and the experience of the Tibetans. It was absolutely memorable—and in the 160-year history of this congregation I would say that there have been a good number of very significant moments—but his presence on that night of April 30 was certainly among the most memorable. He brought with him in his personhood that sense of the divine we all search for, especially when we go into a house of worship, and he made the divine very present.

Is the Dalai Lama Burdened by Knowing How Much Importance Is Attached to His Pronouncements?

Rinchen Dharlo I really don't think he treats as a burden the many questions asked of him to comment on. Again, he also thinks that by answering some of these questions it may be helpful, and he will try to answer them with as much detail as he can. But if he thinks that it doesn't make much sense, then he won't. He's so direct that if he does not want to answer, he will immediately say, "I don't know," or "I don't want to answer this." If he tries to answer, then he takes it seriously.

He thinks that while he is still active—while he still has his physical ability to travel—he should travel and meet people and teach. He said, "There will be a time that I won't be able to travel even though I want to." But so long as he's physically fit, so long as he is strong, he thinks that he should travel, meet people, and be active. Some of us have been telling him that he's keeping too busy a schedule, and he says, "No, I should be."

There was a time in the early nineties when some of our friends had very strongly suggested that he should not travel that much. They were speaking from the political point of view—from the PR point of view—that there was overexposure, that the Dalai Lama has been very popular and that the media has no mercy, that there will be a time when his image goes down, and that he should not now travel. And he said, "You know, I don't care; as long as I feel that my travel makes a difference, I will not care about my image." And he kept on traveling, and until now his image has gone up.

Professor Robert Thurman   He bears his burdens well; he is a strong Tibetan peasant. If you ever saw his mother, they are strong stock. He lives extremely concentratedly and mindfully; he doesn't waste time doing this or that. He has a very positive emotional outlook. He is a highly realized person in that, having realized the nature of life and death to some deep degree, he has a well of basic good feeling in his mind, heart, and being. This gives him energy, like a person who has natural joy even in the midst of difficulties. He is able to find some ground of happiness in the midst of those issues he is very concerned about and working hard at.

Dr. Alexander Berzin   I don't think His Holiness experiences it as a burden at all. His Holiness is very much a bodhisattva. He's totally, totally dedicated to what he's doing in terms of working toward bringing everybody to enlightenment, from a Buddhist point of view, and even if one doesn't look at it from a Buddhist point of view, he's certainly working to better the lot of all beings—not just humans and animals—and so he doesn't see the sense of burden at all.

I'm reminded of one statement that His Holiness made at one of these Western Buddhist teachers' conferences that we used to have in Dharamsala. One of the Western teachers was asking His Holiness about the whole thing of, "Isn't it difficult trying to be a bodhisattva and helping everybody all the time? How can we relax from that and just sort of be more natural?" And His Holiness looked [at him] in great surprise and said, "A bodhisattva never would think to take time off. How can you take time off from being a bodhisattva?" It is something that is just so totally sincere; it's not an act; it's not that you're playing that role and then need time off to be yourself. That's a totally artificial way of looking at it. This is definitely the way His Holiness experiences it—he's totally sincere.

Richard Gere   Two things come to mind. His first commitment is to save all sentient beings in all the universes, and that's a commitment he has made—he will remain in a body so long as there are people suffering, and he will do the work that's needed to remove that suffering from them. So his commitment is much larger even in Tibet. I think that in many ways it's been hard for the Tibetans to understand that he is a creature of the universe; he is not just a Tibetan, and the stature of His Holiness when he's able to be his largest self, this great bodhisattva, obviously makes him more power-ful as the leader of the Tibetan people, as well. But sometimes there is a tension there: many in the Tibetan community expect him to only speak about *Tibet*, that all he should do is to politically engage the problem of Tibet. I, for one—and others—feel that his mission is much larger than Tibet, and his effect on countless more people and beings, in countless more universes, ultimately is more important than just the Tibetan cause, although we all focus, very, very much so, very really and powerfully, on Tibet.

Tsering Shakya   It is difficult, very demanding for him, because some-times his personal wish to purely lead himself to religious and spiritual development and the demand of the world is really in conflict: he is always presented with the problems of the Tibetan community—the factional politics, the rivalries. Everybody will always go to him to arbitrate or to pass judgment, so it must be very hard for him to handle all of that and at the same time to concentrate purely on spiritual issues.

I think the Dalai Lama really feels a very huge burden. Often in Tibetan meetings he says he failed the Tibetan people. Essentially what he means is that his primary responsibility is for the Tibetan people and regaining their freedom, and that has not been successful. Really, every-thing else is secondary. He gets the Nobel Prize and is influential in the West in spiritual matters, but the fact is that he has failed his immediate community, the Tibetan people. I believe that he is fearful of that failure, and also very anxious. He often says when he talks to the Tibetan commu-nity, "I'm doing everything possible, but still I cannot move the Chinese." So, in that sense, I think he feels an enormous burden.

Professor Paul Davies   He's combining in the one person particularly these two difficult duties of, on the one hand, representing his people in their struggle—and doing that with extraordinary dignity—but on the other hand, being a senior scholar versed in traditions of Eastern thought. I'm sure that if he could somehow resign from his office—not that he's likely to do that—that if you could somehow magically take him away from those political constraints and, say, spend a week in some scientific institution—I think that from time to time he visits scientific institutions—and, off the record, let's have a brainstorming session, I think he would be much better valued. But because every word he utters is analyzed and deemed to be full of significance, this makes it very difficult for him to have a knockabout conversation. One of the things I've learned from a career in theoretical physics, in particular, is that best progress is made by people taking their hats and coats off, sitting down, not dogged by the restraints of entrenched positions, but just following ideas wherever they will lead and just trying a few things out in that experimental manner. And that's really difficult for somebody who is supposed to be uttering words of truth that people will seize on. He's only got to say something and there could be a storm of protest. So that makes it really very hard to really get into the mind of the man; it would be so much better to have a complete, off-the-record discussion. But I suspect that that almost never happens.

Dr. Jeffrey Hopkins   He has never complained about such a thing; he is not a complainer in the first place. No, he has a message, and my guess is that he's happy there's a large audience to receive it. I think it's as simple as that. He was asked by a *New York Times* reporter when he was in Indiana in 'ninety-six how he wanted to be remembered in fifty years and for whatever reason—I was sitting in on the interview—he said, "That's against my vows," his meaning being that he took vows not to be concerned about his own reputation and his own self. The reporter had been to many world leaders and asked them this question, so she was intent on getting His Holiness's response to the question and she persisted. And he kept saying things like, "That's against my vows." She'd come back and approach it this way and that way. And finally he turned to her and said, "Now I really think you're *silly*." Now she had a great story there and she didn't write it. She had a great story because here's somebody who for reasons of concern with other peoples was not concerned about himself. It went along a little while longer—she eventually had a separate interview with him and published an article—but in any case, he went on to say that, "Number one, you can't control what people are going to think about you: they may say I'm the Dalai Lama and did such and such wonderful things;

they may say I'm the Dalai Lama who lost Tibet. Who can control what people are going to think and say? And number two, it's against my vows."

Dr. Thubten Jinpa Langri   I am sure that there are occasions when he must feel the burden of being the Dalai Lama quite heavily. Years ago, some of his senior tutors who could speak with him on an equal basis were still alive. As time passes and that generation is no more, he must feel more and more lonely. He also feels the weight put on him by the expectations and hopes of his followers, particularly by the Tibetan community. He is also very aware of the expectations of the audiences he addresses. Quite often he will remark, "Don't expect too much or you will be disappointed." He is concerned that he will be of some benefit to the people who have taken the trouble to come to hear him.

Professor Robert Thurman   Lately I've noticed that the prime minister, who is a very substantial person, has taken a lot of the day-to-day governmental decision-making off him. Now the Dalai Lama says, "I'm semiretired." He can read those books he likes, he's meditating more, he's giving more teachings, which he enjoys and is very good at, all of which proves that when he had all that day-to-day responsibility, it *was* a burden because he's feeling so good about being liberated from some of these responsibilities.

Has He Ever Wanted a Different Life?

Patrick French   I don't think he's wanted a different life, in that I don't think he's ever been lured by sex, which is what takes a lot of people away from a religious, monastic vocation. I suspect that he would have quite liked to have had a quieter life, where he could go on a long retreat, which is something that is part of being the Dalai Lama, part of what he's meant to do. And he hasn't been able to do that because the demands of the modern world are that he's got to be there, ready to appear on CNN if there's some big story related to Tibet.

Lama Surya Das   He is really one with his karma. He gets up every morning, does his two or three hours of prayers, listens to the BBC, and has tea. Of course, some days may be better than others, but I would say that every morning when he wakes up he's aware that he is a Buddhist monk. That's what he's trying to be—to do his prayers and practice in the most pure bodhisattva, *mayhayanic* way. Then he gets into his role as the Dalai Lama of Tibet, and then into his larger role as a world leader and spiritual and social activist. While many of us struggle with self-doubt or inner conflict, he doesn't seem to. He has worked all of that out. He went through a hard crucible from the fifties to the seventies; those decades were very intense for him. He has burst out of many of the personal pre-occupations that other people would normally have. He might get aroused if he sees something sexy on television. I've heard him say that—not that he watches much television—but if he is in a hotel room and the TV is on and he sees something, he'd say he feels "something down there." So he's not inhuman, but that is not where he lives. His energy is not arrested in that level of development, for sure.

The Challenge of Getting Up in the Morning and Being the Dalai Lama

Orville Schell   It must be terribly difficult at times to get up in the morning and have to meet more worshipful people when you are giving all the time and the taking is much more unclear and difficult to define.

Patrick French   He has such incredibly strong spiritual discipline and his religious practice and his meditation is the first thing that happens in his day—it's probably the most important thing that happens to him that day—so I don't believe he has that feeling of take this burden away from me. But I do think that he would, ideally, want more time to go on an extended retreat, or whatever.

Father Laurence Freeman   He does genuinely feel that as a monk he would like to spend more time in practice, and he'd be happy to go back to Tibet as a simple monk, live in a cave, and meditate. He realizes he can't do that, but that is a genuine hunger in him. And that probably gives him the distance, the detachment that he needs from all his other occupations and responsibilities and enables him to carry them off.

Richard Blum   Obviously, he is much more worldly and sophisticated than when I first met him in 1972. But if you ask whether his message has changed, the answer is no. On his sixtieth birthday [in 1995], we had a party for him in Washington. I remarked that at a time when we question our leadership we should consider what the Fourteenth Dalai Lama has accomplished, and I suggested to the members of Congress who were in attendance that a commission be appointed to look for the incarnations of George Washington, Thomas Jefferson, and Abraham Lincoln.

Chapter Three

TORONTO, APRIL 2004

The afternoon of Saturday, April 24, was seasonably cool and a bit windy in Toronto—a light breeze was blowing off Lake Ontario. But it was sunny, and so people were out and about. Many restaurants and coffee houses were filled to capacity, sidewalks were crowded with strollers and shoppers, and the sidewalk outside the main entrance of the venerable Royal York Hotel was abuzz with activity. A huge crowd, composed mainly of members of Toronto's Tibetan exile community, had gathered there in anticipation of the arrival later that afternoon of His Holiness, Tenzin Gyatso, the fourteenth incarnation in a spiritual and temporal institution dating from the mid-seventh century A.D., in which all Dalai Lamas are manifestations of Avalokiteshvara, or Chenrezig, Bodhisattva [Enlightened Being] of Compassion, the bodhisattva ideal being, in the Fourteenth Dalai Lama's own words, "the aspiration to practice infinite compassion with infinite wisdom." His Holiness would be staying at the Royal York during his long-anticipated ten-day visit to this lively, ethnically and racially diverse city.

Norbu Tsering, member, Tibetan exile community of Canada; president, Canadian Tibetan Association of Ontario, official host organization of the Dalai Lama's visit to Toronto, 2004   I accompanied him

60

from the airport to the hotel. He was looking forward to the Kalachakra, his really intensive teachings. He had to be there from seven o'clock in the morning to five in the evening. I saw that he was very tired because prior to his arrival in Toronto he was traveling through America and other cities of Canada. His Holiness has a lot of energy and he doesn't look at his own personal problems; for world peace and for the cause of Tibetans he sacrifices everything.

Annie Warner   On the flight from Los Angeles to Vancouver [en route to Toronto], there was a gentleman sitting in business class who had recently lost his father. He wanted to speak with His Holiness about the grieving process, so His Holiness had him come sit next to him and they had a lengthy conversation.

Norbu Tsering   We had tried to eliminate a lot of people gathering at the hotel because the street is so narrow, and due to the security issues. We didn't want to cause a big problem and recommended that not too many people come. Who could control them? They came—more than a thousand people—and waited, wishing just to get a glimpse of him arriving for his first day in Toronto after thirteen years. Others, non-Tibetans, joined the crowd because they knew almost a week before that he was arriving in Canada; he went first to British Columbia and then he came to Toronto. Anywhere he goes, a lot of Canadians—a lot of non-Tibetans especially—really want to meet him and greet him and say, "Oh, I met His Holiness there; I *saw* him." So it was just overwhelming. I was a bit concerned that there were a lot of people because the traffic was quite large at that time and a car accident or something could happen. Thank God, it went very well.

Some time after four o'clock and running behind schedule—he was already late for a reception in his honor at the hotel—His Holiness alighted from his car amid a whirring of cameras and jostling for position by the media massed there to cover his arrival.

Norbu Tsering   He gave the traditional greeting and, as he passed, he said, "Thank you, thank you." Our security guard tried to escort him inside the hotel, but he just came out and went to the other side of the car and wished everybody well. And on the way in, he shook hands with some of the people who were waiting near the door. We have a special tradition of receiving Tibetans and he was greeted that way and enjoyed that.

Rinchen Dharlo   Wherever he visits, he touches the hearts of people, no matter whether they are his own people or from other ethnic groups. He loves to meet people and if he finds a bunch of people waiting for him at a hotel, unless he is rushed with his time, he would make sure that he shakes hands with as many as possible. And when he shakes hands, he always makes sure to make eye contact with them.

Norbu Tsering   At the reception—technically, it was not the reception with the Dalai Lama because his schedule was very tight and we did not want to bring him down in the late evening because he goes to bed quite early—our Tibetan prime minister in exile was the main guest, and we had MPs, MJPs, local Toronto dignitaries, and our sponsors and media and corporate sponsors.

Sister Mary Margaret Funk   He sure doesn't like receptions. You have to deal with the State Department; you have to deal with the local police, the county police, state police, the CIA. And you have to do all those runs ahead of time, all those security checks—it's just enormously complicated. He's at risk. And then also, after he leaves, people go bonkers: there are so many mentally ill people off their medication. He's aware of all these preparations. But he tries to violate it whenever he can: he gets out of his car and walks through the crowd; he is not fearful about his security.

Pema Chhinjor   One day, the Indian inspector general involved with security came to Dharamsala. His Holiness met with him and said, "I talk to the world about peace, non-violence, and compassion, and the moment I enter the palace, there are people holding guns, saluting me. I don't like this; I'm not afraid of anything because I'm not harming anyone." When we came out of the palace the inspector general asked me, "What does that mean? We think that any political leader, any great teacher, needs security, especially His Holiness. Our guards *have* to be there. Otherwise, how can we protect his life in the palace?"

Coverage of the arrival in Toronto of His Holiness would dominate the airwaves that evening and be featured on the front pages of Sunday's newspapers. The *Toronto Star* would even relegate the visiting Duke of Edinburgh's presence in the city to an inside page.

Nearby, at the new and sprawling National Trade Center, another crowd had assembled—elderly couples; young men and women, some carrying infants, others clutching the hands of toddlers; and teenagers. Most of them were Caucasian or Asian in appearance and many of them were visitors to the city, having traveled from forty-four countries, some from as far away as Europe and Asia. They were standing on line to purchase tickets for the Kalachakra for World Peace 2004, an intensive, ten-day seminar to be conducted by His Holiness starting at seven o'clock the next morning, for which they would pay 380 to 560 dollars per person, Canadian currency.

Annie Warner   In Toronto he would awake precisely at 3:30 in the morning and immediately begin his prayers. Then, at about five o'clock his attendant would bring him breakfast, which is usually pretty substantial since as a Buddhist monk his vow is not to take an evening meal, so he eats only breakfast and lunch each day. He would then continue his prayers and at 6:45 leave the hotel, arriving at the Trade Center in time to begin the Kalachakra precisely at seven. On a couple of days, they began as early as 6:00 A.M. On arrival at the Trade Center, we would drive right up behind the stage. There was no holding time; as soon as His Holiness exited the car he would walk directly onto the stage and begin the prayers for that day. The morning session usually lasted from 7:00 to 11:30. Then His Holiness would break for lunch and conduct brief audiences. He would continue the Kalachakra from one to four then depart for the hotel, his official day at an end. On May 4, the fifteenth day of the third Tibetan month, which is a special observance day, His Holiness decided to go to the Trade Center even an hour earlier and stayed later to offer special prayers in the afternoon. That was remarkable since his days are so long to begin with.

Dr. Alexander Berzin   Toronto was a little bit special because, first of all, it was organized completely by the Tibetan people in Canada, and so you had an unusually large number of Tibetans coming to it. For the Tibetans, it is multidimensional. One aspect is the extreme devotion to His Holiness and the wish to see and spend time with His Holiness, be in his presence, and be inspired by that. I don't think that they are terribly concerned about the teachings themselves that His Holiness is giving but, rather, just to be with him. And also it was a cultural expression of being Tibetan and being with lots of other Tibetans, so it was a multifaceted thing.

Norbu Tsering   Some already had been so many times to his teachings—in India, in North America, and Europe also—and they knew that they wanted to practice more. Some of them come out of curiosity; they want to see him they want to listen to him and know what it's all about, and some people are thinking that he has healing powers—"I want to see him so that I'll be out of my pain"—a lot of mix there.

Ven. Bhikshuni Tenzin Kacho, American Buddhist nun ordained by the Dalai Lama, 1985; resident teacher, Center for the Study of Buddhism and Tibetan Culture, Colorado Springs, Colorado; Buddhist chaplain, United States Air Force Academy   Sometimes people come just because of the celebrity, or the story of the Dalai Lama. I have a friend who was recently ordained as a monk, who's from a very conservative community as well—in fact, his father had been a Catholic monk novice for a short while, before he decided that wasn't the life for him and then had a family. He said he went with a lot of skepticism because he had an opportunity to hear the Dalai Lama at a *huge* event in Chicago, and he said it was just that first night, sitting in the audience and listening to him, that really turned his mind and made him feel that he had to inquire more. That is what occurs for a lot of people as well: they come in curiosity and then they really develop a deeper interest.

The Dalai Lama's Decision to Visit Toronto Given His Many Invitations from Communities throughout the World

Norbu Tsering   We are really a growing community; last time he visited, in 1993, there were only five hundred Tibetan people in all of Canada. Since we made our request, we have almost twenty-five hundred to three thousand people just in Toronto. And also he wanted to visit Canada; this is one of the countries you can feel is multinational and multicultural, where everybody has their own opportunity to practice their own things, whether it's your religion, whether it's your culture, whether it's your home country's traditions. It's not like in China or in some other countries where there are restrictions. I think those are the biggest reasons he decided to come to Canada.

The Kalachakra in Toronto was an almost four-year process. Initially we selected a few of our organization members as a Kalachakra operating committee—for almost two years we were doing the preparations by committee. We have around twenty directors; we distributed different roles to them as to their experience, what they could do, what they could achieve, what we expected they could do better. Since this was all volunteer work, we didn't pay their salary for whatever they did; they even had to pay for their own gas, their own parking, and for two years they had to commit to spend all their weekends. So that is how within the community itself we built the base and the people.

Dr. Alexander Berzin For the Westerners who come, there is the big draw of His Holiness and the inspiration to be with His Holiness, but more and more are becoming sincerely interested in the actual Kalachakra practice—in the actual Kalachakra teachings. Of course, the vast majority are not going to be involved with any actual practice, and the majority will be coming for just the inspiration—what His Holiness calls "neutral observers"—they're not actually ready to take the various vows and commit themselves to a daily practice that are part of an initiation process.

But there is a growing number—you see this each time that this initiation is given—of people who sincerely want to practice. For instance, there's something called an "International Kalachakra Network" that I'm part of; this is something on the Internet—a friend of mine runs the Web site—in which people who are interested in the practice, who do the practice, write in. There are chat rooms, there are various teachings available, different levels of teaching. And after each of these initiations, you get a whole wave of new people coming in. Also there are Kalachakra practice groups that meet regularly around the world—I lead one here in Berlin— and people are setting up more and more of these practice groups with each of these initiations. People come away from it with great inspiration in general. Also it is a social event, so you see people you haven't seen in years if you've been part of the Tibetan Buddhist scene, as it were. And also you come away from it with a greater commitment to the daily practice, which is very helpful.

———

Elsewhere in the city, yet another huge line had formed outside Toronto's pride and joy, its SkyDome. There, people were purchasing tickets ranging from ten to thirty dollars per person to be in the presence of the Dalai Lama during his major public appearance, which would take place following the first Kalachakra session, to hear His Holiness expound on the theme of "The Power of Compassion."

The Attraction of the Dalai Lama's Spirituality
versus His Political Message

Dr. Thubten Jinpa Langri   Initially, people came to see him mostly out of curiosity. As the years passed, particularly after he won the Nobel Prize [in 1989] and his books reached a wide audience, more and more people have taken an interest in him as an important moral voice of integrity. So for many people, whether they are religious or not, he stands as a source of inspiration. Obviously, a significant segment of the public who come to see him are primarily moved by the plight of the Tibetan people, but I believe that the majority of his audiences are inspired by his example as a moral figure.

Norbu Tsering   Most of the time he talks about topics like the power of compassion. It's not political, not that spiritual. It's like he's one of the celebrities, one of the known people in this world; people want to see him and listen to him. That's the main goal of people who are coming here. What is his message here? It's both political and spiritual; it's both things because he's having both responsibilities for the Tibetans.

Sun Wade, spokesman and press counselor, Embassy of the People's Republic of China, Washington, D.C.   [Speaking on April 15, 2004, nine days before the Dalai Lama's scheduled arrival in Toronto] We have already made a representation to the Canadian government; the Canadian government also recognizes that Tibet is part of China and they will not support Tibetan independence. So we are urging them to honor their commitments to the Chinese government. For our part, the Dalai Lama is simply not a religious figure but a political exile who has long been committed to separatist activities, so we urge all countries in the world to honor their commitments to the Chinese people and the government.

By Sunday the weather had changed dramatically. The day had dawned cloudy and chilly, and by the early afternoon sheets of wind-whipped rain were falling. But the storm wasn't about to deter the thirty-thousand-strong crowd that had begun to gather outside the SkyDome early that morning to await entry. The high-tech sports arena, the centerpiece of the complex of steel and glass towers that has transformed the city center, was constructed with a seating capacity of fifty-one thousand and opened on

June 3, 1989. The facility has additional, innovative accommodations: well-heeled guests staying at the hotel that abuts the SkyDome can watch events there without ever having to leave the comfort of their own rooms.

Against the backdrop of this architectural innovation of the late twentieth century, the designers of Sunday's event, promoting an ancient religion and way of life dating from the seventh century, had fashioned a stage set of utter simplicity: a blown-up photograph of the ancient Potala, lit theatrically by the glow emanating from spotlights covered by red and green gels. Called by some "the Buddhist Vatican," the huge, many-tiered building, once the winter palace of all dalai lamas, as well as the political and spiritual nerve center of the centuries-old institution of the Dalai Lama, is today a potent symbol to the vast Tibetan diaspora.

The program was scheduled to begin at 3:30—the now restless media, consisting largely of television crews, had been in place in the press gallery ringing the SkyDome since two o'clock—and the Dalai Lama, who had been over at the National Trade Center since before seven that morning, was to speak at 4:30. By the designated hour, however, only a trickle of spectators had filed into the arena and found seats. Tight security screening was holding up the flow, the media was told, and so there was a rapid exodus from the gallery—to get coffee, to stretch, to chat up one's peers—then, minutes later, a reverse migration to await further developments.

Norbu Tsering   I made the decision to expedite people getting in. Later on we removed the metal detector from the top floor and just checked by the wand, letting people get in faster. Security was an important concern. We were very concerned about his [the Dalai Lama's] security, but we were also concerned about the flow of the people getting into the hall. During our process of meeting, they said, "It's just too hard to get twenty-five thousand people into the SkyDome." We thought at the time it was twenty-five thousand, but then later on people showed up at the gate and a total of thirty thousand people came. Due to the rain and the storm, everything was delayed. Also, the metal detector was a bit slow, so at the first floor, the one-hundred level, we did it by metal detector and at the three-hundred and five-hundred levels, which are very high, we did it by wand, checking individuals one by one.

Annie Warner   Protection was afforded to His Holiness by the Royal Canadian Mounted Police. The motorcade drove into the belly of the SkyDome just behind the stage—we were literally right behind the curtain.

Everyone got out and His Holiness was led through the curtain and to the side of the stage. He was then immediately miked up. We try to minimize the holding time to as little as possible. There was a BBC crew backstage following His Holiness, and they asked him one or two very brief questions before he went on. One minute later, Justin Trudeau took the stage to offer the introduction, so it was very quick.

Finally, at four o'clock, the soft glow of the gels gave way to the intensity of pure white light, chimes sounded, and, to applause from the audience in the now rapidly filling arena, twelve monks from the Namgyal Monastery, the Dalai Lama's personal spiritual retreat in Dharamsala, India, filed onstage and began to chant, their sonorous voices rising and falling in ever-escalating waves. Moments later, as spectators were still streaming in, the monks retreated from the stage and Master of Ceremonies Bill Cameron, a local personality, stepped to the speaker's rostrum to announce that despite the nasty weather, more than twenty-five thousand people were now inside the arena. "There are so many people, so many *different* people, from so many different places," he observed.

Norbu Tsering   That was really unexpected; we were thinking around fifteen thousand at the maximum. In 'ninety-three when he was here, there was not an immediate response from the Canadian people—unlike in America—so initially we were even thinking to have the public talk at the same teaching hall [the International Trade Center] where the maximum is nine thousand people who can be accommodated. But we said, "No, that is going to be really a problem for the logistics, and also we are expecting around fifteen thousand to twenty thousand"—that was what the maximum expectation was. So we decided to have it at the SkyDome, and initially we just sold tickets for fourteen thousand. These were sold within a week. Then we moved to seventeen thousand sold. So, gradually, we kept on increasing the seating level. Right before the event we sold just a very few. Up to the event it was twenty-five thousand, and five thousand came the same day.

We had a variety—from America, from Europe, and from Asia.

Cameron asked the assemblage to remember for a moment the young Eleventh Panchen Lama, who is believed to be coming of age under house arrest by the People's Republic of China, "a captive," Cameron said, "in a struggle not of his making . . . the second-most important religious figure in Tibet . . . the center of international controversy because Communist control [of Tibet] is paramount." Following performances by representatives from the Tibetan Institute of the Performing Arts, the stage was prepared for the Dalai Lama's entrance; a large white wing chair was placed at the center of the platform for his use.

Rinchen Dharlo   His Holiness's office doesn't pay much attention to the decorations; it's all the local organizers, unless they have made the stage in such a way that he does not like. For example, most of the high-ranking Tibetan lamas use silk brocade that they put on chairs and when they travel they even put it on car seats. The Dalai Lama doesn't want to do that. On several occasions I've seen people, when they arrange teachings, decorating with silk brocade, flowers, and that kind of thing. He doesn't like that, and we always make sure we don't have that kind of thing. Otherwise, it's very flexible. In some places the local organizers want to make it very comfortable and look very luxurious, and we always have to ask them to take it out. And if there's a meeting of twenty people in a conference, the Dalai Lama always says, "Don't put a special chair for me."

As Cameron once again stepped to the rostrum to introduce Justin Trudeau, the twenty-nine-year-old son of the late Canadian prime minister Pierre Elliott Trudeau, who would, in turn, introduce His Holiness, a hush fell over the audience, which had grown to nearly thirty thousand.

Norbu Tsering   The Tibetans in Canada remember his father's time, the first time Tibetan refugees were accepted in Canada, when about fifty Tibetan refugees were invited to settle in Canada. We had great leaders, like the Trudeau family. Justin Trudeau lives here and is active in educating the world and he knows about the Tibetan cause also, so we invited him to introduce him, and within an hour he said, "No problem, I'll do it."

Justin Trudeau   He and my father had had an awful lot of respect for each other. They only met once, actually, but I know they experienced a very good connection. Because of the connection between my father and so many of the Tibetan immigrants in the 1970s in Canada, I was asked if I would be interested in introducing His Holiness. I said "Yes!" immediately.

Trudeau observed in his introductory remarks that the "development of new technological advances sometimes just creates new ways for us *not* to get along with one another. That is one reason it is such a pleasure to introduce someone who knows how to get along just fine with just about everybody." It is also a challenge, he acknowledged, "because finding the right words to introduce His Holiness proved significantly more difficult than I expected. Our really good words sometimes seem all used up. Love, how strong a word is love when it's so easy to say, 'I love my shampoo'? Freedom is all about the right kind of convertible, or SUV if you happen to live in the Himalayas," he added. "Fulfillment? That's a word that seems to be linked to the right brand of yogurt."

Trudeau then recalled a lesson his late father had taught him—the value of silence, "a moment to think, a pause to plunge into our own depths, an absence of the constant noise with which we surrounded ourselves, a respect for the constant, superficial dizziness that assails us throughout our waking moments. Silence seems to be the one luxury we all too often forget to grant ourselves." But now, Trudeau observed, "we gather by the thousands in silence to listen to His Holiness, to open ourselves to what he has learned during *his* silence. Every one of us—or our ancestors—came to this land in search of something better. We cherish hope, compassion, acceptance. We're just not nearly as good at it as *he* is. We lack the strength to radiate goodness across oceans. We struggle with the logic of being nice to people who hate you; for the most part . . . the power of true compassion seems far from us."

His excitement building at the prospect of learning from the monk who is widely known as the "Ocean of Wisdom," Trudeau enthused: "If the responsibility of each of us is to draw from the knowledge from the world around us and integrate it into our lives, then we would be hard pressed to find a better source of wisdom. It is with deep humility and simple joy that I have the honor of welcoming His Holiness the Dalai Lama."

The moment the crowd had been waiting for was at hand: the Dalai Lama strode onstage to a prolonged standing ovation punctuated by whistles and shouts, the expression on his round, friendly face reflecting his pleasure at being there, and acknowledged the tribute of his audience. He then turned to embrace Trudeau and the two exchanged *kata*—the *katak*, a white silk scarf, is the traditional, and highly symbolic, Tibetan gift of welcome. So effusive was the Dalai Lama's response to the younger man's introduction that he appeared to be greeting a dear friend of many years' standing. That was not the case, however.

Justin Trudeau   When I got there to present him, he was involved back-stage in a number of interviews and filming, so I didn't actually even meet him before I went onstage. I went up and introduced him. He then he walks onstage—it was the first time I had ever met him.

With Trudeau's departure from the platform, the Dalai Lama gestured to the crowd to be seated and settled into his white wing chair. The arena became quiet. Just as His Holiness uttered his first words of greeting in his deep, sonorous voice, however, his microphone emitted a dull thud that resounded throughout the SkyDome. His Holiness, clearly relishing this unscripted moment of high-tech malfunction, chuckled, his initial response becoming a hearty belly laugh. Then, half coughing, half laughing, he exclaimed, "Good evening to everybody!"

Dr. Thubten Jinpa Langri   The microphone kept switching on and off; it may have been too sensitive. Also, the sound people were not certain whether it was my or His Holiness's microphone that was not working. On top of that, the program was delayed due to security considerations, and I think that the delay made the sound people quite nervous.

Annie Warner   What was funny about that was that the people back-stage were so incredibly precise—I think they had three different mikes on His Holiness and three on the translator and they had cords running every which way. It took them longer than it usually does to mike His Holiness and the translator, so after all of that effort, for it to then malfunction was humorous to His Holiness.

The audience loved that moment too, erupting in applause, then fell silent as His Holiness began once again to speak, saying, "Dear Brothers and sisters, I am extremely happy for this moment to be together . . ." Then, for the next hour, this self-described "simple monk" delivered his message of love, compassion, and spiritual uplift—a message unencumbered by excessive verbiage or profound philosophical insights, but punctuated by frequent chuckles and not a few belly laughs, to the rapt, one could say transfixed, assemblage.

Observing that "mentally, emotionally, physically, we are all the same," His Holiness spoke of humanity's shared potential—"the potential of good, the potential of bad"—chuckling as he expressed his belief that "no one is one hundred percent bad," and declaring that "everyone wants a happy life—happy days and nights, even dreams, including long life—and everyone has every right to be a happy person . . . even animals; they don't know what is the past, what is the future, but they want a happy life." But, he cautioned, "a happy life does not come independently, or come without cause; every event comes due to its own causes . . . so, similarly, pains and problems also happen because of causes, conditions."

Then, endearing himself to the audience by acknowledging that "my English is bad, I'm now getting older and my *English* is also getting older," His Holiness called upon his translator, Dr. Langri, for assistance and continued his address for a time in the Tibetan language.

Dr. Thubten Jinpa Langri   When he is giving a general, public talk, outside the context of formal Buddhist lectures, he prefers to speak in English because that gives him more direct communication with the audience. Every so often, if he wants to convey a more complex point, he will switch into Tibetan. But his English vocabulary is amazingly good and his comprehension is very good.

Dr. Jeffrey Hopkins   He has a definite charm when he speaks in English. In 'seventy-nine, when he first came to the States, I began interpreting for him in public lectures. My own opinion was that the lectures worked best if he spoke the first half in what was then even more broken English, and if in the second half he spoke Tibetan and I translated. I think the reason being, one, its charm—being able to hear it the way someone with that level of English would put it; there's a directness, a connection—and then I always felt it was important for the second part to be in Tibetan because people could then perhaps hear the crispness—the clearness, the mental agility, would come through. His Holiness has an unusual power of speech in Tibetan, which if he spoke English it would knock over the whole world, it seems to me, but that's an exaggeration, of course; the whole world never goes anywhere together. Some people, listening to his English and then contrasting it later to my translation of his Tibetan, would occasionally ask me, "Did he really *say* all that?" because they got the impression that he was a wonderful guy, very kind, very open, but somewhat simple— incapable of great complexity. Of course, that is completely not the case.

Dr. Alexander Berzin   When His Holiness speaks in English, he comes across quite differently than when he speaks in Tibetan; when he speaks in Tibetan, he speaks, probably, the equivalent of the queen's English and he is an elegant, elegant speaker with the largest vocabulary of any Tibetan I've ever met; he expresses himself extremely clearly and fully. Whereas in English, he comes across much more simply—he doesn't have that range of vocabulary or construction—so he does come out sounding more simple in the West. But he does have the same range in Tibetan: when he speaks to uneducated Tibetans, he speaks on a very general level—usually with very loving advice to his own people—and when he teaches, he usually teaches to the highest level of the masters who are there because he's the only one who is basically more realized and more learned than they are. So I think it's primarily a language factor. He has humor, by the way, both when he's speaking in Tibetan or in English. This is part of the general Tibetan character—almost all of them are like that.

Professor Robert Thurman In Tibetan, his voice is much more resonant and he is much more confident and strong. He resorts to translators, even though they are not perfect, to convey more subtle areas of thought. Very often, unfortunately, these thoughts come out in a very tortuous way, where the listener gets lost in the translator's mind so that they get the complexity, but not the Dalai Lama's emotional impact. When you listen to him give these more complex lectures in Tibetan, it is a very amazing intellectual experience. This is because the Tibetan language is a marvelous vehicle for intellectual thought. It is derived from Sanskrit, which is the greatest of all philosophical languages.

T. C. [Tsewang Choegyal] Tethong In Dharamsala he wanted to practice his English so he wanted me to speak English with him. He would say something in English and I would answer in Tibetan—somehow, it didn't seem appropriate to me to talk to His Holiness in English—and he would really get disgusted with me.

Reverting once again to the English language, His Holiness said that his interest lies in promoting religious harmony but that "Sometimes religion is causing more trouble. But if you utilize religion properly, then all religions make a better, happier person."

Turning to the occupation of his homeland by the People's Republic of China, the Dalai Lama, displaying the humbleness that is a hallmark of his worldwide outreach, said, "I have nothing to offer you, just these few words: I lost my freedom, my own country—the majority of my life has been spent outside my own country, living as a refugee." And elaborating on his self-image, he described himself as "a simple monk," confiding, "That's very true. When I studied, I was a lazy student; my knowledge is limited—my knowledge of math, geography, is almost zero."

His Holiness then spoke of the centrality of compassion in his life, noting that "it brings inner strength and self-confidence; with self-confidence you can deal with any problem without losing hope . . . warm-heartedness is the most precious thing." Compassion, he added, "is not based on others' attitude to oneself . . . compassion is unbiased; ordinary love is biased." By extension, he observed, "Peace is not just the absence of violence; peace is the expression of compassion. If there is compassion, peace will come."

Addressing the current issues of military conflict, violence, and terror-ism, His Holiness characterized war as "legalized violence in ancient times" and observed that today there is "a new reality: everything is inter-dependent," hence "destruction of your enemies is destruction of your-self." The only way to deal with our differences, he said, "is through dialogue; there's no other way. The best way is compromise, taking account of the other's interest." Observing that "the twentieth century was a century of violence—we learned that we cannot solve problems"—His Holiness expressed his aspiration and view that "the twenty-first century should be a century of dialogue, compassion, self-confidence and recogni-tion of others' right." Then His Holiness said, to another round of applause, that while he respects contemporary world leaders, "I think our leaders should have more compassion." Pointing to his own head to drive his point home, His Holiness warned, "If a politician goes a little nuts, it's very dangerous."

His Holiness also offered his views on animal rights and marriage and then spoke of his early years as the designated Dalai Lama: "When I was four or five years old and my elder brother six, sometimes we would fight," he recalled. "My weapon was my name; my brother was always crying—the younger brother bullying the older brother. But it was without losing our respect or family love, with much happiness."

Concluding his formal remarks, the Dalai Lama then responded to questions posed by members of the audience, which were written out on cards and brought to him on the podium. Regarding other desired qualities for humanity, he responded, "Knowledge, realism; negative emotion cre-ates problems." As to the source of "all your energy," he confided, "Good sleep—not less than seven hours, sometimes nine or ten hours—and I'm a good Buddhist. No solid food at night; then I'm very hungry [the next morning]." As for his way of coping with human emotions, he said, "I cannot claim I have real peace in my mind, but when some heartbreaking news comes, then in a short while it will go. Sometimes I feel like the ocean—a wave comes, but underneath the ocean is very calm." It is important, he added, "to cultivate the habit of watching one's own thought processes. Usually when we develop anger, try to separate and look at anger and see all the negatives of anger. . . . When sadness happens, try to look separate from the sadness; when you separate, the disturbance is less." When the question of the Dalai Lama's return to his homeland was raised, to a wave of applause with the query, "How can we help you to go home?" His Holiness, with another of his characteristic responses—a lighthearted answer to a serious question, in this case the issue at the core of his raison d'etre—said "Buy one ticket from here to Lhasa."

"But the reality is more complicated," he acknowledged to a peal of laughter. "Tibetans put a lot of hope and trust in me. I consider myself a free spokesman for the Tibetan people; my presence outside is useful to them." The situation inside Tibet, His Holiness suggested, "begins to change . . . so because they trust me I have the responsibility. . . . My approach is not separation, not independence, but meaningful self-rule . . . meaningful implementation of autonomy. My approach is not the disintegration of the PRC but in time things can change. But I appreciate your showing your serious concern for us. We need your help. Thank you." With these words, His Holiness put his palms together once again and, to a standing ovation, strode from the stage.

The Dalai Lama's View of the Toronto Meeting

Norbu Tsering   I was with him for eleven days, and for two or three days I got the opportunity to travel with him in his limo and give him reports of the community in Canada. He was asking questions and I thought: Wow! There are leaders who don't have a clue to what is happening today in Canada to the Tibetans, but he has up-to-date information and he's asking those questions—this is our leader; he knows who we are and what we are facing. And if he knows the problems, then he is able to do something, based on the information he has.

He was very busy, but he was enjoying those eleven days, and he said, "Everything went very well; you guys did a good job." It's such an inspiration and motivation. He mentioned that it was very well organized, and especially it was very transparent to everybody who has study spirit. Also, he knew that there were rumors that some of the organizers make big money, and people think that it is His Holiness who makes the money. We are not individual groups; we are not individual families; we are not individual politicians. We are just like all Tibetans, so it is very transparent to everyone how much money we made and what our intention was too, and what we are going to do with the surplus money. And he was quite honored that Tibetan people volunteered, put in two years' effort, and made this event very successful. He was pleased and afterward he said that from now on, wherever he goes, he wants this type of account taken and made very clear to everybody how much money you made and what your financials look like, and if there is a surplus it is not for your pocket, but it is for the Tibetan development projects.

Annie Warner   His Holiness always knows the capacity of the venue and is usually briefed on how many tickets have been sold and how many people are expected. He may make candid comments concerning the event to a senior adviser in the car going back to the hotel, but once he arrives at the hotel, his attendant will accompany him to his suite, prepare some broth and tea, and ready him for sleep, so once he arrives back at the hotel the day is over.

Norbu Tsering   I got the opportunity to serve His Holiness the Dalai Lama during the Kalachakra, to hold the Kalachakra here, and the people who attended are all very happy and satisfied. For me it's one instant in my lifetime to get such an opportunity to make this event, as much as possible, more successful, and a comfort for the Buddhist people who are coming from Tibet and are very close to His Holiness. From day to day, I do not contribute directly to the Tibetan cause and for His Holiness, but I've put in more like ten years to make this happen, so, personally, it was a great achievement, a great satisfaction, and a great opportunity for me to serve at this time.

———————

That evening, the Dalai Lama retired to the solitude of his quarters at the Royal York Hotel. There he prayed and then retired early, as he has done for practically his entire life, a life that began in a remote Tibetan village seventy years ago in another time—a time of relative peace and independence.

PART II

Beginnings

Chapter Four

FROM TAKTSER TO LHASA

During the spring of 1938, a search party of senior Buddhist lamas sent by the Tibetan government to fulfill a sacred mission arrived at Kumbum Monastery in the eastern Tibetan province of Amdo. The group, led by Kewtsang Rinpoché of the Sera Monastery, had braved the rigors of their journey of several months from the capital, Lhasa, located in south central Tibet, to the remote area to discover the incarnation of Thupten Gyatso, the Thirteenth Dalai Lama, who had died in 1933 at the age of fifty-seven.

The search party had had no hesitation in traveling to Amdo. Three years earlier, the then newly deceased Dalai Lama's remains had been placed in a chair in a Sitting in State ritual, his head facing south. Soon, his head somehow shifted to face in the northeasterly direction, toward Amdo. Then one day, the regent, Reting Rinpoché, while gazing into the sacred lake, Lhamoi Lhatso, located in the southern part of the country, had a vision: he saw the Tibetan letters *Ah*, *Ka*, and *Ma* on those waters, as well as the image of a three-tiered monastery adorned with a turquoise and golden roof. There was a path running from that holy place up a hill. Then a small house with odd gutters came into view. The regent had no doubt: the letter *Ah* represented the northeastern province of Amdo and *Ka* the Kumbum Monastery, which had three levels and a blue-green roof.

The search party next set out to find a hill and a house with the strange gutters of the regent's vision. Arriving in the village of Taktser [Roaring

79

Tiger in the Tibetan language], they came upon a flat-roofed, stone-and-mud farmhouse with gutters constructed of juniper wood. Not wishing to reveal their mission just yet, the lamas asked the owners of the modest house if they could spend the night. They did, and passed the evening making friends with the youngest of the family's five children—a sixth child would be born years later—a sweet-faced, nearly three-year-old boy named Lhamo Dhondrub [Wish-Fulfilling Goddess], who upon seeing Kewtsang Rinpoché, cried out, "Sera Lama, Sera Lama!" The lamas departed the next morning but soon returned, bringing with them not only some of the late Thirteenth Dalai Lama's possessions but also things that had never belonged to Thubten Gyatso, which they showed to the toddler. He immediately picked out the Thirteenth Dalai Lama's own possessions, crying out as each item was placed before him, "It's mine." The lamas knew that their search was over: they had identified the Fourteenth Dalai Lama.

Discovering the Fourteenth Dalai Lama

Patrick French   There are certainly a lot of stories in Tibetan culture of children being coached in a particular way, or of parents saying, "Oh, this child is definitely the reincarnation of whoever, because he said 'I want to go to such-and-such a monastery,'" so there are examples of that. If that happened in the case of the Dalai Lama, it's not recorded. The only thing that even hints of that is the fact that he is often described as coming from a peasant family, which is technically true, but his older brother was already identified as a high reincarnation, and his uncle, his mother's brother, was financial comptroller of Kumbum Monastery, the big monastery at the place when he was growing up. And the Chinese Muslim warlord [Ma Pu-feng], who allowed the Dalai Lama to go to Lhasa, was acquainted with his mother's family. The Dalai Lama's father was a very different quantity, but his mother and his mother's family were people who were already in a position of considerable prominence within that part of Amdo.

It's very interesting, this thing of which identified reincarnations are authentic. Even the Dalai Lama himself recognizes, or would say, that there are a fair number of Tibetan reincarnations that don't appear to be authentic. But then you come up with the question of: Do they choose that child because that child has been sent something through some sort of karmic method? Or do they choose that child because he has charisma? And clearly in the case of the Dalai Lama, you have the description, which

I quote in my book, of Basil Gould, the British official at his enthronement in 1940, saying, "I have never seen anybody assume more complete and natural control of great assemblies." And an official back in London wrote "a flight of imagined fantasy" in the margin [of the official's memorandum], as if to say how ridiculous that a child of five or six could have that effect. And yet he did. What I suspect is that when the search party, the group of monks, is going to find a reincarnation, they look for children who do seem to give off some kind of intense energy, light, power—whatever you call it—and clearly, from those descriptions of the young Dalai Lama, objective descriptions, not from people within his own circle, even as a young child that charisma was there.

Ven. Nicholas Vreeland   If one asks whether His Holiness has some intrinsic quality that has made him what he is, we have to be careful in using the word "intrinsic" because we do not consider that that was a quality intrinsic in him. It was a quality that this particular little boy had, that another little boy *didn't* have, not that he had it intrinsically. In other words, the qualities that little boy had were the effects of a whole series of causes—spiritual development over lifetimes. That little boy was the result of all of that spiritual evolution. Yes, that child is unique; he possesses—embodies—the qualities that make *him* the Dalai Lama rather than someone else.

Dr. Howard Cutler   People are born with a certain personality and temperament. He has an innate, genetic-type temperament that has been very conducive to his role. Based on what he has told me—and what I have observed—a large part of *who* he is is a result of the systematic training of his mind throughout his life.

Professor Robert Thurman   It is a remarkable test of his own personality that he was able to withstand the shock of being designated the Dalai Lama. The process of educating a reincarnate lama in the Tibetan Buddhist system is quite remarkable. Maybe all the recognitions are not correct. But those that are, when it really is *the* person, are like child prodigies, like little Mozarts—it's as if you've found a little Mozart who has already written a million symphonies in ten previous lives. Then you are not surprised when they start writing a symphony at age five. To Buddhists, a phenomenon like Mozart is another real proof of reincarnation. The Dalai Lama was clearly a kind of Mozart of philosophy, psychology, and spiritual practice.

Lama Surya Das   His Holiness jokes that the *tulku* system is only 50 percent accurate and that he's on the wrong side of the 50. But he had the best saintly teachers of his time, so it was not likely to produce a spoiled or egotistical or narcissistic, megalomaniac, personality, as so many royal courts do produce. You always have to look at nature and nurture in any upbringing. So if a different boy had been chosen, what would have happened? The nurture might have produced similar results, but some of the nature probably would have been different.

Patrick French   It's the relationship between the young Dalai Lama and his tutors that created the boy who at the age of fifteen took over the reins of state at the time of the Chinese communist invasion. Again, think how many children of that age would be able to even begin to respond to the demands, not only of having to lead a substantial religious tradition but also to take control of their country in a very hostile situation.

Sun Wade   Actually, the Fourteenth Dalai Lama was born in China's Qinghai Province. He was selected as one of the incarnate boys at the age of two. After receiving a report submitted by the local Tibetan government in 1939, the central government ordered the higher authorities to send troops to escort him to Lhasa. And in 1940, Chiang Kai-shek, then head of the central government, approved an absolute decree confirming the title of the Fourteenth Dalai Lama on Lhamo Dhondrub. All those facts say that Tibet has actually been part of China for many years, since ancient times. That's a historical fact.

———————

Several months would pass before official confirmation was received from Lhasa that Lhamo Dhondrub was indeed the reincarnation. He was then taken to Kumbum Monastery, where he was formally enthroned in a sunrise ceremony. His life now changed drastically: separated from his parents, but consoled by the presence of his immediate elder brother, Lobsang Samten, the three-year-old began the transformation from farm boy to spiritual and temporal leader of the people and nation of Tibet. Reunited with his parents and brought to Lhasa in the summer of 1939, after the payment of a large ransom to Ma Pu-feng, the Fourteenth Dalai Lama began his rigorous monastic education at the age of six with the regent, who served as his senior tutor, and his junior tutor, Tathag Rinpoché.

———————

Dr. Tenzin Tethong   Obviously, he was very much a child like another child and he very much wanted to go out and play with other children, which was largely denied, although he did spend a little bit of time with his brothers. And then, as he has stated, many of the older people who worked in his household—the people who were cooking or cleaning his rooms—often played with him, almost like children, and he has often remarked how wonderful they were and how they not only played as children, but they played as equals and didn't just submit to him because he was the Dalai Lama. So he was raised as a normal child but, of course, denied full childhood experiences. As a young man, when he started to speak and teach, he sounded very much like his tutors. In a sense, both of these tutors were really literally and physically giving the best of what Tibetan Buddhist education had to the young Dalai Lama and they were very successful.

As for his political responsibilities, I don't think there was any prescribed system to train him or bring him into the political world, but he gradually started to understand how the different institutions within the Tibetan government functioned, simply being exposed to it as he was growing up and interacting with many of the older officials, even though he did not start to deal directly with government issues until he was sixteen or seventeen. Prior to that, he was dealing with officials who were assigned to him as personal attendants, or somebody whose position was akin to being the lord chamberlain. Through these people he did get some sense of the politics and formal structure of Tibetan government.

Dr. Howard Cutler   When I showed His Holiness photos of the Potala [during Dr. Cutler's visit to Dharamsala in the 1980s] that I had taken in Tibet, he looked at one and said, "I remember that in this wall there was a hole where a large owl lived and my masters used to warn me that if I didn't study my lessons, this owl would come and pick me up and carry me off."

The Tibet of the Dalai Lama's Youth: The 1940s and 1950s

Tibet, a remote outpost of myth and fascination in the West for centuries, has attracted the interest of such diverse personalities as Helena Petrovna Blavatskaya [1831–1891], the eccentric Russian-born woman who in 1875 founded the Buddhist-influenced Theosophy Movement in the

United States and claimed to have visited Tibet in search of mystical fulfillment—a claim that has never been proven—and the Nazi hierarchy. The genocidal Adolf Hitler even went so far as to adopt and pervert the use of a Buddhist symbol of good fortune, the swastika, as his ultimate emblem of brutality. And during the winter of 1938, Nazi Reichsfuhrer Heinrich Himmler sent a five-man team of German scientist-adventurers to Lhasa to bolster the Nazi theory that the people of Tibet were the true descendants of the Aryans, Hitler's "Master Race."

Various Western governments have also been attracted to Tibet, albeit for very different reasons, the British interest having been strategic rather than mystical. The remote Land of Snows was not only the gateway from China to the jewel in the crown of their empire, the Indian subcontinent, but, more importantly, served as the buffer between Great Britain and an increasingly aggressive Russia. In 1903, at the behest of Lord Curzon [George Nathaniel, first Baron and first Marquis Curzon of Keddleston, 1858–1925; viceroy of India, 1899–1905] the British government sent a military expedition to Lhasa to negotiate with the Thirteenth Dalai Lama. The expedition, led by the quintessential British Empire hero Colonel Sir Francis Younghusband [1863–1942], an explorer known for his daring exploits through unmapped territory on the Chinese-Indian border, turned into a bloodbath in which several thousand Tibetan soldiers were killed. The splendidly arrayed expeditionary force, which included Indian troops, then rode into Lhasa, where they were greeted with claps and shouts—unknown to the conquering force, the Tibetan way of showing displeasure or worse. The Thirteenth Dalai Lama fled for a time to Mongolia, and the British cast about for other interlocutors, whiling away their time playing gentlemen's sports, and on August 19, 1904, making history of a sort by playing the first recorded game of football [soccer] on Tibetan soil. Later, they would impose a treaty on the Tibetan government in which British India would establish both a mission and telegraph facilities, paving the way for a much larger presence, including diplomats and civil servants assigned to the mission.

Prior to World War II, however, very few Westerners had been allowed to enter the vast, icy, and mysterious Himalayan country, whose isolation stemmed in part from an enormous geological event that had occurred 25 million years ago. At that time, the Indian subcontinent had smashed into the Eurasian land mass, raising the sea floor many thousands of feet to form a plateau the size of all Western Europe. For millennia, that once temperate plateau would be forced even higher, creating the forbidding climate and thin air of the largely inaccessible nation. Tibet would remain isolated well into the twentieth century, despite the progressive

Thirteenth Dalai Lama's attempt to modernize his nation in the face of stiff opposition from both its political and religious leadership.

Robert Ford   There was a lot of suspicion in the thirties of the Thirteenth Dalai Lama, who wanted to modernize. He bought three motor cars, and they arrived but were never used—things like this. They had the post and telegraph service up to Gyangze [Tibet's fourth largest city], which was run by Britain, and then from Gyangze up to Lhasa by the Tibetans, installed by the British. So it was a very slow process in that they for centuries had been cut off—a self-imposed isolation from the rest of the world. Only a handful of Tibetans had been to India; the vast majority had no idea of what the rest of the world was like. And so the radio was something quite magical in the sense that it could bring voices and sounds from another planet, almost. But from time to time, under the threat of pressure from outside influences, Tibetans started to think about having some idea of what was going on in the outlying districts. For instance, when I went to Chamdo, before I arrived there, the only communication between Lhasa and Chamdo was by courier. Riding night and day, changing horses very frequently, it would take ten days for a messenger to arrive with communications from Chamdo to Lhasa and vice versa.

Tsering Shakya   By the 1930s, near the end of the Thirteenth Dalai Lama's rule, Lhasa was changing; Tibet was changing. There were a growing number of young Tibetan children—children of Tibetan aristocrats—who were being educated in British public schools in India by the Colonial Service, and young aristocrats were going to military academies run by the British. And also, material culture in Lhasa was changing: motorbikes were introduced, cinema halls were being built. There were Indians—Ladakhi Muslim merchants—who were bringing these things in. Somebody would say: oh, it's a very good idea to set up a photographic studio.

Sometimes people tend to stress too much the isolation of Tibet. Compared to a lot of places, yes, it was isolated, but at the same time, it was not as isolated and cocooned as people assume. There was incredible transaction and things going on in Tibet—people coming from all over the world to Tibet. When people tend to talk about Tibet being isolated, you assume only if they haven't been there that it's closed. But then there were Mongols and people from St. Petersburg, Russia, coming; people from all over the Buddhist world were coming—Japanese, Chinese, Thais; merchants from Armenia, Iran, and Afghanistan were coming.

Lowell Thomas Jr., son of the late world traveler, broadcaster, and writer Lowell Thomas; participant in expeditions around the world; participant with his father in the 1949 trek to Tibet as the eighth American to be received by the Dalai Lama in Lhasa; author of *Out of This World*, his account of that expedition   We got the impression that they felt if they opened up those trails to make them suitable for planes, trucks, whatever, to come in, that their culture would be wiped out, their religion would be badly damaged, their whole way of life would change. And the leaders there knew enough about it that they just didn't want to have that come in and spoil the culture that they had had for God knows how many hundreds of years, going way back to the creation of the First Dalai Lama in A.D. 700. They did not want to get into the industrial age; they liked the way their life was going, and they felt that if they prayed hard enough, and often enough, that the Lord Buddha would take care of them. And when they died, they would be reincarnated, perhaps on a higher level if they had been good Buddhists, and if not, on a lower level, maybe coming back even as a louse, which, I think, they considered about the lowest living form. They just wanted nothing to do with our culture, really, but they did need help; they knew what was coming from the communists.

Robert Ford   Technically, I was the first paid employee of the Tibetan government. I took up with me some radio equipment left over from World War II. This was the days before the transistor, so the equipment wasn't that small, but it was small by those standards—equipment that had been used for the long-range penetration groups into Burma. It was all taken up by mule, of course. There were no roads, there were only tracks—there were no motorized vehicles at all—everything had to be carried by people or by mule, and this is how we carried our equipment.

Life in Tibet was one surprise after another and it was so absolutely fantastic and thrilling, particularly to a young man in his twenties. When I arrived in Chamdo, of course, there was no foreigner; no Westerner had lived there. The only Westerner who had been there was the British consul in Eastern China, and he in 1917 had traveled, actually, from China and got to Chamdo, where he stopped a war between tribes of the Chinese and the Tibetans. So there wasn't much to read about Chamdo, but I knew I was going to a part of Tibet that many Tibetans didn't know. It was part of Kham, and the Khampas are known as rather fierce people. When I said I was going there, various Tibetan friends of mine in Lhasa said, "My goodness! Is it going to be all right? There are lots of funny people down there"—funny in the sense of being rather dangerous. So this was all new to a young man with a sense of excitement.

Other Visitors from the West

Shortly after the end of World War II, other noteworthy foreigners arrived in Tibet. The high-profile explorer and broadcaster Lowell Thomas Sr. and his namesake son were welcomed in 1949 because Tibet was threatened with invasion by forces of the newly established People's Republic of China, and it was hoped that they would plead the Tibetan cause in the West. Others included Heinrich Harrer, a tall, blond, thirty-four-year-old mountaineer, and his companion, Peter Aufschnaiter, two escapees from a British detention camp in India. And in 1950, Fulbright scholar Frank B. Bessac and several companions who were accompanying a reputed CIA operative on a uranium-seeking mission survived a murderous rampage by nomads on the Tibetan border and were able to make their way to Lhasa.

It was late in the day on January 15, 1946, when the first of the post-war Westerners to arrive, Harrer and Aufschnaiter, glimpsed Lhasa's best-known landmark, the centuries-old Potala, from afar. The two adventurers, who had been trapped in India since the outbreak of the war in September 1939 and had escaped on their third attempt, had just endured a danger-fraught, seventy-day trek, first through British-occupied India and then across the frozen and forbidding wilds of Tibet. They were, understandably, exhausted, hungry, and filthy. Being Austrian nationals and thus regarded by the British bureaucracy as enemy aliens, the men immediately came under suspicion.

Robert Ford Obviously, having escaped from British internment in India, the British looked at them with some suspicion. [Hugh] Richardson was then the officer in charge of the mission and he helped them as much as he could. Arthur Hopkinson, who was the political officer in Sikkim in charge of British India's relations with Tibet, had served in the First World War and he took a very sympathetic attitude to Harrer and Aufschnaiter, in the sense that he knew what war was like, and I don't think it crossed his mind that they were Nazis as such. They weren't prisoners of war—they had been interned. When the Tibetan government said they wanted to expel Harrer and Aufschnaiter, that they didn't want them in the country, then the British government started to press—yes, they were escaped internees and they should be brought back—it was Hopkinson, basically, who said, "Hold on a little while; you don't have to push this so hard. These two chaps have had a hard time. Please let them stay a little while and recover." So he was the element that allowed Harrer and Aufschnaiter to stay in Lhasa.

Patrick French   There are two different points; one is that the film, *Seven Years in Tibet*, is nonsense; it's very different from the book. Then, if you get back to the book, well, that was ghostwritten—certainly the English version was adjusted. Would you have expected Harrer to talk about his own political background, writing a book of that kind at that time? Probably not. And again, it's very easy to say things with hindsight— that anybody who came from Germany or Austria shouldn't have been involved with them in terms of Hitler's rule and the Holocaust. Harrer can say, Well I was in Tibet at the time when the Holocaust was happening. It's a very difficult call; clearly he was, to some extent, part of that system, and that was glossed over until in the late nineties it began to be more widely known. As a historian I find it quite hard to make absolute judgments about people who are part of a regime that subsequently is shown to be evil—whether you can actually say that a person, particularly a young, ambitious man like Harrer, should necessarily have had the foresight to avoid being part of that.

Professor Robert Thurman   He wasn't really a Nazi. He wasn't political; he was just a mountain climber—that's how he got to Lhasa, by this incredibly intrepid journey.

Luckily for Harrer and Aufschnaiter, they were not arrested immediately upon their arrival at the Tibetan border. Instead, they were allowed to make their way to the capital, where they managed to find refuge in the home of a sympathetic and influential Lhasan named Thangme, known to locals as the "Master of Electricity" due to his position as head of the city's electrical works. And thus began Harrer and Aufschaniter's relationship with a nation and its people—a relationship that for seven years would bring Harrer into the very private world of the then ten-year-old boy revered by his followers as His Holiness the Fourteenth Dalai Lama.

Heinrich Harrer   We were the talk of the town when we arrived. We were for the first five or six days under house arrest, not permitted to leave the house of Thangme, who had taken us after we had got permission from the four cabinet ministers, and soon everybody was talking about us. His [the Dalai Lama's] brother, Lobsang, visited us at our place while we were staying at the house of Thangme. He was an officer of first rank; he was responsible for the electricity in Lhasa—and everybody came to visit us. People came every day to see us, among others, the brother of the Dalai Lama, who was a few years older and was His Holiness's best friend. He was a monk too but he was not a rinpoché; he was only a commoner monk. He later came to visit us also in Europe; he was later my very best friend, with whom I went swimming in the river and so on.

We were very much touched because we had escaped, and then we came to Lhasa and we never had hoped to see His Holiness. And the first time that he touched us—usually he had a tassel to bless people, but he blessed us with laying his hands on our heads. It lasted only a few minutes, and I looked up and he smiled at me and I had to continue on because the regent [Reting Rinpoché] was sitting a few yards from the throne.

Robert Ford   I didn't have much contact with the regent as such. They were all rather aloof. One must remember that at that time, their exposure to the West was minimal: when I went there in 'forty-five, at the mission, there was the doctor and his wife and myself. We were the only Westerners. Later, Harrer and Aufschnaiter arrived. From time to time, the political officer in Sikkim would come up, but very infrequently. So it was a very small community, and we mixed at a much higher rank than one would have done normally because we were part of a representative body—the official British Mission—so we were received and entertained by the highest officials. But the regent himself and his tutors generally kept very much aloof. They had their job to do; they didn't particularly seek contact with the outside world.

Lowell Thomas Jr.   It was a place I would have enjoyed going back to again, and probably would have in the following few years if it hadn't been for the invasion. But the Chinese moved too quickly, so I lost that opportunity to go back and there hasn't been another opportunity since, or any time that I'd really want to go, now that the Chinese are in there.

Dr. Frank B. Bessac had arrived in Beijing on a Fulbright Scholarship in 1947. In the fall of 1949, he set out for Tibet in the company of Douglas

Mackiernan, who was on a mission for the CIA, allegedly to find uranium there, and three Russian traveling companions. Six months later, on April 29, 1950, the five men crossed the border into Tibet, only to be met by a barrage of gunfire. Mackiernan and two of the Russians were killed.

Dr. Frank B. Bessac   When I arrived in what is called Tibet, we had seen some evidence of battles coming into the area. But we went eastward where we were met by people who killed three of my friends and wounded another. They shot at me and took me prisoner. And then a day and a half later, the group came that was under orders from Lhasa to give us protection and help. They were very friendly, and then we spent over a week in a little monastic Tibetan governmental house on the plateau where there were Tibetans who twenty years before had been to India and had been educated and could speak English. I settled down and found it very pleasant, except for the problem of my friends, who didn't. Because of my experience of living among other nomadic peoples and knowing how they raided, I felt that this was a rather natural thing. Those people who had killed my friends were of that area; they didn't know that they should come and protect us. I tried to protect them from receiving horrible punishment by the government but was unable to do that. I managed to get it so that the people who had murdered my friends wouldn't suffer terrible mutilations and disfigurations. The Tibetans wouldn't allow the government to execute people, so they had this in mind.

It ended up that, in large part because of my urging, they were whipped in public and removed from their governmental positions; I saw them being whipped. Then they were taken out and stood along the road. I went down that road and saw them standing there and got out and shook their hands to show them that I forgave them. They were thankful that I had done what I could for them, but I don't know what happened to them after that. Somebody told me that they weren't able to go back and assume positions as defenders of the outpost.

When I came to Lhasa what I did after catching my breath was to make it clear to them that I was not an official of the American government, that I wasn't State Department or CIA. They simply set up a number of interviews with various people: governmental people, cultural leaders, and outsiders, such as Heinie [Heinrich] Harrer and Hugh Richardson. And they arranged for me to speak at the General Assembly, their legislative body, where I talked to them at least a couple of times and attended their sessions to know how they were handling things.

The Visitors' First Impressions of the People of Lhasa

Dr. Frank B. Bessac My impression of the people of Lhasa was that they were very friendly, and that the city was a beautiful place. I didn't realize that their feudalism was much more friendly to the serfs than it was in Europe, but I didn't approve of their social organization. I thought that these were people who should be allowed to attain as much as they could in terms of changing the government and their society for the better. But they were friendly people who had a right to do this in terms of their own ethnicity.

Robert Ford Whenever I wasn't on duty, I used to go with Lobsang, a Tibetan member of the British mission who spoke beautiful English and knew English ways, to various places of interest in Lhasa and in the surrounding area. Then, of course, being a member of a very elite mission—there were only three Europeans there—one had invitations to government functions: lunches with the Tibetan government, with all officials of various kinds. And this continued, obviously, when I went as an employee of the Tibetan government. My status has changed, but by this time I spoke some Tibetan—this was two years later—and I was made to feel at home. I was welcomed everywhere, and I had a very privileged existence.

Lowell Thomas Jr. I had the feeling that maybe other cultures, perhaps, had better answers regarding the mysteries of life than even we did in the Western world, and since that might be the case, who are we to thumb our noses at other cultures? And even today, we see what's going on. Who are we to go and try to impose our democracy, let's say, in this case, on another people somewhere else? I've got a lot more respect actually for other ways of life. It's very broadening to one's mind, I think, to travel into countries like that. Before that, I'd spent some time in Turkey and Iran and had already developed that kind of an attitude about other ways of life, other cultures, so I think it was a great reinforcement for me of that basic thinking.

Curiosity among Tibetans about the Outside World

Robert Ford It was so strange to them. Later on, when I went to Eastern Tibet, my boss there was one of the cabinet ministers and we became very, very close. When we were discussing the Chinese threat, he said, "Well, you know, we should have some airplanes." He thought that since I had been in the air force, I'd be able to organize the planes, I'd be able to fly them, so I had to explain that airplanes just don't happen right there; you have to have a whole body of people to look after them, to service them, to fly them. But this was completely incomprehensible. After all, they had very little in the way of an army, anyway, and it was not well-equipped and well-organized, and this was a reflection of their lack of contact with the realities of the twentieth century.

Lowell Thomas Jr.   It was quite an insight—quite an impression—to go into one of those monasteries with thousands and thousands of monks and see them all together, waiting to have lunch, which was barley flour that they would make into *tsampa* [a staple of the Tibetan diet]. It was really quite an eye-opener, such a different society altogether.

Being in the Presence of the Young Dalai Lama

As a young boy, the Dalai Lama enjoyed a life of regal splendor, surrounded by courtiers, learned tutors, and high-ranking government officials in the Potala Palace, a thousand-room structure dating from the seventeenth century. The sprawling, seven-storied palace contained offices, storerooms, a monastery, chapels, and even a prison, and it was Lhasa's key landmark—the first and last sight of visitors to the Tibetan capital.

Yet, as grand as the Potala may have been, it was a forbidding place to the youngster from Taktser who had spent his toddler years sleeping near the kitchen stove in his parents' modest dwelling. In contrast to the coziness and warmth of his family's farmhouse, the young Dalai Lama's bedroom on the Potala's top floor was cold, poorly lit, filled with decrepit furniture, and infested with legions of mice that would scamper across the room and over his bed as the youngster slept.

The Dalai Lama's days were occupied with study—memorization of sacred texts, in particular—and meetings with members of his government. In those years it was a rigidly formulated autocracy dominated by high-ranking families and presided over until 1950 by a regent. There was, however, time for recreational pursuits. The youngster enjoyed playing with a clockwork train set and with lead soldiers. He also engaged in physical activity, jumping and running around his apartment as well as on the adjacent roof, from where he would spy on his subjects with powerful binoculars. Once, as he too enthusiastically swung an ivory-tipped walking stick that had belonged to the Thirteenth Dalai Lama, the youngster accidentally struck his brother Lobsang in the face, causing him to have a permanent scar.

In the early spring, the Dalai Lama would leave the Potala for the more pleasant surroundings of Norbulingka or "Jewel Park," the summer palace of the Dalai Lama, consisting of gardens, small buildings, and a private house shared by His Holiness with only his closest attendants. Even in that relatively relaxed environment, however, he was restricted by protocol from public view save for ceremonial occasions when, borne in his elaborate palanquin [an enclosed litter supported on the shoulders of bearers], he would be paraded before his people.

Gelek Rinpoché, incarnate lama; holder of Geshe Lharampa degree, Drepung Monastery; former monk; founder, Jewel Heart Organization for the Preservation of Tibetan Buddhist Culture In Western culture when we say we "met" someone, it implies we shook hands, sat down, and talked. This is not true in Tibetan culture, particularly as it relates to the Dalai Lama. My privilege was to first *see* His Holiness, rather than chat with him. I was very small—five or six years old—at that time. I remember that His Holiness was traveling, either from the Potala or the Norbulingka to the central temple in Lhasa; the procession went behind our house. There were many people lined up and I was there also. Suddenly, our eyes met. He leaned out of the palanquin and looked at me and gave me a big smile. As the palanquin moved ahead, he turned his body toward me and looked back at me. My mother was standing with me and as she observed the Dalai Lama, she said, "His Holiness likes you." That was my first, memorable, contact with His Holiness.

After I had been recognized as an incarnate lama, I would very often see His Holiness at ceremonies. Of course you could not say, "How are you? What do you think?" So, personally, His Holiness was very restricted. I was able to see him five or six times a year. Occasionally there would be a private audience. These meetings, which usually lasted fifteen to twenty minutes, a half-hour at the outside, were very well organized. A number of elder officials would be standing close by, so you could not say what you wanted. When His Holiness started giving teachings, it was the greatest pleasure to attend these meetings, where we sat very close to His Holiness. He would laugh and joke and make eye contact. That was the context of my contact with His Holiness in Tibet.

The Westerners' First Impressions
of the Young Dalai Lama

Robert Ford   I first met the Dalai Lama as a member of the mission, when the then-political officer in Sikkim, who was in charge of British relations with Tibet, came on an official visit to Lhasa. He was, of course, received by the Dalai Lama and I was part of the entourage. As he reminded me many years later, I was, perhaps, the youngest foreigner he'd seen—I was only twenty-two—and he was a little boy, of course. When I bent my head before him to receive his blessing, he tweaked the hair on the back of my neck. Technically, I was not supposed to look at the Dalai Lama, but I was so surprised at this that I kind of raised my head and looked and I saw a little smile there. This was his personal way of saying, "It's nice to see you and you're one of us."

Later on, from 1947, when I was a member of the Tibetan hierarchy, as it were, I went to all the formal occasions when the Dalai Lama was present and sat in my allocated rank place. The most moving occasion was when I left to go to Chamdo, in Eastern Tibet [in 1947]—this was under the auspices, under the employment of, the Tibetan government—and with my staff I had a private audience with His Holiness. It was kind of a farewell, a departure—"Go peacefully on your way," as they say in Tibet—and this was my farewell audience with His Holiness. In fact, it was the last time I saw him in Tibet. He was a minor and, of course, this audience was ordered by protocol—there was strict and unrelenting formality about *every* occasion. I must say that on these occasions His Holiness didn't speak, so to say that one was "received" by the Dalai Lama, you didn't actually have a conversation with him; you were received and you were blessed.

Heinrich Harrer   I saw him in the road, like everybody else. There were thousands of people looking when he was carried on his palanquin when he was brought from the Potala into the town—there was a big procession—and he peeked out of the window, saw me, and waved at me. And then a few days later—it was the Tibetan New Year—I met the Donyer Chenmo; he was the chief chamberlain of His Holiness and he said, "You're welcome to come to the New Year's reception, which is in a few weeks"—the Tibetan New Year is two months later than ours; I had arrived in January, and in the middle of February was the reception at the Potala. Then I was called to the Potala, and in the meantime there were clothes from the Tibetans, so we were dressed quite well. We stood in a line like everybody else, not in the masses; they gave us permission to stay in the row of the very first people after the ministers—when meeting His Holiness at New Year it was subject to protocol, and we were in the first row after the ministers to reach His Holiness. Then we got a *katak* from the Donyer Chenmo, which we presented to him. The Dalai Lama was sitting very high up, much higher, and we were standing forward. Usually no one is looking up, but we looked up and then he smiled at me and blessed me by putting his hands on my head. But then I had to continue because the regent was sitting there and he was a very much feared person. It was the first time he touched me; it was only three weeks after I had arrived in Lhasa.

Lowell Thomas Jr. He was fourteen that year. He was pretty remote. He smiled at us; obviously, he was curious about total strangers from another part of the world. He did not speak to us, of course, nor were we allowed to speak directly to him. My father's impressions were the same as mine— that he seemed to be a very intelligent, bright-eyed young boy. We just felt that he seemed to be burdened enormously. To me, he was smiling, but he was very quiet. And he was surrounded, of course, by officials—the regent, for example, and the lord chamberlain. And then it was suggested that the Dalai Lama would pose for pictures inside this very dark palace where he was. They let us set up outside, in the Dalai Lama's private garden, and then we were able to take some pictures of him, 16-millimeter movies, while he was sitting on his throne, surrounded by beautiful flowers and again by his staff.

Dr. Frank B. Bessac The Dalai Lama was about fifteen in 1950. I wasn't allowed to interview him, but I saw him and he just looked like a nice young man who was thoughtful and pleasant. He gave the impression of being an intelligent young man who was interested in seeing me and felt very friendly, but we weren't allowed to—we didn't have any time to sit down and talk things over. He wasn't allowed at that time to have interviews with outside people.

Of the early postwar visitors, Harrer would have the most impact on the young, impressionable Dalai Lama.

Harrer's Relationship with the Dalai Lama's Family

Professor Jonathan Mirsky   He was parted from his mother very young and raised by rather severe tutors, and the people he got on best with were the servants in the palace and in the summer residence. I think that one of the reasons he liked those two Austrians who came to Lhasa during the war was that he had a kind of normal relationship with them.

Heinrich Harrer   She [the Dalai Lama's mother] visited us. She had just had a young child. They [court officials] came one day with the invitation from the family of His Holiness, and we said, "When can we go? We are in the house all day; we are not supposed to leave the house of Mr. Thangme." So then they said, "If the family of the Dalai Lama calls you, then you can certainly go without any hesitation." So we went, the first time we left the house of Thangme, and came to the house of the Dalai Lama, which was just below the Potala. Then we were ushered into the third floor and there, on a very high level, was sitting his brother, [Thubten Jigme], Norbu Rinpoché, the father of the Dalai Lama, and the mother. They received us in European fashion. After we left visiting the family of the Dalai Lama, his mother gave us a big cover made of sheep wool, which is common, instead of a sleeping bag. And she gave us also a bag full of rice and another bag full of tsampa—it was about forty kilos; and then a big leather bag full of butter—the butter was sewn up in a Yak hide because it had come a thousand kilometers from the Himalayas.

When we left the house and came back home everybody knew, of course, that we had been visiting the family of the Dalai Lama, and in the procession home, the Sherpas were carrying our loads of tsampa and we were sort of *personae gratae*—we were suddenly somebody and everybody could visit us. So this was the very beginning of meeting the family of the Dalai Lama. Afterward—I didn't know at that time—but Lobsang went right away afterward up to the Potala and they brought His Holiness because he could visit him any time, and it was probably an order of His Holiness when the mother said to me, "His Holiness the Dalai Lama wants to meet us." So it was ordered by His Holiness the Dalai Lama. A few days later, we were invited once more.

Lobsang was very kind because he came to visit us more often. In the meantime, we had moved away from Thangme's house to Tsarong's house. When we stayed in Tsarong's house we were free to move in the town, and our first visits were to the four cabinet ministers—one after the other. But the connection with the Dalai Lama was only beginning. The next time I met him was when he came in the procession from the Potala into the Norbulingka, which is two miles distant. Thousands of people were lining the roadway where he was carried in his sedan chair. He just looked out from the window and waved at me. That was the first contact. I didn't see him for the next year or so.

The Young Dalai Lama's Personality and Interests

Heinrich Harrer   He saw us with his binoculars—he watched us from the Potala roof when we were swimming or playing in the garden in the big park. There I introduced a shower. I became very intimate with the whole family of the Dalai Lama. Then one day, it was, of course, years later, there was all this ice skating—I introduced skating—and every time his brother, Lobsang, told him what we were doing, which you could see only with binoculars or not at all. So one day, three years after our arrival, he decided to call for me, via his brother, Lobsang. And then Lobsang said, "Tomorrow you must come with me. We will go up to see His Holiness." That was in the Norbulingka, not in the Potala.

Then [in 1948] the Dalai Lama called for me and asked me whether I could build him a cinema. I was used to never saying no because we were supposed to know everything that was Western. So I said, "Yes, of course I can build a cinema." And so I started building the cinema, not very bad, but not exactly to the truth. And then when the cinema was finished, it turned out it was only a pretense that he called me and said he wanted to have a cinema made. It turned out that it was more or less a pretext for him to meet me. That was the very beginning.

Tsering Shakya   This was not happening because of Harrer. By the 1930s, there were cinemas and photographic studios in Lhasa. Society was changing; the whole society was opening up because of trade, because of the opening to India. The Dalai Lama met with a lot of Tibetans from different parts of Tibet who had traveled to different parts of the world. So it was possible that the Dalai Lama himself would be opened up.

Professor Robert Thurman   Harrer was an extremely important influence on the Dalai Lama, who jumped at the chance of gaining exposure to the West from him. He was delighted to have Harrer there. Harrer was extremely imperfect in the sense that he was not highly educated; he was a mountain climber, a peasant from Austria. Even though Harrer was not that well-educated, and not a thinker, the Dalai Lama was able to learn much about the West and the world from him. Harrer was an important influence, which I recognized when I arrived in India, and the Dalai Lama immediately jumped on me because I could speak Tibetan with him.

Heinrich Harrer   We built the cinema. He had a special place in the summer garden in Norbulingka prepared for it. So I erected a wall, projector, and a screen, and they had only a hole through the wall between the screen and the projector. He sat alone there watching the movie while I was sitting in the little projection room. But he went right away to the room where I was standing with the projector and then—I don't know how long it lasted—we looked at some movies. The first one was about [U.S. Army General Douglas] MacArthur [1880–1964]. He admired MacArthur very much. In any case, when the movie was over, I was standing there, where he was sitting on the floor—no cushions, nothing—and then he pulled me down and I was sitting next to him. There were four people attending him, three monks and the chief chamberlain; there were four people attending him wherever he went and whatever he did. Later on, when we met every day, he waved them away, so we were always sitting alone there.

The Young Dalai Lama's Intellectual Curiosity

Heinrich Harrer   First of all, he was curious about our life. Neither the three monks who attended him all day long, nor the two teachers, nor the regent, Reting Rinpoché, had ever left Tibet, so they couldn't explain anything to him of the outside world. But I had two people who protected my going, supported my going—quietly, not officially. One was the mother of the Dalai Lama—she had also never left Tibet, but she realized that it might be very good for her son one day if he got information—so there was a close connection to her. I stayed over in her house in the Norbulingka, outside the inner wall, and she watched always the big door into the inner wall when the regent left after giving his lectures to His Holiness. When he had left and gone to his own palace, she pushed me out and His Holiness was already waiting and waved at me, and then the door opened— there were two of his guards in front of the door—and I moved in. One day, when I was late, his mother scolded me terribly. She said, "You are late today"—maybe it was ten minutes or so, not more—and she said, "You know how much it means to His Holiness that you are coming, so don't come late any more."

Patrick French   His mother was a huge influence over him even though as a young monk he couldn't be with her as much as he wanted to. But she remained very important throughout her life. His father was very different. He was somebody who you tend not to hear so much about. He was an angry, aggressive, unpopular man. Older Tibetans who remember the period when the Dalai Lama's father was alive really don't have very many good things to say about him. If you read the records of British officials who were in the mission in Lhasa, they describe all sorts of instances of his throwing his weight around, or of people who were supposed to be work-ing for him demanding those things that they weren't entitled to. The obvi-ous thing would be to say that he must have been influenced by that, but he seems so unlike his father. And he also doesn't even necessarily appear to be reacting against his father, particularly. But I suspect that the father figures in his life are people he mentions in his autobiography, and the impression I get of them—in fact, there was one whom I met—they were probably very impressive, wise older men who were the father figures in his life. And I imagine that his calmness is something that he learned from them. I don't know how important his brothers and his sister are to him.

Gelek Rinpoché   As a young man, His Holiness could occasionally see his blood relatives. His brother, Lobsang Samten, was an exception; he was sort of his buddy, so he would see him all the time. Some of His Holi-ness's teachers told me that when they had to be tough on him, Lobsang became the "blame boy"—the teachers would be rough on Lobsang in the hope that His Holiness would be frightened.

Robert Ford   Harrer claims to have been tutor to the Dalai Lama. But to have the formal role of tutor to the Dalai Lama would mean that you are his religious tutor, which, of course, Harrer would never claim to have been. So in that sense, some Tibetans would say—and have said to me— "Well, he wasn't a tutor to the Dalai Lama; his tutors were A, B, and C, and that was it. And this is not correct." And I would say, "Well, look, you know he's using it in a Western sense, not in a Tibetan sense: he taught the Dalai Lama some English and a little bit about Western ways, and, in that sense, he was a teacher."

Heinrich Harrer   I taught him how to shake hands, for instance, which is done in Europe. The Tibetans have a custom: they never touch another person with their hands, like in Europe; there was always a distance kept. To me he talked like this, so we were laughing together. My Tibetan was, of course, later quite fluent, but at the beginning, I spoke only the dialect of the farmers and later I learned quite a lot of the honorific terms. I got more movies from Hugh Richardson; he was the political officer in Lhasa of the British. With him I was very good friends and from him I could get new reels of film to show His Holiness. I will never forget that he gave me once Shakespeare's *Henry IV*—"Uneasy lies the head that wears a crown" [*Henry IV, Part 2*, Act II, Scene 4]. He sent me that and I repeated it very often and he said he could see how a king can be removed. I didn't mention that it could happen to him, but it did happen to him, and I think that no king has had a worse fate than the Dalai Lama—it was exactly what Shakespeare said: "Uneasy lies the head that wears the crown."

He had seen the peace treaty made by MacArthur in Tokyo with the Japanese and he was interested to notice that in Lhasa all the courtiers admired very much the Japanese because the Japanese are Asians. And later on, the Tibetans admired also the Koreans when the Americans were not capable to conquer the line between South and North Korea; it filled them with a certain pride that an Asian nation was capable of opposing a big nation like the United States. In any case, it was self-defeating because if the Americans are in this war and it ends in favor of the Americans, then the Chinese would have been occupied in that war and they wouldn't have been free to move into Tibet. They couldn't understand that. They always said that the best forces in the world have certainly been the Japanese.

Patrick French   I'm sure that he was interested in meeting Harrer, but Harrer probably exaggerates his own importance in the formation of the young Dalai Lama. Clearly, the young Dalai Lama was a curious child. I know that the British who had the mission in Lhasa at that time gave him mechanical toys, objects that he was very excited by. And he liked looking at picture books with photos of distant lands, so he was intellectually curious in a way that went beyond his Tibetan Buddhist training.

Robert Ford   He was a young boy; he was being brought up in all the attributes of Buddhism and spent time studying with his tutor and with others, because he met all the fellow rinpochés from the other monasteries, and he went through the ritual of a young Buddhist monk. Obviously he was a special person, but he had to do his studies like everyone else, and it was a period of great trial for him: it required a great deal of concentration. And, finally, he got the rank of geshe, of doctor—he graduated, as it were—but, of course, he was apart: he was a rinpoché, an incarnate lama, *the* incarnate lama; there were other incarnate lamas, of course, but *he* was the Supreme Being.

Chapter Five

COMING OF AGE IN OCCUPIED TIBET: UPRISING AND EXILE

In late 1949, following the establishment of the People's Republic of China, the People's Liberation Army (PLA) launched a series of incursions into Eastern Tibet. Those forays would evolve in the autumn of 1950 into an all-out invasion by tens of thousands of troops. The now fifty-five-year occupation of Tibet has resulted in the deaths of 1 million Tibetans, one-sixth of the population, while others were routinely tortured or imprisoned for their religious practices and resistance to the Chinese aggression. The occupation also resulted in the destruction of more than six thousand monasteries, which were looted of precious religious and national artifacts; the forced communization of hundreds of thousands of villagers; the devastation of the country's ecosystem, with Tibet being used for the production of nuclear weaponry and as a dumping ground for nuclear waste; and the transfer of ethnic Chinese, making indigenous Tibetans a minority in their own nation. Further, the people of Tibet became subject to the vicissitudes of China's internal political struggles, most notably in the period known as "The Great Leap Forward" and during the Cultural Revolution.

The Chinese Rationale for the Invasion

Sun Wade   Historically, Tibet has been part of China from the time of the T'ang Dynasty, actually, which is from A.D. 618 to 907. The Tibetans in Han had, through marriages between royal families and meetings leading to alliances, cemented political and kinship ties of unity and political friendship and formed close economic and cultural relations. So they had actually laid a strong foundation for the ultimate founding of a unified nation. In the mid-thirteenth century, Tibet was officially incorporated into the territory of China's Yuan Dynasty [established by Kublai Khan, 1215–1294, conqueror of China and founder of the Mongol Dynasty]. So since then, China has exercised several dynastic changes, but Tibet has remained under the jurisdiction of the central government of China. And the government held the power to confirm the reincarnation of all high Buddhas of Tibet. In the autumn of 1911, a revolution took place in China's interior, overthrowing the seventy-year-old ruler of the Ching Dynasty and established the Republic of China. In the previous dynasties, the central government of the People's Republic of China exercised jurisdiction over Tibet. The Bureau of Mongolian and Tibetan Affairs was established by the central government in 1912 to replace the Ching Dynasty's department in charge of Mongolian administration affairs, and the Bureau was responsible for local Tibetan affairs. In April 1940, the Commission for Mongolian and Tibetan Affairs opened an office in Lhasa as the Permanent Mission of the Central Government in Tibet. The death of the Thirteenth Dalai Lama in December 1933 was reported to the central government by the Tibetan local government in the traditional manner, and the Tibetan local government also followed the age-old system: you report in to the central government all the procedures that should be followed in the search for the reincarnation of the late Thirteenth Dalai Lama.

Harry Wu   Way back to the Kuomintang government, they always said Tibet was part of China. In 1991, I went back to China [after having been imprisoned in the laogai system for many years]. There are two [laogai] locations, one in the Takla Makan Desert, the other one in the Gobi Desert. Actually, it's the Chinese Siberia—just like Moscow, they exile people there. My major concern was the laogai system; I know that many people have disappeared in the desert—along the desert are huge labor camps, just like Magadan [the infamous Soviet hard labor camp where many dissidents, including Jewish refuseniks, were imprisoned during the communist era]. So I secretly crossed and they said, "There is a tomb over there; in the Tang Dynasty [A.D. 618–907], a princess married a Tibetan king—this is a very common story among the Chinese. By the Tang Dynasty we had already combined together. So isn't Tibet a part of China? Of course!" I say, "Wait a minute," because on the tomb it very clearly describes the princess—actually she is *not* a princess; she's just a pretty girl selected by the emperor—as Chinese. She is escorted to the Chinese border and then met at the Tibetan border and escorted by Tibetans. The *border!* Then I found a publication from the Beijing authorities, a so-called historical map, from today, the Ching Dynasty, Ming Dynasty, Han Dynasty. Tibet was never part of China; they lie!

Tensions Leading Up to the Invasion

Heinrich Harrer   After the advance of the Chinese communists, I made my report to the Dalai Lama and to the foreign ministers. I had a radio receiver—it was very, very old; I have pictures where I'm sitting next to this radio set—actually I had foreseen when they would go and make their first attack. They moved always in the moonlight, when it was very bright. They moved far into the country they wanted to occupy. I warned the Tibetans and, as you know, they tried to do something. For me it was very difficult because I had to be very careful; some of the Tibetans even considered me a warmonger—that I thought such things would happen to Tibet.

Robert Ford   There was always a sense of fear among a lot of the people. All they knew of the Chinese was their ill treatment of the Tibetans in the 1915 to 1917 period, and there was a great deal of suspicion, so there was always the fear that the Chinese might come. I don't think anyone expected them to come quite so quickly, quite as soon as they did in 1950, having only come to power in 1949.

Gelek Rinpoché   To some people in Tibet, the Chinese invasion was a surprise. They had a strong belief that Tibet was a holy place. It had huge, snowbound mountains that were difficult to cross. But I heard from my parents that the Chinese *were* coming. Propaganda came by radio from China, suggesting that China had military power well beyond what one could imagine: the Chinese could come by air, by water, they could come through the mountain passes. And also we knew what had happened in Mongolia. Then, too, people were flowing in from Eastern Tibet and selling their possessions very cheaply in the Lhasa market. These things were happening in front of our faces, but the government did not wake up. Many officials believed that they could talk with the Chinese. After all, they are human beings. Some officials also considered themselves experts in diplomacy. Some people in the monasteries did not want to disturb the peace. The village people thought nothing would happen to them because they were villagers. The nomads thought nothing could happen to them. So this was the situation Tibet faced.

———————

Historically, China and Tibet were separate nations. Indeed, the Thirteenth Dalai Lama reiterated Tibet's independence in 1913. China, however, both during the years of the national regime and following the establishment of the People's Republic in 1949, desired to incorporate Tibet into its own territory. The large-scale Chinese invasion of Tibet in the autumn of 1950 paved the way for takeover. The Tibetan army was powerless to counter China's overwhelming advantage in both troops and weaponry, and by 1951 Lhasa itself had come under Chinese occupation.

The government of Tibet's appeals to the United Nations, as well as to its traditional allies—Great Britain, India, and the United States—for assistance in stemming the Chinese aggression went unheeded. At the UN, there was little interest in placing the issue of Tibet on its already crowded post–World War II agenda. Further, the organization and those nations that normally might have sympathized with Tibet's plight had by then become engaged in a major military action on the Korean Peninsula.

In an attempt to deal with the developing crisis, the Dalai Lama and his government made a strategic, temporary move to Dromo, a town in southern Tibet that is close to the Indian border. During His Holiness's stay in Dromo, the Chinese initiated political discussions with a delegation of Tibetan officials headed by Ngabo Ngawang Jigme, the displaced governor of one of Tibet's easternmost provinces. On May 3, 1951, under Chinese coercion and without clear guidance from the Dalai Lama, Jigme signed the Seventeen Point Agreement, which, in essence, mandated Chinese sovereignty over Tibet.

The Dalai Lama, on learning in a radio broadcast of the signing of the agreement, expressed deep shock, declaring that the terms were "far worse and more oppressive than anything we had imagined." Whatever the circumstances surrounding the creation of the Seventeen Point Agreement, as well as the issue of whether Jigme possessed the authority to sign it, the People's Republic of China had created a legal pretext for control of Tibet.

In 1987, at a meeting of the U.S. Congressional Human Rights Caucus, the Dalai Lama articulated a Five Point Peace Plan to resolve the decades-long conflict with China. Stressing peace and human rights, the plan called for respect for the Tibetan people's human rights and democratic freedoms. The Dalai Lama proposed that Tibet become a non-violent, demilitarized zone. Under this plan Tibet's natural environment would be restored and protected.

Rinchen Dharlo   My native town is right at the border. The Chinese did not come right away after they invaded and signed the Seventeen Point Agreement. The Seventeen Point Agreement was signed in 1951. I think the first group of Chinese arrived in my native town sometime around 'fifty-six and they were there for a little over a year. Then, all of a sudden, all of them left our native town and people were happy; they thought that now the Chinese were going back to China. But then there was a revolt in Central Tibet and the Chinese soldiers were deployed to crush the uprising. We did not know anything about this.

The Chinese March into Lhasa

Gelek Rinpoché   I very well remember the day the Chinese soldiers arrived in Lhasa. They came behind my house, carrying a huge banner and photos of Mao. They had a marching band as well. The people of Lhasa were on the street to see the arrival. There is a funny thing in old Tibetan culture: when you clap, it means "Get out of here! Get lost!" But when the Chinese saw the residents of Lhasa clapping, they assumed this was a public welcome. So when the Chinese distributed propaganda photos and films of their arrival in Lhasa, the whole world thought that the people of Tibet were welcoming them. But the Tibetans were saying, "Get lost! Get out of here!"

Pema Chhinjor   The Tibetan freedom fighters were very innocent; they didn't realize how powerful the Chinese were. At the same time, China, for political reasons, did not want to use all of its force. The world was watching what China was doing to Tibet.

The Dalai Lama Gets On with His Life
during the Occupation

In 1959, as he faced the certainty of exile, His Holiness, who had begun his religious education as a small boy and was now in his early twenties, sat for his rigorous, day-long final examinations at the Jokhang Temple in Lhasa. During the morning session, he was examined by thirty scholars on logic; in the afternoon, he debated with fifteen scholars on the subject of the Middle Path; and in the evening, his knowledge of the canon of monastic discipline and metaphysics was tested by thirty-five authorities— all sessions conducted in the presence of twenty thousand monk-scholars.

Geshe Lhundrup Sopa   I was the partner of the examiner when His Holiness took the examination for the geshe degree in Tibet. His examination was, in some ways, not like that of other, more ordinary, geshe exams. It was a bit different, formal. Usually at the exam, there are abbots of the great monasteries—government officials and scholars. They will grade the examination. When His Holiness took the exam, representatives from the major monasteries were selected as examiners. It took all day—morning, noon, and evening—so three times he had to take examinations on many, many different topics. He answered all the questions very brilliantly; even my own questions were brilliantly answered. Of course, everyone expected him to do very well: he had prepared for a very long time; every day at the Norbulingka, scholars from the great monasteries would debate with him, so he was well-prepared. In that instance when I was the partner in the examination of His Holiness, there was no time to form a personal relationship, but I had the impression that he was a great scholar and a most intelligent and compassionate person. Later, when I left Tibet and came to Dharamsala, I had the opportunity for a more personal conversation with His Holiness. And again, my impression was that he was intelligent, kind, and a Dalai Lama such as there never was before.

Professor Jonathan Mirsky   I was in the back of a car with him many years ago here [in London] and I'd been reading about the examinations one has to pass to receive the geshe degree. He said he found it extremely difficult and that he was rather lazy, and when it got to a few months of when he was going to have to take this exam, one of his tutors said to him, "You know, it's going to be awfully embarrassing if you fail this exam." Since he'd already been identified as the Dalai Lama, they could hardly take that away from him, but it would be embarrassing if he failed these exams in Buddhist doctrine. And he said, "Suddenly I felt something working inside me and it became very simple for me to study: that was the first time I really, truly believed that I felt the Thirteenth Dalai Lama—who was a very scholarly man—inside me, making it possible for me to take these exams." That, at least, was a story of his that made me realize that as a young man he had had some doubts about himself.

Professor Robert Thurman   He was isolated in Lhasa. He would hear gossip from the janitors in the Potala and the Norbulingka. He didn't like injustice. He would look down through his spy glass at the people in the prison beneath the Potala; he felt sympathetic to them. He was already making reforms, especially once the Chinese came. That is why he did not flee initially. He tried to bring reform in collaboration with the Chinese, but he found that they were insincere: they were not actually trying to liberate the Tibetans from some former social structure; they were just trying to occupy and annex the country.

Geshe Tsultim Gyaltsen, holder, Lharampa Geshe Degree [highest degree]; author; founder and spiritual director, Thubten Dhargye Ling ["Land of Flourishing Dharma"] Center, Long Beach, California [so named by the Dalai Lama]   Before 1958, we had the Seventeen Point Agreement. It said that the Chinese could not attack the policy of the Tibet government and also they couldn't disturb the monasteries. Then, just before His Holiness took the examination with the great monastics, we had tremendous fear, and also secretly thought about whether he would be successful or not because the Chinese would make difficulties with the Tibetan government, so we started to worry.

Gelek Rinpoché   In Dharamsala [where the Tibetan government in exile was established], the situation completely changed. Unlike previous Dalai Lamas, he made eye contact with people. In the old style, the Dalai Lama looked up in the air rather than *at* people. There was also a bureaucracy that was placed between the Dalai Lama and the people. The more the Dalai Lama was hidden from people, the more important the bureaucrats became. But even before arriving in India, His Holiness began the changes during his last years in Tibet, after he assumed control of the government at the age of fifteen. He worked to change the bureaucratic system completely. In Tibet, there was a huge gap between the government and the people, like the difference between hell and heaven, so this fifteen-year-old boy tried to pick up the work for change begun by the Thirteenth Dalai Lama. But the Fourteenth Dalai Lama's changes were met with tremendous obstacles and opposition from the old Tibetan bureaucratic level, as well as from the Chinese. In India, he was able to make changes so, finally, he could function the way he wanted to.

The Lives of Other Tibetans under Occupation

Gelek Rinpoché   I was between eighteen and nineteen. The Chinese had given me the rank of editorial board member of a newspaper. I received a salary but I never spent a single day in the office. My education was religious in content, one which did not emphasize writing at all. The Chinese would also give gifts, and one of my teachers would say, "These are poisons and one day they will demand to know where they are, so you can't touch them." And we put the gifts away.

Arjia Rinpoché, the only Tibetan high lama of Mongolian descent; former abbot, Kumbum Monastery; reincarnation of Lumbum Gye, father of Tsong Khapa, founder of the Gelupa sect of Tibetan Buddhism; founder, Tibetan Center for Compassion and Wisdom, California   When I came to Kumbum Monastery, I was very young, two years old. I was so young that I can't remember everything. But one thing I very much remember is when His Holiness came to our monastery. I was very young—five or six years old. That was before 1958, so our traditional roles were still there, so all the rinpochés and monks in the monastery hosted His Holiness in a welcoming ceremony. When His Holiness came, he gave me lots of candies—obviously, kids like candy—so I was very excited and happy. He gave me so much and I was so young so I couldn't handle it, and some of it fell down to the floor. Then everybody was laughing and His Holiness was laughing. I remember that picture until today.

Life in the Monasteries

Geshe Tsultim Gyaltsen   I was seven years old when I started in the local monastery. When I was sixteen, I wanted to go to the great monastery, Sera, near Lhasa. I had a very strong wish to go to Sera because my local monastery and Sera debated the same texts, with the same lamas, the same teachers. The next day, we went to Ganden Monastery. Immediately, I changed my mind.

Arjia Rinpoché   I was the rinpoché [abbot] of the [Kumbum] Monastery. The monks have rinpochés, which are reincarnations of the father of Lama Tsong Khapa. When I grew up a little bit—I was four or five years old then—I can remember a little bit. At that time my daily life there was mostly with my two brothers and some assistants. And then, also, every day I had to recite prayers, so it was very difficult for me. I tell the truth: I didn't like to say the prayers all the time, so it was very difficult for me. Even so, I said the prayers. In the morning, when I got up, I had to go to Buddha's altar and say the prayers, do the prostrations—that was our routine. Then, later, there was a class, even though I was very young. Then I said some prayers. I played a lot, and then I wrote a little bit. Also, my teacher was very kind, so he gave me other education, like how to deal with daily life, how to be kind to other people. So mostly at that time, my daily life was very simple and easy. Then, when I grew up a little bit— when I was seven or eight years old—my schedule was better settled. Of course, every day we said the prayers, we studied a lot, and also I had some kind of social contact with people, like monks who came to me, asking questions—that's a traditional idea. Although I couldn't handle that and I had to ask my teachers right away, even so, I had to do the procedure.

When I was young, I liked to draw pictures and later I was very much interested in architecture. So then my uncle, who was the previous Panchen Lama's teacher, supported me in studying architecture. Then, later, after the 1980s, he taught me and I worked with him and did lots of three-dimensional Kalachakra mandalas [sacred diagrams used in visualization and meditation] work there. That gave me a good chance. Later, after 1990, I became an abbot of Kumbum Monastery, and during that time we did a big renovation in Kumbum, so I had a good chance to practice my architecture. Usually I do designs for the temples and *stupas* [repositories for relics]. Also, I did a three-dimensional Kalachakra mandala and when I was exiled here, I built one here. [This mandala has been on display at the Smithsonian Institution in Washington, D.C., and at Tibet House in New York City.]

Abrupt Changes in the Late 1950s

Arjia Rinpoché   In our place in 1958 there was a big change. Kumbum Monastery is in Eastern Tibet; that's far away from Lhasa. In our place, until 1958, everything was fine. Afterward, the Chinese government all of a sudden changed the rules and closed the monastery—that was called

"The Great Leap Forward"—so, one day, all of a sudden, we had a big meeting in the monastery—it's a ceremonial area. At that time, we had three or four thousand monks there. Then there was a big meeting—everybody went—and then, all of a sudden, the workers, the Chinese officials, the cadres, and the soldiers came and called for the reform of the religion. They arrested lots of monks, and then there was no more religious life in the monastery. My teachers, my assistants, the housekeepers, and everybody except me were arrested. I was sent to a Chinese school with somebody else, who was a stranger, so I had to stay with him. The monks worked in the fields.

Harry Wu   In 1959, when the People's Liberation Army marched to Lhasa and put down the uprising, I had already received a so-called tag as a counterrevolutionary Rightist and I was separated from the people, I was isolated as an enemy of the people and the government. And the Chinese authorities organized a big exhibition to try to educate the people. They said: this is politically necessary; we will liberate the people there. There is a slave system in Tibet and Tibet is ruled by someone like the Dalai Lama, so we want to bring the people back to the socialist liberation and we will be together with the Mongolians and Tibetans, free. And we had no chance to read any information, or truth from the course book, or publications. We were always told Tibet was part of China; we believed it was part of China; we agreed that this was a scandal, a kind of international, imperialist allegation, trying to separate our motherland, take away Tibet— the British were doing that; and right now the Americans are doing that. The majority today would agree with that.

Gelek Rinpoché's Escape

Gelek Rinpoché   I was always an anticommunist in my blood, thinking that they are here to destroy us. I knew very well what had happened to Mongolia. I knew when the Chinese would have power there was no way I could remain. In 1959, a number of my classmates who came from Eastern Tibet told me what would happen. They said, "They will arrest all of you—your kind of people. If you go into forced labor you will be lucky, so you'd better go now." But I had not yet completed my studies.

On the day of the uprising [March 10, 1959], I saw my parents for the last time. From the Drepung Monastery I saw large truck movements— the road was filled from east to west—so we knew that something had happened that night. I went to bed and was awakened at 2 A.M. by the sound of gunfire. People started getting up and putting lights on. They were uneasy and tried to find out what was going on. There was a soldier present who knew how to receive mirror signals. That day, I stayed in the monastery but in the evening I knew I had to leave. I had put aside many boxes of Chinese silver coins and a bagful of Indian currency in my desk. I never took it. Instead, I ran to the mountains. There was no place to hide since the Chinese were throwing up firecrackers to light the area. So we kept on going from village to village. Finally I reached my family's estate, where there should have been many mules. But the khampas had taken them. I stayed there for ten days. At one point, a Chinese helicopter flew overhead and started firing; the bullets hitting the ground near me were like water boiling. Eventually I was able to leave, although when the villagers saw me they cried and begged me not to go: there were armed Chinese soldiers on the other side of the river. Then someone led me across the mountain. All told, I traveled for one month.

The Dalai Lama Flees

Shortly before ten o'clock on the evening of March 31, 1959, the Dalai Lama, three months shy of his twenty-fourth birthday, and nearly ten years into his role as political and spiritual leader of his conquered people, disguised as a simple soldier, made his way from the shrine dedicated to Mahakala, his personal protector divinity, into the chilly night air. First, though, he walked around the building, stopped to imagine his escape, then returned for a moment to the shrine's entrance, where he imagined his return to Tibet. Then the admittedly frightened young man—the thought of capture by the Chinese terrified him—removed his glasses and stepped outside, to be met by two soldiers who escorted him through a huge crowd, and, accompanied eventually by more than three hundred Tibetan freedom fighters, endured a perilous journey to India, during which he had to cope with terrible weather and illness, not to mention the constant threat of discovery by the Chinese.

Pema Chhinjor   I was at a freedom fighters' camp in the southern part of Lhasa. There was communication between the camp and the Norbulingka, but the information was top secret so that nobody would know that His Holiness was leaving. Only our high leaders, including my brother, knew of His Holiness's plans.

Geshe Tsultim Gyaltsen   Normal people didn't know. But then, four weeks after His Holiness left, we all knew. Then many people did not want to stay in the country; they wanted to escape; they thought it would be terrible in our country because His Holiness had left. I, myself, also wanted to follow His Holiness.

I wasn't thinking about my studies; I was thinking about how to escape from the Chinese—to be free of the soldiers. Everybody was like that. I had only some books and texts for study—that's all, nothing else. I left from Ganden. I went through the Himalayas to South Tibet—many thousands of refugees got through that way. The roads were not open at that time because of the very deep snow. We didn't have a choice. Before there was a narrow road that some people knew and were first, and then we followed those people through the mountains. We were up in the mountains for two days. Chinese soldiers tried to have a round-up at the border, but one day before they came, we saw the border with India.

Pema Chhinjor   We were told to hold our positions to keep the Chinese troops from intercepting His Holiness. We knew how to operate in the mountains; some of the Chinese troops had breathing problems because of the high altitude. The freedom fighters were able to keep the Chinese from capturing His Holiness and his entourage before they arrived at the Indian border. Although the Chinese had destroyed Lhasa and occupied the land, they, in the words of a Chinese officer, "lost the battle" because His Holiness escaped.

Richard Gere   His Holiness told a story once that I recount quite often, but it's very moving to me. We had shown His Holiness the movie of his life, *Kundun*, by Martin Scorsese. We had all seen the movie—it had been out for about six months before and everyone had seen it at least once—but at the screening, we were pretty much watching His Holiness watch the movie. When it was over, I asked him if there was something he wanted to say, and he made a joke. He said, "Well, they got *the glasses* all wrong." It was funny, but we could all tell it was something he really didn't want to talk about right then, so we adjourned to another room and had tea and cookies and we all talked—a lot of old friends of his were there who had been on the scene for quite some time.

After everything had relaxed a bit and we had greeted each other, I said, "Is there anything you'd like to share with us about the experience of seeing this movie?" There's a scene at the end where His Holiness finally makes it to Indian territory—which, I think, was Sikkim—to safety. He was brought there by the Khampa horsemen, and in the movie he waves goodbye to them, watches them ride away, turns his back on Tibet, and looks toward India. "Well," he said, "That moment was a powerful moment for me in my life, as I watched those Khampa horsemen who had saved me and were the patriots of our country. As they rode away, I knew that I would never see them again"—he never did—"and when I turned away from them and turned my back to Tibet and looked toward India, I looked around me and I didn't have a friend in the world." And then he looked around the room with us and he said, "Now I have friends everywhere."

Tsering Shakya   The decision to leave is essentially the fact that for the Dalai Lama and his court the pressure had become intolerable: whether to side with his people or to cooperate with China. By cooperating with the Chinese they would antagonize the very people who, as their rulers, they are responsible for. It was an extremely difficult, uncompromising position that the Chinese put the Dalai Lama in because they were looking for a figurehead through whom they could rule the country. The Dalai Lama and his entourage, the court, just felt that he could not be the figurehead; they had to lead the people. And if that was not possible, they had to flee the country.

Gelek Rinpoché   Before the Chinese actually came, there was a feeling that if this happens there is no way the government headed by the Dalai Lama can remain in power. But after the Chinese came, Tibetan government officials thought they could talk to them, and almost ten years of dialogue ensued. But Tibet was being squeezed day by day. His Holiness would have liked to have had a dialogue in the hope of avoiding bloodshed because he knew extremely well—as did every Tibetan leader—that there was no way to challenge China by force. The Tibetan government tried to get support from the world community, including the United States and Great Britain, a country that was very familiar with the situation. But the Tibetans failed to receive any tangible, reliable support. There was some hope that the United States would help because of anticommunism. The CIA did try something but it was too little, too late, although the Tibetans did organize a resistance.

Pema Chhinjor   Many of the freedom fighters were discouraged that His Holiness was leaving Tibet. When it was certain that His Holiness had reached India, Tibetans had to decide whether to remain and fight, or to flee the country. Once the Chinese learned that His Holiness had reached

India, they launched a strong military assault, with artillery and aircraft dropping bombs—they didn't worry about killing civilians.

Rinchen Dharlo   In 1959, when His Holiness left Lhasa, there wasn't a single Chinese in my native town. When we learned from the radio that His Holiness was fleeing and that on the way he fell sick, people here—everyone in my native town—were crying that His Holiness had fled. At first when they heard that he had left, everyone was crying. Then later, when they learned that he was sick, people really began to worry and they were all worshipping—burning incense and lighting butter lamps and saying prayers—and then after a few days we heard that he had made it into India and he was well, and people were smiling.

Had the Dalai Lama Not Fled, Would He Have Eventually Been Imprisoned?

Robert Ford   I think he was much too important in Tibetan terms to have had that experience—to have had that sort of pressure. Of course there was pressure on him, and this is why he left: he could see that the only way he was going to help preserve Tibet's culture, Tibet's religion, and Tibetan customs was to leave and to set up an alternative government and a separate Tibetan community, which would be free to practice its religion and observe all its customs. It's just speculation, but I don't think it could have been in Chinese interest to have diminished too much his role. But, of course, they could have tried to manipulate him. They could have used all the subterfuge and what have you and kept him a virtual prisoner.

Patrick French   If the Dalai Lama had remained in 'fifty-nine—the rumor put about at the time that he was about to be captured and killed, I think, was untrue—I don't think that would have happened. But, almost certainly, once the Cultural Revolution got under way he would have suffered a similar fate to the Panchen Lama. He would have had to undergo public struggle sessions—public humiliation—and he would probably, from about the mid-1960s, have been put under house arrest; he would have been simply taken out of circulation. In all that period of the sixties and seventies nobody would really have known what had become of him. The interesting point is, once the Cultural Revolution comes to an end, you have the explosion of the Gang of Four; then you have the period in the early 1980s when the Chinese Communist Party is looking for somebody within the Tibetan system to do business with. Obviously, the Dalai Lama would have been the person they had to, if you like, negotiate with. It's very hard because it's hypothetical, but I do think there would have been a great benefit to the Tibetan people in the 1980s to having the Dalai Lama physically inside Tibet. That would have made a lot of difference. The great difficulty all the way along with the negotiations of the last twenty-odd years is that their primary interlocutor has been in exile.

Tsering Shakya   Certainly during the Cultural Revolution he would have really suffered. But I don't think the Chinese would have executed him because they did not do that with all the other high lamas, like the Panchen Lama. One of the main problems with China in Tibet is that the Chinese know in their heart-of-hearts that they don't really have legitimacy to rule in Tibet, and they know that their presence in Tibet is not only questioned by the Tibetan indigenous population but by the international community and also within the Chinese community. So they always need a figurehead in Tibet through whom they rule the country. So if the Dalai Lama had not left Tibet, they would still have needed him as a figurehead. One thing about the Dalai Lama is whatever sort of view he had about the conditions—the backwardness of Tibet, or the cruelty of the society— really the vast majority of Tibetans have an immense emotional, psychological, and social attachment to the institution of the Dalai Lama, and they do believe he is the legitimate ruler of Tibet. And his position is not there because he's elected, or he has acquired power. It is there because of history and the institution. To get rid of that institution, unless there is a total social revolution among the people, it is not possible; people will continue to believe that. The problem is that his presence is so strong—conspicuous by his absence—that it is stronger than it has ever been at any point in the history of the institution of the Dalai Lama, because he is not there. Inside Tibet, he has proportionately become almost a biblical mythology of the return of the king; the people are waiting for the return of the king even though he has been demonized by the Chinese government—the Chinese government says he is feudal lord, a serf-owner—but the majority of the people do not accept any of the points made by that government, and they look to the fact that he is outside Tibet.

Lama Lobsang Thamcho Nyima   When I was a youngster, living in a large monastery in Amdo [in the 1980s; Lama Lobsang had entered the monastery at the age of seven], my greatest wish—along with all the other monks—was that His Holiness would return as soon as possible. Even young Tibetans who grew up after the Chinese invasion had a great feeling for His Holiness. We believed that when he returned, he would unite all the Tibetans, and we realized that the Chinese feared his great potential to influence his people.

Living in Daily Fear Following the Dalai Lama's Exile

Arjia Rinpoché   In 1964, they called for "social education," so all of a sudden the situation got worse. At that time, they even arrested the Panchen Lama, too. Then the situation got worse and everybody had lots of fear. They sent us to a very difficult place to work, due to hard labor. When we came back to the monastery, we had to study. They pursued the political campaign for one year and four months, so I had a very hard time. Everybody had fear, and was scared: we had to study and we had to denounce His Holiness, of course, and His Holiness the Panchen Lama, of course, and then lamas denounced the lamas—sometimes lamas got into trouble and we had to denounce them physically, not just verbally; you had to go there to denounce them. So at that time, it was a hard time again.

Tsering Shakya   One thing you remember is that everybody was very frightened—that there was tension in each household. I remember that in my family, everyone was very tense; my parents didn't say anything in front of the children, and they always told us not to say anything to outsiders because at that time, although I didn't go to school—my sister did—every morning when you went to school, the children each had to report something. It was called "public criticism"; you were supposed to criticize bad conduct of your family or your neighbors or your classmates, and you were supposed to correct your bad behavior. But what happened was that children would get up and say, "My mother has a picture of the Dalai Lama and she's a reactionary and she opposes the party and the motherland." And, of course, the teacher would then report this to the police, and the police would come.

Arjia Rinpoché   I'm a nomad kid; my parents are nomads. I have eleven brothers and sisters, so when I became a reincarnation, during 1958, the "Great Leap Forward," when they made classes—like poor or rich— because of me, then our family became the "bad class," which is rich. Physically, we were not rich—our family was okay, but not that much. It was because of me that my parents became bad people, so in 1958, they arrested my father; unfortunately he went to jail and never came back—I think he died somewhere but, so far, we haven't gotten the true information. Someone just sent a message to us saying: "A person has died who looked like your father." That was the only information. Then later, my uncles, my other brothers, and my sister-in-law—a lot of people went to jail. And my mother passed away in 1990. My brothers and sisters are still in Tibet; some are monks and some are just lay people. The first time I came here, I really couldn't contact them because I was very afraid—I was not afraid for myself, but I didn't want to make trouble for them. Today, sometimes I do, but not directly. They sometimes call me from some-place—maybe they use a pay phone. My family lives on a very high mountain so they don't [often] call me. We have some kind of connection, but not often.

Tsering Shakya   My mother had the idea of leaving Tibet because the Dalai Lama had left. The heart of Tibet was not there, so she wanted to go out of Tibet. And when we got to Nepal it was not our final destination. She just had to go where the Dalai Lama was, to see him, and to find out what was happening to the rest of Tibetan society. So the fact that we were going to Dharamsala, we knew we were going there because the Dalai Lama was there. By 1967, there were not many Tibetan refugees coming across the border; the trickle of refugees had stopped because by 'sixty-two there had been a war, the borders had been tightened, and both sides of the border between India and China were already closed and highly militarized. So by 1967, when we were allowed to leave as Nepali citizens, we were among the very few people who were able to come out of Tibet at that late stage. So when my mother went to Dharamsala it was like bringing fresh news from Tibet of what was going on.

Arjia Rinpoché   Of course, the Cultural Revolution was the worst. Then the monks were all sent to the fields to work or put in jail or put in some kind of dam construction. I returned to Kumbum—in 1966 I was seventeen years old—and I had to work in the fields, of course, and had to do hard labor. Fortunately, I didn't go to jail, but at that time, no matter whether you were in jail or not, the situation was almost the same. I'm a nomad kid, maybe they would send me to a nomad place. But they decided not to because some monasteries became kind of "life museums": people like the Red Guards could come and study and learn, so they had to have some kind of museum to give negative education. They would say: "This was a bad place; bad guys used to live here and they used to torture people and hold them as slaves." Then later, of course, they turned to cultural heritage and so they needed people there and I was one of the people in the life museum. Then I worked in the fields and at the same time in the monastery. So at sixteen years, I did hard labor—I'll never forget; that was the hardest time in my life.

Lama Lobsang Thamcho Nyima   At that time [the 1980s], the Chinese repression was very harsh. In Amdo, Chinese officers would visit the monastery to determine how many monks lived there. We would have to hide when they came. At the same time, we were able to learn from great lamas.

Rinchen Dharlo   When that happened, Tibetans were very much looking forward to the rest of the world—people in the free world—governments of the free Western countries; we thought that the rest of the world would not remain silent because the kinds of suppression, the kinds of atrocities, were so much that there would be something. In that way we kept our spirits high; we always hoped. But then the Cultural Revolution did not remain that long and, on the other hand, we were also able to inform the rest of the world how our people in Tibet were treated.

"It is a remarkable test of his own personality that he was able to withstand the shock of being designated the Dalai Lama. . . . It's as if you've found a little Mozart who has already written a million symphonies in ten previous lives." —PROFESSOR ROBERT THURMAN

Young Lhamo Dhondrub, the future Fourteenth Dalai Lama, as a toddler in Taktser, the small village in northeastern Tibet where he was born on July 6, 1935.

"There was a very important speech made in 1954 by Mao to Chinese commanders and soldiers going to Tibet. . . . He was very perceptive; he knew that he needed the Dalai Lama to rule the country." —TSERING SHAKYA

"His Holiness is an incomparable model . . . of how one should deport oneself in relationship to a hostile adversary." —ORVILLE SCHELL

Chairman Mao receives a *katak* from the Dalai Lama during His Holiness's visit to Beijing, 1954.

"Thubten Norbu always believed in total independence and he always said that we should settle for nothing short of total independence." —RINCHEN DHARLO

"I had foreseen when they [the People's Republic of China] would make their first attack." —HEINRICH HARRER

The Dalai Lama's eldest brother, Thupten Jigme Norbu (*left*), presiding at a meeting in Vienna on July 30, 1959, during which Chinese aggression in Tibet was denounced. Before the Dalai Lama's escape to India, the Chinese had tried to subvert Thupten Jigme Norbu, offering to reward him to kill his brother if he were to resist their indoctrination. At his left is Heinrich Harrer.

"Annette was the first person to invite him to the Congress of the United States . . . now he has entrée to the White House, the State Department, and to the congressional leadership."
—REPRESENTATIVE TOM LANTOS

Representative Tom Lantos and the Dalai Lama exchange greetings during the Congressional Human Rights Caucus, 1987.

"When I was in charge of the house we rented for him in Dordogne [in southwest France] in the late 1980s to teach at our center, some of my best memories of hanging out together with him were when he would be walking around at five or six in the morning, looking at flowers."
—LAMA SURYA DAS

The Dalai Lama and Lama Surya Das, Dordogne, France.

"Sitting behind him [the Dalai Lama] the whole time was this row of geshes. . . . frankly, all of the geshes are old men, obviously in their seventies and eighties, and they seemed to doze off during the session." —Rabbi Irving Greenberg

From left, front row: Dr. Blu Greenberg, Rabbi Irving Greenberg, and the Dalai Lama engaging in Buddhist-Jewish dialogue, and behind them the sleeping geshes, Dharamsala, India, October 1990.

"The U.S. president did not specify in what capacity they were meeting with him [the Dalai Lama], but Clinton met him not in his Oval Office but in Mr. Gore's office— that was mainly not to anger China." —Rinchen Dharlo

President Bill Clinton accepts the Dalai Lama's *katak* as Lodi Gyaltsen Gyari, Special Envoy of His Holiness the Dalai Lama, and Vice President Al Gore look on, April 27, 1993.

"The Dalai Lama may not have known who he [the late Fred Rogers, the popular host of the PBS children's program, "Mr. Rogers' Neighborhood"] was . . . he may have had some idea of who he was, but not like most kids who grew up with him." —RABBI A. JAMES RUDIN

Rabbi A. James Rudin, *top,* and Mr. Rogers, *right,* look on as the Dalai Lama greets the audience, Greensburg, Pennsylvania, November 11, 1998.

*"He said, 'I will
pray for them.' And
that year, suddenly,
the team's fortune
turned around:
they went right up
to the top and won
the league."*
—PROFESSOR
JONATHAN MIRSKY

Professor Jonathan Mirsky honors the Dalai Lama with a unique
katak, the Tottenham Hotspur scarf.

*"They were quite
surprised to find
somebody who was
so much on an equal
level as an intellec-
tual, in the way of
debating, arguing,
and discussing."*
—DR. PIET HUT

Dr. Piet Hut and the Dalai Lama during the Dharamsala Scientific Dialogue, 1997.

"We were passing some of the old Tibetan stalls along the way and I saw the thankas [Tibetan paintings] hanging there and so I said to him [the Dalai Lama]—we were talking about the Tibetan refugees and how they made their living—'I want to buy one of those thankas to take back to our center in London.' He looked at me a little strangely and we drove on." —FATHER LAURENCE FREEMAN

The *thanka* of the birth of Christ, commissioned by the Dalai Lama, painted in Tibetan form by Buddhist monks, and presented by His Holiness to the World Community for Christian Meditation during the Way of Peace Pilgrimage to Bodhgaya, 1998.

"When we arrived, he made the presentation to me for our community [the World Community for Christian Meditation] of this big tube . . . he took it out of the tube and gave it to me beautifully wrapped in Tibetan cloth and as I unrolled it, he said, 'Can you guess what it is?'"

The Dalai Lama presents Father Laurence Freeman with the Nativity *thanka*, 1998.

"He indicated how pleased he was to meet me and to be in this great house of Jewish worship. . . . I made the gesture indicating that he should precede me . . . he grabbed my arm and made it very clear at that moment that I didn't have a choice and that I was going in before him; he was in absolute command." —DR. RONALD B. SOBEL

Participants in the International Campaign for Tibet's annual Light of Truth Award ceremony, Temple Emanu-El of the City of New York, Thursday, April 30, 1998, honoring Martin Scorsese and Melissa Mathison. *From left:* John Ackerly, Lodi Gyari, Rinchen Dharlo, Richard Gere, Mr. Scorcese, His Holiness, Ms. Mathison, Professor Robert Thurman, and Dr. Ronald B. Sobel.

He shakes your hand and bows—and when he looks at you, you have the feeling that he can see into the depths of your soul." —ANNETTE LANTOS

Annette Lantos and the Dalai Lama in Washington, D.C., 2003.

"There's a great picture of the two of us on the steps of his house in 1972 and then another one taken in 2002, in the exact same place, and I have put them together. I had two of each made; he has the other set. For those who think that he's been materially advantaged by the fact that he's become such a prominent figure, he's still living in the same house he was thirty years ago and, clearly, wearing the same clothes."
—RICHARD BLUM

Richard Blum's set of photographs of himself and the Dalai Lama taken thirty years apart and inscribed, "To Your Holiness, thirty years and we've just begun."

"His Holiness lives according to what he teaches . . . he embodies it and, specifically, his whole attitude of compassion; that's one of his basic teachings." —VEN. THUBTEN CHODRON

"He was looking forward to the Kalachakra, his really intensive teachings. He had to be there from seven in the morning to five in the evening." —NORBU TSERING

The Dalai Lama at ten o'clock on the morning of April 29, 2004, three hours into that day's Kalachakra teachings, Toronto.

Chapter Six

DHARAMSALA: THE EARLY YEARS
IN "LITTLE LHASA"

T. C. Tethong   In the early days of exile, His Holiness had the very difficult problem of encouraging the refugees to resettle. In the early 1960s, His Holiness sought land from the Indian government so that the refugees could leave the road camps [where many of them worked and lived and where conditions were very harsh]. Prime Minister [Jawaharlal] Nehru [1889–1964] wrote to the governors of the Indian states, requesting land. But it was very hard to get the refugees to resettle. First of all, few Tibetans prior to 1959 had ever been south of Calcutta or Bombay. Secondly, they were not used to the heat and tropical climate of Southern India. They felt more comfortable in the Himalayan region, near the Tibetan border. They believed: we are going to get back our country any day and we do not want to be left behind. They wanted to be as close as possible to Tibet. This went on until the mid-to-late 1960s, when, as a result of the Cultural Revolution, more refugees arrived and we were able to convince many people to resettle in the south of India.

Geshe Tsultim Gyaltsen   Nobody was hurting us. But when you're hungry, you think about food. Actually, we thought about when we would see His Holiness in India. Also, we were quite happy because after we crossed the border, the Indian government gave us rations because we didn't have anything with us.

His Holiness was great—everything was for the people. He had ideas

129

about how to make a success for the monks and ordinary people. So when we arrived at the refugee camp, His Holiness gave a message: Everybody do what you do; monks continue to study and practice as you did in Tibet. Whatever skills you have from Tibet, we need you to continue to do them in the refugee life. He came to Dalhousie a few times and gave us ideas. And he went to other camps also. That is why Tibetan refugees were successful and the monks were studying and practicing.

T. C. Tethong   The first batch of refugees was single males, many of them freedom fighters. Later, when people heard that the Dalai Lama had come to India, they also began to come. Ninety percent of them were either nomads or farmers or villagers. They did not speak Hindi and lacked varied skills. Our concern was how to obtain gainful employment for these people. One solution involved handicrafts. But this could only employ five hundred people at most and we had eighty thousand refugees to deal with.

There was a man named Maurice Friedmann, originally from Poland, who had come to India as a follower of [Mohandas K.] Gandhi [1869–1948]. Maurice was very close to His Holiness, as well as to India's leaders, and he advised His Holiness that the refugees should be settled on the land. So Nehru wrote to the chief ministers of all of India's states, asking for donations of land. Three states responded with offers; the most accessible parcel was in Mysore State. This parcel of three thousand acres of land north of Mysore City was all jungle, infested with wild animals, including elephants. The Indian government helped in reclaiming the land, a process that required years of manual labor. Some relief organizations provided bulldozers, others food. One of these groups was the American Emergency Relief Organization, which was organized by Lowell Thomas [Sr.]. The Swiss provided technical cooperation and supervision; they suggested that the refugees grow maize and that was quite a success.

When we were developing the settlements in the South, [His Holiness] would come every year, spending two to three weeks, giving a teaching, visiting the hospitals, and walking across the fields. That is part of the reason we succeeded; we had a leader who took full interest and whom the people trusted. When he first visited the Tibetan settlement in South India, we were all living in tents. It was arranged that he would stay at a government guest house in a nearby town. But he said, "I will stay in the camp." The security people were concerned. The Indian officials wanted him to be comfortable, so he stayed the night in the guest house. But the next day, he came to the camp and stayed in a tent we had erected for him. He said, "I came to see my people and I want to *live* with them."

Tsering Shakya   The thing I remember most is being ill most of the time—having sores, having lice—and also lack of food. I never felt satisfied; I was always hungry. But when we went to Mussorie it was slightly better because the schools were usually situated in these country houses the British colonial officers would build as their summer retreat, and they were never meant for schools. There were so many children; in one room we had about twenty people sleeping on the floor, or in bunk beds. And there was no playing area, so we had to build our own playing field; it was a lot of labor. A lot of the children had to board at the school because when the majority of the Tibetans came out in 1959, the India-China relationship was really tense. The situation got worse, and by 1962 there was a war.

Pema Chhinjor   When I left Tibet in 1959—I was fourteen and was a freedom fighter—and came to India, some of my family remained in Tibet. It was only after twenty years that I was able to communicate with them. It was very hot in India; there was a lack of food and I came down with tuberculosis. I was taken to a British hospital in Bombay, where I spent one year in recuperation. I didn't know anything about politics. The hospital opened a school for the Tibetan patients and it was there, under a tree, in the evenings, that I learned Hindi and English. I then went to college and became a teacher.

First Meetings with the Exiled Dalai Lama

Norbu Tsering   I was around eight years old. It was not really a close encounter; it was just being in the general public and noticing him and getting a special blessing from him. It was the first time I ever had his blessing. Being a Tibetan, I met the Dalai Lama several times during my childhood. We always praised him because he was the incarnation and our spiritual and political head. It gives me great satisfaction whenever I see him. I feel very calmed down and cool. It's just like you are seeing *God* Himself.

T. C. Tethong   I had met him when he came to India in 1956 and gave my family a brief, private audience. I was a teenager at that time and His Holiness asked me about my studies. At Mussorie, the first question His Holiness asked me was, "How's your spirit, down or up?" Like any young person, I replied, "My spirit is high." Of course, I was apprehensive and a little frightened at meeting His Holiness. But he broke the ice in a very friendly way.

Rinchen Dharlo   I met His Holiness in 1959—I guess it was some time around December—the same year I left Tibet. First I left my native town with my father and spent a few months right at the border. After six months, my mother and my younger brother and another sister were able to leave Tibet and join us. From there we came to Katmandu, Nepal, and when we arrived in Katmandu we learned that His Holiness was visiting Bodh Gaya [the site of a pilgrimage by Tibetan refugees], so we went to Bodh Gaya, and two days after we arrived, His Holiness arrived and there were thousands of people in line, waiting for him. We waited there for about an hour and then finally he came. He was only around twenty-five at that time and I was eleven years old, and it was very exciting; all the people who were waiting on the two sides of the road cried—first of all, they were not able to catch him because he was in a car and some of them were able to see him, whereas the majority of the people could not see him. But then he walked to the corridor of the guest house where he was staying, came out, and waved his hand. I found him very young, charming, and energetic. I felt very lucky; the majority of the people who were waiting for him just did their three-times prostrations—I also did—and all of them were crying because it was soon after we had left our country—the loss of our country. That was quite an experience.

Tsering Shakya   I remember being taken to see the Dalai Lama as a little boy, with my family, and sitting there, and being told by my mother how to behave—I was not allowed to say anything—so I was frightened to be going there; I didn't want to go there because they had told me so much about what not to do, not to say anything, not to move! My first impression was that he was very big—as a child he looked as if he was a towering figure. We are sitting on the floor and he is on a raised cushion, so you are always looking up. But I remember he had a stern face and was talking very earnestly to my brother and to my mother, who was crying all the time; she was reporting on what she had seen in Tibet. I think the Dalai Lama might have said something to me, but I don't really recall very much.

Professor Robert Thurman   He was a charming young man, much more slight than he is today. He seemed very high strung and did not radiate the sort of calm and the massive presence that he has today, but he was very alert and aware of *you*. I really liked him, although at the time I was very attached to my own teacher, who was an elderly Mongolian lama. In India, I was assigned to study with the same teachers that the Dalai Lama had—we were sort of like classmates; he was only five or six years older than I was. At the time, I wasn't looking at him as a major guru, but we liked each other and got along very well. He had not had a Westerner like myself, who spoke Tibetan fluently, to discuss Western subjects. I would try to ask Buddhist questions and he would divert the conversation, telling me to take them up with his teachers. Then he and I would talk about Freud or physics or another subject.

The Exiles' Early Hopes of Returning to Tibet

Rinchen Dharlo   We always expected that we would be able to return to Tibet soon. That was why my parents had chosen to stay in one place for two years—hoping to go back to Tibet. And then when this did not happen they came down to India, as did many of the families of Tibetan refugees. Almost all of them had stayed in border areas in the beginning, and later they were told by His Holiness to come down and get settled, and that's how they came. Then afterward, everyone was looking to go back; they thought that His Holiness would be able to find a solution to the situation with the Chinese government. That did not happen. But then, in the meantime, everyone got busy—the Tibetan government started establishing settlements. And no matter how successful we have been in exile, still the Tibetans in exile are looking to go back to Tibet. That's also my goal.

Richard Gere   The idea of impermanence is not just language to them; they've embraced this to the heart of who they are. Things change; everything changes; everything is in a constant state of change and the thing that allows you to be in the moment, whatever it may be—more specifically, the human condition—that however bad it is right now, it won't remain this bad forever. I think, also, they have a basic belief in the goodness of people. They were a nomadic people—they were quite fierce, actually—before they became a Buddhist country and that nomadic trait, or aspect of them, allowed them to swim through any culture that they've come in contact with. I don't think there's ever been such a successful exile community—certainly this recent.

Setting up the Government in Exile:
Young Exiles in Service to Their Community

T. C. Tethong   We had a very loyal staff. Only about ten of us spoke both Tibetan and English. Everyone worked for a minimum salary and was very dedicated. I was very happy. All I had was a bedroll and a steel trunk for my belongings. Nobody complained: if we were told to go to South India, we went; if we were told to go to a refugee settlement in Northeast India, we went.

Pema Chhinjor   [At the time Pema Chhinjor became a teacher] I became political: I was a founding member of the Tibetan Youth Congress, as well as a member of the organization's steering committee. Many years later, I stood for election to the Assembly of People's Deputies and I won. Then I was elected to the cabinet and served as security minister for four years. The opportunity to serve under the guidance of His Holiness was the best achievement of my life.

T. C. Tethong   In 1959, when His Holiness was at Mussorie, I was asked to perform volunteer work at the first refugee camp established by the Indian government. I served there as an interpreter until I came down with a violent case of dysentery. When I recuperated, I received a call from His Holiness's brother-in-law, who told me that the office of His Holiness required English-speaking Tibetans to help out. I went up to Mussorie and met His Holiness at the house that had been provided to him by an Indian industrialist.

My father had been in the Tibetan government service during the time of the Thirteenth Dalai Lama: he had fought in the area of the China-Tibet border, was military governor of Kahm Province, and later was a member of the cabinet. So His Holiness said to me, "You are a son of a man who has performed significant service. I expect that you will be very suitable." It was exciting to work in the office with senior government officials who had come with His Holiness from Tibet. It was awesome and scary for us young people who were just coming out of college.

Moving the Government to Dharamsala

T. C. Tethong   Many things changed after His Holiness moved to Dharamsala. There was some grumbling by those Tibetans who thought that Dharamsala was too secluded. It was a beautiful place, if a little out of the way, in those days. At first he stayed in a bungalow with just the bare necessities. But when he decided to build a new residential area, and a new Temple, Tibetans felt relieved.

I remember His Holiness giving a talk, saying that we have to remain Tibetan, maintaining our ideology and culture. At the same time, we have to resettle ourselves. We don't know when we are going back. While we hope this will happen as early as possible, we have to be practical. We have to think of our children. We cannot live from hand to mouth all the time. Then he added that if we are able to go back, these buildings can be used by the Indian community or by Tibetans who want to stay. So he managed to convince the Tibetans to resettle, and I consider this a major achievement.

In Dharamsala, all of the ministers who had escaped with His Holiness in 1959, as well as other important officials, worked on the upstairs floor, while those of us who spoke English were situated on the first floor. In addition, there was an official that the Indian government had deputized to work as a liaison with the Office of His Holiness. Our main task was to deal with the barrage of media people seeking both information and audiences with His Holiness. While there had been a rudely organized government in Mussorie, the setup in Dharamsala included departments for religious affairs, home affairs, refugee affairs, education, and security for His Holiness.

In Dharamsala, the former ceremonial aspect was very much reduced —an audience would be just *an audience*. When His Holiness met people, even heads of state such as Nehru, an interpreter and one or two senior officials would be present. It was very informal. I had to be present at cabinet meetings in order to take notes. In these sessions, five or six people would meet with His Holiness and tea would be served. Communication was still formal but the whole environment was simplified. The hardest thing for us in the beginning was getting used to sitting on chairs in front of His Holiness. If he were sitting on a large sofa, he would often ask someone to sit next to him, and sitting next to him would be dreadful for us. At first, when we sat facing him, we would bend our heads low, but then we got used to it. Yet even nowadays, when, for example, I meet His Holiness in a hotel suite, it is still difficult for me to sit next to him. That is because of the reverence generations have had for him as a spiritual as well as a political leader. Perhaps it is easier for young people today. I have seen some of them coming for an interview who would not hesitate to ask His Holiness straight questions, whereas, in those early days, we did not ask him *any* questions, even though His Holiness *wants* you to ask questions.

Dr. Tenzin Tethong   I started to spend time in Dharamsala; I worked as an interpreter and as a secretary, mostly writing letters in English, translating documents. I did some work in the education office, as well. And then I started to work with my brother and another friend and we started a Tibetan language magazine; we thought a lot of the refugees in India needed information, in Tibetan, about the new world that they were in—

most of them had probably come out of Tibet for the first time ever and were literally stuck in these refugee camps with very little information about the outside world. Dharamsala was in those times a place where a lot of people passed through, primarily, of course, to see His Holiness and His Holiness's two tutors. So we got to know a lot of younger people and we began to talk of, and be very conscious of, the fact that younger Tibetans needed to be somewhat more involved within the community because, again, it was a time when anybody, especially the younger people, who had picked up English or some Indian language or some new skills basically were going out, either to Nepal or Bhutan or, if possible, to Europe and North America, where the best opportunities were. So we thought it was good to try and get younger people involved within the community. And so that led to a conference of young Tibetans from all over India and Nepal, primarily, and as a result of that conference, the Tibetan Youth Congress, an organization that is quite active even today, was established.

Rinchen Dharlo   After finishing school, I was one of the young people who volunteered to serve the Tibetan community. There was a paper mill—a paper factory—in Bhopal and a carpet factory in Simla, where I worked for six months. Afterward, there was a carpet factory where I was asked to work in the office. The carpet factory was established mainly to try to make money for the refugees. The carpet factories could employ a lot of people.

Then, from Simla, I was called to Dharamsala and I was asked to go to Nepal. There was another carpet factory and I was told to be the manager. When I arrived in Katmandu, Nepal, the carpet factory was already closed due to mismanagement and was under the supervision of the Nepal Red Cross Society and the Tibetan Office in Katmandu. We wanted to restart it, but somehow it got delayed. Instead, I ended up working in the Tibetan Refugee Welfare Office in Katmandu. I continued to work there for another four years. And then the Dalai Lama's representative who headed the office was transferred to India and I was told to be the acting representative.

It seems I did well, so then I was appointed as the full-fledged representative of His Holiness in Nepal. My main responsibility was to look after the social-economic welfare of the Tibetan refugees.

The Newly Exiled Dalai Lama's Administrative Style

Rinchen Dharlo   He was very much involved. At that time, the Tibetan government in exile was very, very small. In the small parliament we had only seventeen members; today we have forty-six. And in the cabinet we had four ministers and the Tibetan Refugee Welfare Office in Katmandu was under the Home Department at that time. Only the offices of Tibet in New York and Geneva—only these two were under the International Relations Office. At that time, we did not have that many offices of Tibet around the world and in the Tibetan Refugee Welfare Office in Katmandu we did not do much in the political area; mainly we looked after the refugees, to try to give maximum employment to the refugees. And for the Tibetan refugees in Nepal, those who wanted to go to India to meet their relatives, the welfare office took care of their travel documents, and then also to see that the children got a proper education. Whenever we had orphans, or semiorphans, or whenever we found parents who were not able to take care of their children, we always took them to India and got them admitted into the Tibetan Children's Village and the Tibetan Foundation in Mussorie. At the same time, new refugees kept on coming from Tibet—not that many, an average of about fifty a year, and we always took care of them.

I was directly responsible to the minister and secretary of the Home Department, who would discuss within the cabinet, and then His Holiness got his reports from them. But whenever I went down to Dharamsala—in those days, we were required to go to Dharamsala once in two years; that biannual meeting was necessary, but then I used to come to Dharamsala much more than that, most every year—so whenever I was in Dharamsala I had an audience with His Holiness. He was very gracious in giving time. At that time, His Holiness was looking not to travel as much as he does today, so it was much easier to get an audience with him.

Sending Representatives Abroad

Dr. Tenzin Tethong   In 1973, I was sent to New York, where the exile Tibetan administration had an office from the early 1960s as a permanent appeal at the United Nations. This was set up after 1959, and I worked several times with the UN General Assembly, where the Tibetan issue was discussed—in 1959, 'sixty-one, and 'sixty-five. This office had been set up, to a large extent, with considerable support, encouragement, and even some help from the United States. But by the time I was being sent—literally to try and keep the office open—U.S. policy had already changed considerably: Nixon had already gone to China, the Chinese were already coming into the United Nations, and, actually, the United States didn't want the Tibetans to be around anymore, either as an embarrassment or an irritant to the Chinese. We were being encouraged to basically shut down our operations.

This was something that His Holiness and the exile administration weren't eager to do, and so I was sent literally to keep the office doors open. I ended up reaching out to people who I may have known, or had connections to, when they visited India. This would include some young scholars, some university professors, and even some young people who came as travelers and hippies to Dharamsala and that part of the world.

I slowly tried to see if these people would help us keep the Tibetan issue going. In New York at that time there was a small Tibetan community of maybe less than a dozen people and maybe another dozen or so in New Jersey. Altogether in the United States, maybe, at that time there were three hundred to four hundred Tibetan people at the most, scattered in just a few cities and, in some cases, just one person—in Alaska, Florida, in Idaho. So that's what I did, and tried to get each Tibetan to somehow become a little more involved, and, in many cases, one or two of these individuals would start a little group, or have a name like "Friends of Tibet," and would help us by trying to draw attention to the Tibetan issue—whether it was writing a letter to their newspaper or trying to get their congressperson or senators involved. One of the more public things that I was able to do was in 1975, when I was able to bring the Tibetan Performing Arts Group in Dharamsala on a tour of the United States and Canada. Again, this was a somewhat simple thing to do, but for the longest time there was nobody seen to support such a thing. First of all, it wasn't commercial and, secondly, even on a noncommercial basis, very few cultural or educational groups were eager to sponsor or help anything Tibetan because, obviously, in those times, everybody was careful not to offend the Chinese in any way.

Rinchen Dharlo I was his representative in Nepal for ten years—from 'seventy-eight to 'eighty-seven—and in 'eighty-seven I was asked to go to New York and to head the Office of Tibet. So I came to New York in May of 'eighty-seven. That was my first visit to the West, and it was quite a big cultural shock to be coming from tiny little Katmandu city to New York. That was a great challenge for me. And then it also happened at a time that interest in Tibet was growing in the Western Hemisphere.

A People in Exile: Escape, Fortitude, and Survival

Tenzin Gephel My parents escaped to India in 1959, along with tens of thousands of Tibetan people. When my parents arrived in India, at first they did very hard work in road construction because they did not know the language; they did not know the place. When they learned the language a little better, they started doing some small business, and that is how until now they lived in India. My mother passed away after she escaped to India—at that time, so many Tibetan people died, because of the weather, because of illnesses that developed in India, and a lot of people died on the way to India; my mother was one of them who died because of the Chinese Revolution. My father is still alive; he's healthy.

Tsering Shakya   My personal history is different from that of most Tibetan refugees because we didn't come as refugees. My ancestors were Nepalese people who were doing trading in Lhasa. They had been there since the sixteenth century. But Nepalese merchants had enormous power in Tibet and they were not subject to Tibetan laws because [as a result of the] Tibetan–Nepal war in the eighteenth century Nepal imposed extraterritorial rights, which meant that Nepalese trading communities in Tibet were not subject to Tibetan law and they were exempt from various taxes. When the Chinese took over Tibet in 1950, they decided which country's citizen you were. We were given an alternative: to take up Chinese citizenship or Nepalese citizenship. My mother decided she would choose Nepalese citizenship, so we were expelled from the country. But some members of my family said they would have Chinese citizenship and they had to remain there.

In 1967, when I was seven years old, my family left Tibet and went to Katmandu. From Katmandu, then my family went to Dharamsala, and from there I went to the Tibetan Refugee School in Mussorie, in the North of India. In 1972 I got a scholarship to come to study at Rugby, one of the private schools in England, in Hampshire. The headmaster of that school was the son of Sir Basil Gould, who was the British representative [in Tibet]. He was helping Tibetan children to come to school. He sponsored six students—I was the youngest—to come over to school.

Rinchen Dharlo   My native town is very close to Nepal and used to be a barter trade center. The main road takes less than twenty-four hours to cross the border. But at that time the border was guarded. First my father and I—only the two of us—escaped, and after six months, my mother, younger brother, and another sister were able to join us. But still, my grandma and two other sisters had to stay back, and they were able to join us only after a year—it was very difficult. So for two years we stayed in a very remote place, right close to the border, hoping to go back to Tibet; we never thought that we would have to be in exile that long. We knew that His Holiness was in India and many of his close associates were also in India, but we did not know anything about the rest of the Tibetans.

There, in that remote place, we suffered a lot because of malnutrition, lack of medical facilities, and shock from the loss of our country: my mother died at the age of thirty-two, my grandma died, a cousin died, and then a younger brother and another younger sister—five members of my family died within a period of two years. Although I was eleven years old, I had to work very hard; almost every day I had to go to fetch fuel and wood. Several times I went to work in the fields of the Nepalese farmers, who paid us in grains.

Then, after two years, two representatives from His Holiness toured the northern borders of Nepal and these two Tibetan government officials gave us the full information, saying that now His Holiness is in India and he has established the Tibetan government in exile, and that if we came down to India we would be taken care of—the children would go to school and the young ones could get a job. So after my mother died, my father decided to leave Nepal, and he took us to India. That's how we entered into schools established for Tibetan refugees.

It was all very forested; there were only two houses in McLeod Ganj [the Tibetan enclave in upper Dharamsala]. We landed at the place where there was a bus stop, and all of us spent the night there. We stayed there for two weeks on the same ground; we cooked our meals—we put our cooking utensils on three stones and collected dried wood from the forest. One of my cousins and two of my younger sisters were admitted to the Tibetan Children's Village, but my younger sister, another brother, and I were too old to go to the school at the Children's Village. My father wanted me and my brother and sister to go to school and he was insistent—if he wanted something he would see that it was done—so he approached the Tibetan officials and was told that the Indian government had established schools for the Tibetan refugees but admitted only children who were documented refugees in India. We had just come from Nepal and so we were undocumented, and there was no other way to get admitted. My father began to inquire as to how we could be registered as refugees. He was told that in a city a hundred kilometers away he could get some kind of a permit saying that we were new refugees. Then he left me, my younger brother, sister, and cousin and he just said, "I'll be back within a week." He left and for ten days he did not turn up, and we were crying all the time; he did not speak the language and we were so worried that he may have gotten lost—you know the difficulties in India when you don't speak the language. After ten days, he showed his face and was waving a piece of paper. The very next day, he went to the education department and the three of us were admitted and sent to a school in Simla with a group of about twenty-eight other young children. As the bus departed, my father just waved good-bye and left for Nepal.

My father came back to India after two years. By the time I was in school I was able to write to whomever I wanted, and I sent several letters. Fortunately, he got all of them. I and two of my younger brothers and sister were in the Simla school and the two youngest sisters and a cousin were admitted to the Tibetan Children's Village in Dharamsala. There was no communication between us, although it's only twelve hours by bus. I didn't see my youngest sister for many years. When they were in Dharamsala, one of them got adopted by a French-speaking Swiss family. The younger sister pleaded that she also be sent with her, or that someone else be adopted in her sister's place. But there was no one who would listen to the young child, and the two of them got separated. I met my sister who was adopted only in 1981—after almost 20 years. She had already forgotten her language—she spoke a few languages; French was now her mother tongue, and she spoke Swiss German because she studied there. In addition, she spoke Romanian, and then she learned English in order to be able to communicate with her brothers and sisters. Then, while she was learning English, she met a Tibetan young man and they fell in love and they got married, and by the time I met her she was able to speak a few Tibetan sentences.

Why Were Tibetan Children Adopted Abroad?

Rinchen Dharlo   The Tibetan Village was started by the older sister of His Holiness, and then afterward the Tibetan Children's Village received funding from many individual families from the West, and many wanted to adopt. At that time, there were many orphans, as well, so His Holiness and his sister thought it would be good for the children to be adopted, so a policy was made. I think at least sixty or seventy children were adopted into families in Switzerland, and some were sent to children's villages in England. Then in the late sixties, when His Holiness went to Switzerland, he was very sad to find that so many of them had come to see him but they had already forgotten their language. And then the Tibetan government made a policy not to give up children for adoption. Those children who were adopted by Swiss families in the late sixties forgot everything, but then in the late seventies and early eighties, they came back to the community; they tried to research their roots, they learned the language, and in the eighties they were the people who took to took to the street to rally to demand human rights in Tibet. And today, many of them are living within the Tibetan community.

Gelek Rinpoché   For the first ten to fifteen days in India, we camped; there was no food. The first civil place we reached was an old Tibetan monastery in northeast India. We then went to a transit camp where it was very hot and many people died. After a year, I was asked to join a group of ten young lamas to complete our studies and learn how to communicate with the West. His Holiness selected me to come to Dharamsala, where I worked in various capacities: I was a teacher and then a principal. Then I was selected to go to the United States to study English, cultural anthro- pology, and political institutions at Cornell for one year. When I returned to India, I worked in Tibet House, in Delhi, and also taught a crash course in Tibetan to Indian military officers.

Nobody said the transition to exile was easy. My family in Tibet was very wealthy. For example, we had two automobiles at a time when there were only four or five in the whole country. Apart from my family, I had personal wealth, yet I am happy to be out. Do I have attachments? Sure, but my attachments do not pull me back. When I moved from one place to another in my early days in India, I was happy to get a ride in a garbage truck.

I twice dreamed of going back to Tibet to collect my ritual objects, but I have been able to leave this without hardship or difficulty. That is because of Buddhism. Do I feel bad? Sure. Did I miss my parents? You bet! Did I miss my car, horses, mules, silver coins? No! So an ordinary per- son like me was able to do this. For an extraordinary person like the Dalai Lama it is hard. He is, of course, extremely sad about what happened to the Tibetan people. One of his teachers sent a poem to us from Mussorie:

> The beautiful, peaceful land of the snow of Tibet
> What is happening today, good or bad
> We could never understand everything
> My heart is aching
> How can I remove this pain from my heart?

So you have the sadness of the people and their suffering. Power is imper- manent—you have it today; you don't have it tomorrow. Buddha told us that twenty-five hundred years ago. So this made me very adaptable to any culture. The Dalai Lama's ability to adjust to a new situation comes from the Buddha; his strength comes absolutely from Buddha.

PART III

Spiritual Saint or Political Troublemaker?

Chapter Seven

TAKING THE DALAI LAMA'S POLITICAL MESSAGE REGARDING CHINA ABROAD

Dr. Alexander Berzin   One of the things that certainly has propelled the movement is that you can't separate the Buddhist teachings from the agenda of the plight of the Tibetan people—that in going around and teaching in the West, there's always been this agenda, not just by His Holiness but by others as well, to increase awareness of the Tibetan situation and somehow try to bring about world opinion in terms of pressuring the Chinese government to allow more freedom of culture and religion.

Father Laurence Freeman   It is difficult to separate them because he is a symbol—a Christlike figure, actually—of a crucified people. And he is a symbol of the possibility of a nonviolent response to that kind of persecution. He's popular in a way because he symbolizes how human beings *could* be—how political and religious leaders could be; how all of us could be as individuals in dealing with violence or rejection. He has this joyfulness in suffering, not that he enjoys the suffering, but he's joyful *in* the suffering that he has to go through. He doesn't, which is very wise, impose that suffering on the audience that he's with, and he's quite selective about the occasions and circumstances in which he speaks about Tibet. That wins people's respect and affection.

Dr. Howard Cutler   He told me that becoming a refugee had had an important impact on him. It had galvanized him and made him understand what is important in life. It reaffirmed his Buddhist belief and practices because Buddhist teaching involves change, suffering, and the idea of impermanence. He told me that of course it would have been better if the Chinese had *not* invaded Tibet. But he thought that if he had remained in Tibet under the old system, he probably would have ended up being highly complaisant, performing his spiritual practices in a routine manner.

Dr. Jeffrey Hopkins   Definitely he wants to communicate his message about love, compassion, altruism—how this works to help the individual family—and going from small areas to international politics is definitely at the core of what he's doing, but certainly, there's a political message that goes with this because Tibet is the home of these teachings. And if you consider how much Tibet was known in 1979, when he first came to the States, and how much it's known now, he has accomplished an unbelievable amount.

Tsering Chakya   The people who are concerned with human rights come from a different element than those who are concerned with spiritual development. People who are engaged in the Free Tibet campaign are not necessarily the same constituency as the Buddhist spiritual community. In fact, they are often antagonistic and a different set of people. In my experience, having been engaged in the Tibetan campaign all this time, I noticed that the people who are the most spiritually oriented Buddhists tend to be less concerned about the immediate problems of human rights, whereas the more liberal ones—the people who are working with Amnesty International—tend to be less spiritual and are concerned with the immediate issues of human rights. In fact, it's not the same constituency at all. That's why Tibetan popularity can tap into both resources. There are always different issues that become fundamental in mobilizing people, and certain issues for a decade have dominated. In the 1980s the anti-apartheid movement dominated. And before that it was human rights in Eastern Europe, and Jewish refuseniks. Now the human rights issue in Eastern Europe has more or less disappeared, not that there are no human rights abuses now, but people don't see it as urgent. And the antinuclear campaign movement has disappeared. So in this way, Tibet has been able to sneak up the ladder of priority for people. It's not so much that suddenly the Tibetan issue is worse, it's simply that some issues, either through success or change, are no longer the issues they were before.

The Dalai Lama's First Visit to the United States

Richard Blum   I had visited Tibetan refugee camps in 1968 and was immediately attracted to the people. I admired them for their kindness and fundamental spirituality. I also wanted to help them because of their abject poverty. I became very friendly with the director of one of the camps, who asked me if I would like to meet His Holiness. I said, "What? Are you *kidding*? Of course," so in 1972, I went to Dharamsala and sat in on two meetings with His Holiness before I had a private audience with him. The other meeting involved a group of Tibetans who had escaped and who treated him as if he were really a Godlike figure. In return, he was very kind, very gentle. In my first meeting with him, we talked about his coming to the United States.

I came back to see him again in 1978, when Diane [Feinstein] was chairman of the San Francisco Board of Supervisors. The State Department took the position that since His Holiness was not a head of state, proper security could not be provided. I then got the then-mayor, George Mosconi—he was assassinated soon after and was succeeded by my wife—to offer security if His Holiness came to San Francisco. So Diane brought him a letter of invitation and we lobbied the Carter administration to allow His Holiness to come, and a year later he arrived in San Francisco.

Dr. Tenzin Tethong   I was able to make arrangements for His Holiness to visit the United States in 1979. That was a big, key event as far as Tibet is concerned. There had been suggestions of possibilities and plans for His Holiness to visit the United States from the early sixties on, and a large part of that might have been driven by possible official U.S. encouragement—that it might be a good way to show support for the Dalai Lama or the Tibetan issue if it suited your success.

At the time I was beginning to make the preparations in 1977 and 1978, there was no official support or encouragement of any kind. Of course, before his first visit, very little was known about the Dalai Lama—there had been just a few newspaper reports here and there—and so we put together a string of old invitations to His Holiness from some Buddhist groups, a few colleges, a few church-related groups and we had very little official support for really putting this together properly, so we also had to make sure that in every locale we had volunteers to help us with everything from driving to security—to do as much as we could to insure His Holiness's personal security. And in the fall of 1979, His Holiness was able to make his first visit, which lasted almost a month and a half. He visited many cities and many Buddhist groups and universities, and in most of these places he basically gave short talks on Tibetan Buddhism and also spoke about the exile situation.

His Holiness was not totally ignorant about the United States because, obviously, he had met many Americans through the years, especially in exile—many American scholars and diplomats and journalists had come to Dharamsala or met him in many places—so he was not unfamiliar with American matters. But I think that when he came to the United States he was impressed with the fact that Americans were quite welcoming, not in a very formal or superficial way, just naturally quite open and friendly.

He also felt that Americans were quite open to listening to *his* views, which were, quite obviously, Tibetan and from a very strong Buddhist point of view. So he enjoyed that visit very much. And, of course, he visited a wide range of people—there were one or two long-standing invitations from some small colleges and universities, one of which I remember, Carroll College, in Waukesha, Wisconsin. There was no particular tie with Carroll College other than that a former alumnus, a writer who had met His Holiness and had extended that invitation many years earlier. Then he also met with several scientists and scholars—people who were studying the mind and the body—in several universities. And some of the university visits were very good because His Holiness had the opportunity to visit Harvard and the University of Virginia.

And then he had a wonderful visit with the Kalmyk Mongolians in New Jersey—Mongolians who had drifted to the European part of Russia many centuries ago and essentially were stranded there for the longest time and came as refugees after the Second World War and resettled in New Jersey.

After His Holiness's first visit, of course, the profile of the Tibetan issue became much more visible. Right from then His Holiness was not only able to attract attention in general but he was able to win over a lot of people because His Holiness was more than just an interesting figure, and, in fact, he had something valid and important to say. Through the years, even in Washington, His Holiness was able to meet an unusually diverse group of congressional leaders who became very sympathetic and supportive of his work and of the Tibetan issue. I think that many would say that in recent years the Tibetan issue has become one of the best issues on Capitol Hill because it has support from almost the whole political spectrum.

The Five Point Peace Plan

At a meeting of the U.S. Congressional Human Rights Caucus, held in Washington in 1987, the Dalai Lama articulated a Five Point Peace Plan to resolve the decades-long conflict with China. The plan advocated respect for the human rights of the Tibetan people; abandonment of the policy of transferring ethnic Chinese into Tibet; turning Tibet into a demilitarized zone of nonviolence; protecting and restoring Tibet's natural environment; and the commencement of negotiations on the future status of Tibet.

On June 15, 1988, addressing a gathering in Strasbourg, France, the Dalai Lama elaborated on the Five Point Plan, suggesting the creation of a fully self-governing, democratic Tibet in association with the People's Republic of China. The Five Point Peace Plan, combined with his Strasbourg proposal, constitutes the Dalai Lama's "Middle Way" approach, which he discussed in February 2003 during an interview with the BBC, stating, "I am not seeking separation or the independence of Tibet from the People's Republic of China. All I want is genuine self-rule for Tibet within China. This is my Middle Way approach."

Paula J. Dobriansky, undersecretary of state for global affairs, U.S. Department of State; special coordinator for Tibetan issues   In our exchanges with the Dalai Lama, he has indicated to us that he seeks cultural and religious freedom in Tibet. We have said that very publicly and we have said it privately—*that* is what we support.

I'm the third person to hold the position of special coordinator. The first two were at the assistant secretary level. This [the George W. Bush] administration felt that, first, it was important to elevate the issue because of its very nature. In my position as undersecretary, I take into account a broad range of issues—human rights, humanitarian, environmental; there's a multidimensional component, if you will, to what I do. In dealing with Tibet, one of the areas that we have discussion with the Chinese on is human rights. But this position was created in order to facilitate dialogue between the Dalai Lama and his envoy and Chinese officials. The feeling was certainly that by elevating it, one, it demonstrates the importance we attach to the issue; secondly, it also encourages a focus, very specifically, on facilitating dialogue between the Dalai Lama, his representatives, and Chinese officials because the assistant secretary level is where you have, for example, engagement on U.S.–China human rights dialogue. So there was an attempt to have a focused look at this and to try to also underscore the importance that we attach to the issue of Tibet.

Professor Robert Thurman   He has always said that to finalize the arrangement there would have to be a plebiscite of the Tibetan people *in*

Tibet. He has said he would lobby and use his considerable prestige to see that they agree to legitimize China's control of Tibet in exchange for genuine internal autonomy. The other sticking point is that in order for him to negotiate this, China would have to reunite the other two provinces of Tibet—where two thirds of the Tibetans live—with Central Tibet. Some of his supporters think that he shouldn't offer such an autonomous status. They feel that he should insist that Tibet is historically independent, and that China's control over Tibet is illegitimate and has no standing in international law. The Chinese maintain that in order for them to talk to the Dalai Lama, he would have to concede that Tibet has always been an integral part of China. This is obviously an untruth that he cannot subscribe to because he won't utter a lie.

Paula J. Dobriansky   When His Holiness visits the United States, it is specifically in his capacity as a religious leader, and he speaks to the issue of the importance of religious and cultural autonomy in Tibet. That is the context in which we engage His Holiness. In this administration, President Bush has met with the Dalai Lama several times. The Dalai Lama has also met with Secretary [of State Colin] Powell on several occasions, with Deputy Secretary of State Richard Armitage, and with me, as well, as both undersecretary of state for global affairs and as special coordinator on Tibet. In addition, when there are discussions with Chinese officials, the issue of Tibet has been discussed at all levels. The issue, specifically, of the importance of religious freedom and cultural autonomy has been raised and discussed by President Bush, first with Jiang Zemin and also now with Hu Jintao; by Vice President [Dick] Cheney during the course of his meetings; and by other high-level officials throughout this administration. We also have a variety of fora in which other issues are raised, such as, when we have our U.S.–China dialogue, which is at the assistant secretary level, cases relevant specifically to Tibet are also raised; human rights cases are raised and discussed in that forum, as well as the Panchen Lama.

In the last few years, the Dalai Lama has sent senior representatives to China in an attempt to generate dialogue on the issue, most recently in September 2004. At the same time, the Dalai Lama continues to press the cause of Tibet in the West. He is handicapped, however, due both to China's growing economic power and the aggressive advocacy of those of Tibet's ardent supporters who view the Middle Way approach as being too conciliatory.

The Dalai Lama's Appearance before the
Congressional Human Rights Caucus

Rinchen Dharlo   In 'eighty-seven he had his first political visit to the United States. I arrived in New York in May and at that time there was a plan to have him visit the United States, so I had to request that my predecessor stay back and help me to coordinate his visit. His visits included Atlanta, Indiana, and Washington, D.C., during which time the U.S. Congress wanted him to inform them what were the aspirations and hopes of the Tibetan people. So he prepared his Five Point Peace Plan, which he announced in Washington, D.C., and which received an enormous amount of support from other countries—mainly from parliamentarians and intellectuals.

Representative Tom Lantos [D-CA], Member, U.S. House of Representatives, 1981–; founder and cochair, Congressional Human Rights Caucus; ranking Democratic member, House International Relations Committee   Annette [Mrs. Lantos, executive director of the Congressional Human Rights Caucus] started it and I helped her; she was the first person to invite him to the Congress of the United States. We met him in a little conference room with a handful of colleagues. And she shepherded these various visits. On his more recent visits, you have huge numbers of members of Congress and the administration eager to be in his presence, to meet with him, and to be part of the Tibet spirit. Now he has an entrée to the White House, the State Department, to the Congressional leadership, and, indeed, to every segment of American society. So he has made enormous progress.

Annette Lantos   We met the Tibetan community [during a visit to Nepal] and were exposed for the first time to the tragedy of the Tibetans. We had known about it from what we had read in the newspapers, but in meeting with them we saw to what extent they depended on the support, love, and teachings of the Dalai Lama. It became apparent to us that this is a man greater than life, with values that can sustain people under the direst circumstances, so we became very interested in having his voice heard in Washington. We negotiated the invitation for a whole year after our trip to Nepal. That was the first time he had a platform within any official segment of the U.S. government to expound his Five Point Peace Plan. It was quite an experience.

It was quite difficult to persuade members of Congress to attend the briefing. They did not want to jeopardize their relationship with China. The Chinese ambassador came to our office the day before, pleading that we stop the meeting and saying that we could seriously harm the relationship. The State Department was establishing a relationship with China, and we also had a visit from the State Department, urging us not to go ahead with the meeting. But my husband had the independence and the freedom to do it.

In fact, the meeting took place with five or six members of Congress in attendance. The only media representative there was a summer intern working for the *Washington Post* on Capitol Hill. She took an amazingly wonderful photo of the Dalai Lama and my husband greeting each other. That photo took up half of the front page of the *Washington Post*'s Metro Section. That was the first time that the Dalai Lama burst on the U.S. political scene. Later, of course, there was tremendous interest in his presence in Washington.

Dr. Tenzin Tethong   Within days, Chinese government officials in Tibet started to again publicly accuse His Holiness of disrupting the peace. And the Chinese not only tried to inform the people in Tibet of the wrong deeds of the Dalai Lama, but they were trying to get the Tibetans to oppose or protest the Dalai Lama. And something of the reverse happened: not only were the Tibetans not willing to go along with that, but the first of the many demonstrations started taking place in Lhasa—there were some very major demonstrations by monks and nuns in Lhasa—and one in which a police station was burned. So all of that became very high-profile news events, and it was covered extensively all over the world.

It happened just within days of His Holiness's speech and so at that time not only was there a lot of attention but many of the congressmen and senators who had since his first visit started to speak out and be concerned about Tibet were expressing their willingness to be more supportive, more helpful.

At that time we didn't have any ongoing relationship with any of these congressmen or people in Washington, and His Holiness thought that it was time to try to do some work in Washington, D.C., itself. I was told to see if I could do anything, so right after that I started to work on exploring this, speaking with friends and all kinds of people about what can and what should be done in Washington. Of course, in one way, I was always wearing the Tibetan-Government-in-Exile hat, but often that was just only a title, or a credential I could take because the Tibetan government had very little resources to do anything in the United States in terms of dollars.

So what we had to do was to establish a presence in Washington; we had to find a way to create a structure that would not only be a proponent for Tibet but find a way to support it as well. So after a lot of consulting and speaking with friends and groups and others I went forward and established what is called "The International Campaign for Tibet," an effort meant to indicate that we were going to educate the international community about the conditions in Tibet and to find ways to resolve it. So then I started to set that up in Washington and while I was organizationally on the board and head of the International Campaign for Tibet, I was also continuing as the Special Representative of His Holiness.

The Impact of Winning the Nobel Peace Prize

The Dalai Lama's repute in the West was enhanced when in 1989 he was awarded the Nobel Prize for Peace.

Rinchen Dharlo When he got the Nobel Prize, I was with him in Southern California. The day before, we came to know that he and the Czech, [Vaclav] Havel—he has some kind of personal relationship with President Havel—were the finalists. And there was also the very strong rumor that he was the winner. Then the day when he knew that he was the winner, he felt that Havel should have won—he was very impressed with his work. He got up that day very early, as usual, and said his prayers, and then he turned on the radio to try to get the news of who was the winner. Then he said, "Turn it off." First, he was curious—he was very much interested in knowing for himself—but then he thought that was not a good motivation: as a monk, he should not be concerned with his fame. And he turned off the radio. The next day, at a news conference, someone who was interviewing him asked whether he was excited, and he said, "There was some excitement, in the morning. I turned the radio on but I turned it off later."

Adam Engle In the early 1990s, I asked him what winning the Nobel Peace Prize meant to him. He laughed and said, "As far as I am concerned, it really doesn't mean *anything*, yet I am aware that it helps me in getting attention for the Tibetan people."

Richard Gere There was certainly a sense of naïveté about him. I honestly don't think he had any idea of how powerful the Nobel Peace Prize was. In his lifetime, he's gotten an endless series of awards. There are very few giants on this planet and he's one of them so, of course, he's gotten all the humanitarian awards and the honorary doctorates in his life. But I don't think he realized that that was of a different order or how his life would change, not just in terms of how he was being perceived, but also in the extreme pressure on his time and energy after that. His job is to help people—his only reason for being here is to *help* people—and since that happened, the opportunity to help people, and to be effective, has increased enormously. Obviously, the demands on his time to be meaningful and helpful have also increased, so as he's gotten older, the irony is that he has much more demand on his time and energy.

The Official Reaction of the Chinese Government

Sun Wade   We have to know just who the Dalai Lama is. When we talk about the Dalai Lama it's important to bear in mind two points: one is that we have to look at the Dalai Lama from a historical perspective; and also we have to look at this issue with a complete perspective. Historically speaking, the Fourteenth Dalai Lama has been the core representative of Tibetan feudal serfdom, which he calls the opposite. At that time a great number of serfs have been economically exploited and they have suffered inhumane treatment. It was only after the peaceful liberation of Tibet that we have abolished the serfdom system, and actually the situation in Tibet has been fundamentally improved.

The Dalai Lama, in order to maintain the interests of an overwhelming minority of serf owners—they actually broke the agreement with the central government in that they instigated the armed rebellion. And after the rebellion, they fled abroad. In the past forty years, they have used foreign forces, and the Dalai Lama has engaged in a number of activities in splitting the motherland and undermining stability and development in Tibet, and also he has undermined the interests of the Tibetan people. These are historical facts, so we think that the issue of the Dalai Lama is not a religious issue; instead it is a political issue. The Dalai Lama is *not* purely a religious figure; he is a political exile who has long been engaging in activities that are separating the Chinese motherland.

Professor Jonathan Mirsky   That's just a lie, and they know it's a lie. Look, they cannot talk to him. Every now and then, emissaries of his go to see them—people like Lodi Gyari [a key associate of the Dalai Lama] and others, who are friends of mine—but the fact is that these negotiations don't mean anything; they mean *nothing*. The Chinese got the message in the early eighties when those three delegations [went to Tibet]. They suddenly realized that it hadn't worked in Tibet—that the Tibetans still longed for the Dalai Lama to come back. And that's how they treated his sister, who was in the first delegation.

They know there's no point in negotiating with them because the moment he goes back, the whole situation in Tibet would change, and even become rather violent, so they will never do it. And they see very low-level people; they see people in the United Front Organization; they never see really important officials, and nothing much comes of it. Lodi, who is a very skillful diplomatist, always tries to put the best light on it, but the fact is that there has never been any change. The only time there was ever a change—and it was before any of these delegations—was when Hu Yaobang [1915–1989], then the general secretary of the party, went to Tibet in May of 1980 and apologized to the Tibetans for bad Chinese treatment over the years, and he said that the Chinese would now suspend all tax demands in Tibet. It was a very full apology, and that was one of the reasons why, not very long thereafter, that Hu Yaobang was purged. The next year, I went to Tibet for the first time and I spoke to members of the Chinese cadres there, and they were furious with Hu Yaobang for having said this; they felt that he had humiliated them. And after his purge, I went to Tibet more times and now that Hu Yaobang was off the scene, these Chinese cadres in Tibet and in Szechwan were delighted that this had happened to Hu because they felt that that apology would weaken China's position in Tibet.

Sun Wade   The second point that we have to bear in mind when we talk about the Dalai Lama is that we not only have to listen to what he has to say but also watch what he has been doing—that is very important—the Dalai Lama has been talking much about the so-called fraternity of human rights and he mentions the interests of the Tibetan people. But we should always bear in mind that the Dalai Lama has been the representative of a feudal serfdom system in the forty-five years since he fled Tibet. He has never made any contribution to social progress in Tibet, and he has never done anything for the Tibetan people. Instead, in recent years, the Dalai Lama's group has conducted many acts of infiltration into Tibet, and in the past few decades, they have been involved in all kinds of explosions and assassinations. These kinds of acts definitely have undermined the stability and development of Tibet.

Harry Wu   The Dalai Lama is always the enemy; all religious leaders are enemies of the Communist regime. You have to know what the definition of communism is. I'm not a political science scholar, okay? My view is simple: communism is two things, no private ownership and privacy, and no religion. That's it! That's why, when they came to power they abolished private ownership; nobody has privacy at all; all the people's lives, jobs, are controlled by one hand, and they eliminated all religions—Christians, Buddhists, whatever.

Representative Tom Lantos   The vast economic and military entity that China is still totally lacks moral authority. And while the Dalai Lama is not in the business of either military power or economic power, he has a quality that the Chinese can only *dream* about in their wildest, wildest dreams, namely to develop at least the tiniest moral authority. The Dalai Lama has *total* moral authority and the Chinese government has none, so, in a sense, they are not dealing in the same currency. But it is self-evident that the Chinese want desperately to bask in the reflection of what the Dalai Lama exudes, which is a set of values and the admiration of the whole world.

Other Political Travels:
The Dalai Lama's Meeting on July 17, 1996, with British Foreign Minister Sir Malcolm Rifkind

Sir Malcolm L. Rifkind   Like everyone else, I found him a very spiritual sort of person. But I was taken slightly by surprise because he combines a spirituality of manner with a very simple sense of humor; he giggles a great deal—a lot of laughter, a lot of fun—and that's an unusual combination with someone who also has very serious things to communicate.

There were just the two of us—there may have been one other person there, but I cannot be certain—but certainly it was primarily a discussion between the two of us; I do not recollect anybody else making a significant contribution. We had received indication that he was in London and would welcome a meeting. My officials in the Foreign Office advised against my seeing him—this was at a time when Britain and China were going through very delicate negotiations on Hong Kong—and there was considerable concern that if a British minister were to receive the Dalai Lama, the Chinese would take that as an unfriendly act, and that that could damage what for Britain at the time was a much more important question, of making progress in the Hong Kong negotiations. I took the view that although these were valid arguments, it was not acceptable that a foreign government—in this case the Chinese government—should dictate who a British minister should or should not meet. But in deference to the views of my officials, we reached a compromise—that I agree to see him, but that the meeting did not take place in the Foreign Office, in my ministerial office. The meeting took place in Number One Carlton Gardens, which is the official residence of the foreign secretary—in other words, in the house that I normally lived in—rather than in my office. This gave it a more of an informal nature, rather than a formal meeting. I did this in order to reassure my officials that I was sensitive to the wider implications. We made it clear; it was made public that there had been a meeting—the meeting was not kept private in that sense. The Chinese made some very angry comments, but they did not have the slightest impact on the British-Hong Kong-China discussions. So from that point of view, it was all very satisfactory.

Sun Wade   We are strongly opposed to those meetings. All the countries of the world recognize Tibet as part of the Chinese territories, so we are strongly opposed to those kinds of meetings with the Dalai Lama. By the way, the Dalai Lama recently has also said that the Tibetan issue may be resolved within the framework of the People's Republic of China, and also within the framework of the constitution of the People's Republic of China. So, actually, we hope that the Dalai Lama will match his words with deeds.

Rabbi A. James Rudin   You do this just to keep your issue out there. From his point of view, he's representing a disposed people and he wants to go back [to Tibet] and so he keeps on. There must be some relationship with the Chinese that Blair and Chirac and the Bushes and Clinton all knew that wasn't going to cost them anything [to receive the Dalai Lama]. And the Chinese by now must understand that the Dalai Lama is good currency in the United States, and they can't punish France for doing it—there hasn't been any real punishment. But they tried to discourage him in Israel.

While the Dalai Lama has visited Israel twice, in 1994 and 1999, he was not received officially by the Israeli government. In 1994, however, he met in Eilat with Yossi Sarid, then minister of environment, and in 1999, he was received in Jerusalem by both Mr. Sarid, who had become minister of education, and by then-speaker of the Knesset Avraham Burg.

Yossi Sarid   Since I must follow my conscience, it was very important for me to see the Dalai Lama. He is a man of peace, he cares for education and for the environment, and since my career was developed on these same issues, I believed that we had something to talk about. He said the right things about Israel. He was positively impressed by his visits. He is very polite; apparently he was not upset when in 1999 he was not officially received by the government—at least he did not mention it in our conversation. He did express appreciation for the very fact that we met. In the end, we interpreted our meeting as one between an Israeli minister and the Dalai Lama. I had no hesitation in meeting him when he came to Israel, even though the Israeli Foreign Ministry did not like the idea that a government minister would receive the Dalai Lama. I was told that, God forbid, bilateral relations between Israel and China would be spoiled as a result of the meeting. I told the Foreign Ministry officials that *I* was taking responsibility—that if the relations are important enough for both countries, I don't think, with all due respect to myself, that my meeting with the Dalai Lama would harm these relations. When the president of China [Jiang Zemin] was in Israel [in 2000], I didn't notice any bad feelings over my meeting with the Dalai Lama. On the contrary, he met with me and we signed an agreement for cooperation in the field of education. Our receiving the Dalai Lama did not at all harm Israel's relations with China, which remain good. That is not to say that I am satisfied with the status of civil and human rights in China, but China is a very important country. We have our relations, which are good and improving.

Justin Trudeau   When one looks at geopolitics, certainly where Canada is concerned, you can't understate the complexities involved sometimes. Canada—and my father in particular—has always enjoyed very good relationships with China; my father was the one who recognized China and went to China even before Nixon did. And that's always been something very, very strong, the relationship between the PRC and Canada. But at the same time, I don't think that the relationship and the respect for the Dalai Lama that we have imperils our relationship with China. It's just that China is in a position where it hates to be told what to think or what to be or how to be and really tends to react strongly to people meddling in their internal affairs. I don't think there's any question that at the top levels the

Chinese know there needs to be change and accommodation; it's just that for saving face and for their own strength, they need to be the ones who are responsible for the change. So any time people meddle in what they see as internal affairs, they get a little bit snippy. But I don't think that there really is a tremendous contradiction, and when one looks at the history of China versus Taiwan and the way we've managed to skirt around that issue and yet enjoy good relations with everyone—as in we, the world—I don't think it's as big an issue and a deal as the Chinese feel they should make it for image's sake.

Harry Wu   China is huge, gigantic. Their leaders were welcomed to the White House. Okay, I understand they were changing because the system was unreasonable. Later I found that people said, "Well, China is quite interesting; China is a good place to go, to travel." I went to Yale University, Harvard, and Stanford. People think China doesn't have a gulag. There's the Evil Empire; China is the Angel Empire. The first time I passed over the check-in point at San Francisco International Airport, I said: "I'm free; I'm *free*." But later I found out I'm not free; I'm *not* free. When I spoke out, when I showed people, the left here did not want this. China, you killed my mother; you killed my brother; you almost killed *me*. What did I do? If I'm a free man, I just want to tell about it. What is it you want of me?

The More Militant Stance of Some of Tibet's Supporters in the West

Professor Robert Thurman   There is a range of people in the West. Some are more aggressive, some less aggressive, and some don't even care because they think it is just a lost cause—that it is *finished*. Others feel that while the Dalai Lama is very nice spiritually, he is confused geopolitically and, therefore, they don't think there is any hope—the majority is like that. There are some young, frustrated, fire-breathing Tibetans who say they want guns and want to do something. But so far, except for a couple of self-immolations, there have not been violent acts or terrorism among the Tibetans who chafe at the Dalai Lama's policy of nonviolence. Then there are some rightwingers who would like to use the Dalai Lama in an anti-China way, although they are now fewer in number. The Dalai Lama never allowed himself to be a pawn of those people.

Orville Schell   The Dalai Lama has been more conciliatory. Whether that is a successful, practical strategy or not has caused much debate. It is true that the Chinese Communist Party does not respond as some other organizations might to a sense of moderation, mediation, and trying to work things out in the liberal mode, which, of course, is His Holiness's posture toward them. But I also think that, quite apart from whether it is the best tactical strategy to push, cajole, or influence, His Holiness is an incomparable model—not necessarily in a purely practical way—of how one should deport oneself in relationship to a hostile adversary.

Sir Malcolm Rifkind   It reflects a number of considerations. It reflects his own personality, which is ultimately a spiritual personality and, therefore, he is prepared to take these things to some extent in a slightly fatalistic way. Secondly—it is one of the few things that the Tibetans and Chinese have in common—to play a very long game, and to recognize that when you're dealing with the history of countries and of nations, then you have to measure these things in years and, sometimes, in generations, not just in weeks or months. Thirdly, as commentators in America, or in Britain, or elsewhere in the West, we can afford to be more radical in our advice because we're not living there: it's one of many issues for us; for the Dalai Lama it's the well-being of his own people, and he has to take that into account in a much more careful and cautious way. And he has very limited cards to play. He has obviously rejected violence as a means of promoting change and that is admirable, but, of course, it also severely reduces the short-term threat that he represents to the Chinese position. It may make his long-term position stronger—you can meet violence with violence but when you have a resistance of a nonviolent kind, that is something that the Chinese may welcome in the short term but may find more difficult to resolve satisfactorily in the longer term.

Representative Tom Lantos   He's more *realistic*. He is prepared to have a flexible and moderate approach because he's convinced—and I believe correctly—that only such an approach is likely to yield results. Being more royalist than the king in this instance will not lead anyplace. I, personally, fully support his approach.

Patrick French   There was a moment in the early-to-mid-1980s when rapprochement was possible. Then in the late eighties and the early nineties, with the collapse of the Soviet Union, the people around the Dalai Lama saw that communism was failing and that Western support for the Free Tibet movement was growing, and they decided, perhaps understandably, that they were going to try and see whether they could use that foreign support primarily, not American support, to get some kind of nego-tiating leverage against the Chinese government. And that failed. So, really, since the early nineties Tibetans inside Tibet are facing nothing but repression, and negotiations haven't gone anywhere for the last fifteen years. So although voters in the United States or in Britain will probably turn out in numbers to vote for the Dalai Lama going back to live in the Potala, that doesn't necessarily cut any ice with the Chinese Communist Party. I don't think they're particularly interested in what people like you or I are thinking. That's not how they work. The problem of growing up in a democratic society is that you assume you can change things politically, but it's not that kind of system; they're just not interested.

Paula J. Dobriansky   The issue of influence here is that it is in the mutual interest of the Tibetans—and in particular, the Dalai Lama and his envoys—as well as the Chinese, to try to forge an understanding and to try to reconcile differences. And the reason is because when you look at it from the Tibetan side, what His Holiness has specifically said that he is looking for is simply economic improvements and equality for Tibetans; he's look-ing, naturally, also for cultural autonomy—in other words, preservation of the very essence of the Tibetan culture—as well as the ability of Tibetans to be able to pursue religious freedom. And, also, he mentions the impor-tance of the environment—that he is very concerned about environmental degradation in Tibet. Finally, he has also indicated how he would like to ensure that, just like in other parts of China—for example, when you have an inflow of Chinese into Hong Kong, they actually have a framework of rendering visas—he's looking for a comparable approach in the case of Tibet. Now it's in the Tibetan interest to have reconciliation because these are things that affect people's lives. Also, Tibet is part of China, so for that reason you also want to have productive members of society.

On the Chinese side, His Holiness has been very clear in terms of what he has put on the table as a means of reconciliation. Toward this end, I think it is in everyone's interest—here the Chinese have a very clear indi-cation of what His Holiness is looking for—so something could be said for dealing very directly with His Holiness on these issues and knowing what issues you're dealing with. So there is a real incentive for engaging now along the lines of these issues, which are not only in the interest of Tibet but also in the interest of China itself.

Richard Blum   He moderated his stance in 1989 when he said he was no longer seeking independence but was perfectly willing to have Tibet become an autonomous region of the People's Republic of China. The Chinese often ignore that statement. My guess is that there is a difference of opinion concerning what constitutes autonomy. In my last meeting with Jiang I said to him, "If you and His Holiness were in the same room, you would like him."

Dr. Alexander Berzin   I don't think he has moderated. His Holiness is extremely realistic and practical—that's a term that he uses over and again when he speaks in Tibetan—and so he's just looking at the reality of the situation and what is the best that they could hope for. I don't think that he would like to go further in his position but is reining himself in. His Holiness, from the experience I've had with him over all these years, is totally sincere—he's not playing games.

Annette Lantos   I have never heard him say anything bad about the Chinese; he always has great compassion for them. He would never sanction violence in the pursuit of any cause, including the liberation of Tibet. Because he cannot sanction violence, that has caused him many problems. For him, the means and the ends are the same. I can applaud that. But, of course, I am not a politician.

Richard Gere   His Holiness is filled with forgiveness. He's also a man of justice. But, from the Buddhist point of view, karma is its own sense of justice. Karma has to ripen; what affects our future is our present actions. Love and compassion today will ultimately reap greater rewards than any kind of violence or stridentness now. His Holiness's approach is basically that. Clearly, he speaks the truth about what's going on, but it's pointless to put up roadblocks.

I had something important happen to me one day. I was speaking at a rally in Washington and I was using all the touch points that I believed in, talking about fascists, communist leaders, totalitarian thugs, et cetera, who had been abusing not only their own people but, clearly, the Tibetans. There was a woman who spoke after me, Mairead [Corrigan] Maguire, the Nobel Peace Prize–winner, and she said, "You know, Richard, if you don't mind me saying, you might want to think again about being so angry, and calling people these really heavy names, because some day you're going to have to work with them toward the peace and it's not going to be skillful to have that impediment in the way." She was very right about that. His Holiness is a leader who speaks to leaders; there are others of us whose job, maybe, is to be more strident and more vocal, but a man of His Holiness's stature functions in a different way.

Professor Jonathan Mirsky I was present for that great speech at Strasbourg. First I went to Dharamsala to read some drafts of the speech and then I went to Strasbourg to see him, and he gave the speech in which he said, "We no longer insist on independence for Tibet; what we want is a great measure of autonomy." Now for some of his followers it was disappointing and for some—people in the Tibetan Youth Congress, in Delhi, who I used to see there or would come here, this was not a word they would have used. This was almost treachery, and they felt he had fallen into the hands of the Chinese. Not that he was cooperating with the Chinese, but that he had given up the great struggle for independence. This is one of the reasons why the Chinese act in such bad faith, because they always say that the Dalai Lama—the "criminal Dalai Lama," the "splittist Dalai Lama"—insists on independence. He hasn't insisted on independence since the middle eighties; he's an autonomy man.

Sun Wade We have not only to listen to what he has to say but also what he has been doing in the last few years. And the fact of the matter is that he hasn't basically changed his position for Tibetan independence.

Annette Lantos The Dalai Lama has great leverage but it is *invisible* and *unenforceable*. But it will prevail; in the end, an unfair, unjust, repressive tyranny will fall. I believe that Chinese communism will eventually implode from within, as communism did in Russia. The Dalai Lama has great patience; he has a different sense of time.

Father Laurence Freeman He certainly could dialogue with representatives of the People's Republic of China. He's probably much more astute and experienced politically now than he was as a young man when he was taken in by Mao. In a way, the Tibetan approach is almost naïve in the circumstances, but their naïvete is their strength as well, and it's their purity. And, of course, it's the basis of the great support that they do get from the West.

He knows and he's said to me, "They don't trust me." Everybody else in the world thinks he's the most honest man there is, but the Chinese believe that he is cunning and manipulative and they just don't trust him, so he feels that—it's a very astute insight; he may or may not be proven right—that the changing Chinese attitudes toward Tibet will come about through the Chinese intelligentsia exerting an influence over time on the Chinese government, and also through the Christians in China.

Rinchen Dharlo   He is someone who respects other opinions; he has always had differences with his older brother, Thubten [Jigme] Norbu, who is in Bloomington; Thubten Norbu always believed in *total independence* and he always said that we should settle for nothing short of that. There was a huge difference of opinion between the two brothers. He always says, "I don't agree with my brother. But still we are very close to each other, as brothers."

Pema Chhinjor   In a referendum, 62 percent of the exile community voted to accept the wishes of His Holiness in dealing with China. We can talk about freedom, but how are we going to get it? China is becoming stronger economically and is a large market for the rest of the world.

Dr. Howard Cutler   Like everything else in his life, his approach to China goes back to what he believes is most consistent with Buddhist thought. Thus he developed the Middle Way approach, which is not one extreme or another. His moderation stems from his natural compassion and tolerance, his desire as a human being to be conciliatory—to bring all parties together. That is what he is like as a person.

He is also a very practical guy; he doesn't have unrealistic expectations. As a result of the unique opportunity he has had in meeting political and business leaders from many nations, he has had an amazing practical education in how the world works. Today, despite some opposition to his views on China, he is holding the Tibetan community together by virtue of the great respect that all Tibetans have for him. But it is difficult to know what will happen when he's no longer there.

Dr. Jeffrey Hopkins   In an interview with William Buckley on *Firing Line*—it was conducted at Middlebury College as I remember, in their converted chapel—Buckley didn't even get the idea that His Holiness opposed what the Chinese were doing in Tibet, His Holiness was so soft-spoken about what was happening. His way is not to be too harsh in his statements, I think, as an appeal to the Chinese leadership so they can see that this is someone they can deal with.

Pema Chhinjor   We were able to obtain some important Chinese documents indicating that in thirty years a total of thirteen million Chinese will be settled in Tibet. Tibet is a good place to ease China's problem of overpopulation. Tibet is also important to China because of its very strategic position in Asia. Given these factors, the Middle Way approach of His

Holiness is the best answer. We know that other countries will not support Tibetan independence but do agree with his Middle Way position, which will, at least, allow for the preservation of Tibetan identity, civilization, and culture. The Middle Way envisions genuine self-rule, with Tibet living under the Chinese Constitution.

The Chinese should have no second thoughts about that, but they are still wedded to their old, negative slogans concerning His Holiness. Tibetans are not Chinese and the Chinese are not Tibetans—Tibetans don't speak the Chinese language and they don't eat Chinese food or wear Chinese clothing—yet they are willing to live under the Red Flag and Constitution. The Chinese refuse to accept the Middle Way because they fear the Dalai Lama. If he comes back to Tibet under self-rule, they know that the Tibetans will want to listen to his teachings, seek his blessings, and follow him. On top of that, many in China will want to go to Tibet to listen to His Holiness.

Rinchen Dharlo Their [China's] national interest comes first, so that's why it's difficult. We have not been able to even get a simple resolution passed in the Human Rights Commission in Geneva condemning the human rights abuses in China, as well as in Tibet. The United States has always sponsored a resolution and the European nations, including the Scandinavians, have always cosponsored such a resolution, but in so many years we have not been able to get this resolution passed, mainly because of the Chinese government's influence over developing countries.

Sun Wade There is no basis whatsoever to claim Tibet as a so-called independent country. In recent years, the Dalai Lama's group and other organizations in the West have tried to distort the facts and make unwarranted accusations against China's religious policies in the name of human rights and religion. So we think this is a kind of interference in China's internal affairs. The fact of the matter is that no country in the world recognizes the so-called Tibetan exile government. And, of course, we definitely do not recognize the so-called Free Tibet movement or any other relevant illegal organizations.

Representative Tom Lantos I certainly don't anticipate seeing any change in the Chinese leadership as, obviously, the current leadership is the young leadership, and that young leadership is likely to stay in office for a long, long time. So to whatever extent we can anticipate changes, those changes will come at a glacial speed.

Sir Malcolm Rifkind   There have been different stages in the British position. The first was, obviously, when we ruled India, and any views that we had about Tibet and about China were colored by the implications for the Indian Empire. From Britain's point of view, the existence of Nepal, of Bhutan, and if there had been an autonomous Tibet that would have been useful and desirable, but it was not in itself some fundamental requirement; it was understood that Tibet came within China's sphere of influence. And as India was part of the British Empire in those days, we could hardly object to Tibet's being part of the Chinese Empire. In the latter stages of the relationship—that is, in the last twenty-five years—Hong Kong has been the main preoccupation of successive British governments up till 1997, and therefore whatever sympathy and admiration we had for the Dalai Lama as a person, and for the plight of his people, we saw our prime duty as to try to help the people of Hong Kong. And as we could not have by ourselves or, indeed, with others, changed the status of Tibet, we tended to keep it as a low-key issue in terms of our own public position.

Arjia Rinpoché   His Holiness himself—and lots of people—want him to go back to Tibet. He will take this Middle Way and more compromise, maybe. If he goes there, the situation will be different. In China, of course, sometimes the political issue and their policies are so strong. But if you compare it to before, there is a big change in China—lots of freedom there; socialism and communism are almost gone—so there has begun a kind of capitalism. But, on the other hand, lots of Tibetans think he doesn't need to go back because the Chinese government will never talk to him, so there's no way to compromise—the Middle Way is just a saying—so that's why the movement is slowed down.

Dr. Tenzin Tethong   There are those who think that, unless you're absolutely clear about Tibet's complete independence, anything else you do is harmful to Tibetan interests, and some of those who call for complete independence say that His Holiness's suggestion about the Middle Way of resolving the issue is harmful. But I don't agree with that. While I do profess this basic trust about the Tibetan people's rights, I think what His Holiness is doing should not be seen as harmful to Tibetan interests, but that His Holiness is doing something that will advance the Tibetan people's situation: he is dealing with the realities of a people who have been suffering rather drastically for the last forty or fifty years.

He has personally received support from hundreds and hundreds of people coming out of Tibet. And then he's also aware of the extent of changes taking place in Tibet and how the very survival of the Tibetan language and culture is also at great risk, and so he has the great responsibility, before trying to provide luxuries for the Tibetan people, of at least trying to save Tibet at this stage. So whatever he proposes, in terms of creating a dialogue and some new relations with the Chinese and a new structure whereby the Tibetans can have a complete say in matters that affect them, is definitely going to help the Tibetan people. So the whole debate from those who take a hard-line position may be helpful in terms of drawing some attention to the fact that Tibetans feel quite intense about how independent they want to be—there may be some merit in that—but other than that, on a practical, realistic level, nothing constructive really has been offered.

Mickey Lemle   He can't storm the barricades. What he *is* doing—to be totally nonviolent—is very smart. He has said, "If and when we get Tibet back, we are still going to be neighbors with China." If something doesn't happen during the lifetime of His Holiness, there is a serious question of how much Tibetan culture will survive. The issue for Tibet is how long it can sustain the population transfer. Right now, the language of upper mobility is Chinese; there is intermarriage; the culture is disappearing. My own view is that Tibetan Buddhism is a world resource. It is the spiritual equivalent of the rainforest and, like the rainforest, it is disappearing very quickly, before our eyes.

Pressing Tibet's Cause with Western Leaders: The "It Can't Hurt" Strategy in His Many Meetings

Rinchen Dharlo   Whenever he meets with these political leaders, I've never seen him ask of these people to punish China, to impose sanctions, or to sponsor resolutions condemning China; he doesn't ask for these things. I've seen him asking people to communicate with China, not to exclude China. He always says, "Bring China to the mainstream of humanity and let them learn." He wants them to engage in dialogue, and he encourages them to do more on human rights and negotiations, not only in Tibet, but for all of China. This is the way he communicates.

Actually, outside India, his first meeting with a political leader was in 1989 when he met with the president of Costa Rica [Oscar Arias Sánchez]. And then his second meeting was with the Mexican president.

And the next year, he met with President Havel, then President [George Herbert Walker] Bush. And then he was received by many presidents and prime ministers around the world—except in some of those countries with whom the Chinese pressure worked.

The Dalai Lama, being a statesman, a famous person, some of them just wanted to meet him. For many of them it did not matter whether he was viewed as the head of the Tibetan government in exile or as the spiritual leader of Tibet; they just wanted to meet him. Some, like Tony Blair and the Canadian Prime Minister [Paul Martin] met him as a religious leader. The U.S. presidents did not specify in what capacity they were meeting with him. Clinton met him not in his Oval Office but in Mr. [Al] Gore's office. That was mainly not to anger China.

Professor Abelardo Brenes   When he came back in September 2004, he explained his position regarding China, but he didn't seem to be making a public appeal for action. I did not experience optimism from His Holiness. But His Holiness did mention his hopes for democratization in China itself. *That* is his great hope.

Sun Wade   If the Dalai Lama is really willing to solve the Tibetan issue within the People's Republic of China, within the framework of China's constitution, it's quite natural for him to admit that he insists on the current system of regional ethnic autonomy even though this system of regional ethnic autonomy has been inscribed into the constitution of the People's Republic. But the Dalai Lama has never talked about that; he's not willing to talk about the current political system. Instead, he's spending much time talking about the so-called political status of Tibet and he's trying to propagandize those proposals in the international community, so as to mislead the public. So whatever he has said, one thing is clear: the Dalai Lama has been changing tactics, but his position regarding independence for Tibet has not changed and he has not changed the essence: to split the Motherland of China.

Dr. Jeffrey Hopkins   He's extremely well aware of the destruction of Tibetan culture, the death of so many Tibetans, and I think you have to look to his persistence in visiting countries, in meeting with the political leaders of those countries, to understand how dedicated, persistent, and unstoppable he is. And I say this because everywhere that he goes, the Chinese government objects beforehand to that government and complains that he should not even be allowed in the country. I think we need to notice that the Dalai Lama does not step back and say, "Oh, okay, I'll stay at home," or, "I'll go to those few countries where it doesn't matter." He doesn't force himself on others, but he's persistent and he doesn't get upset when the Chinese pressure is too much for some country. Some people could say he's too kind, but in his own kind way, he is *very* persistent on making connections with world leaders everywhere.

Annette Lantos   They [the Chinese government] are threatened by what the Dalai Lama symbolizes—an authority greater than any worldly authority. Deep down, people who deny the reality of anything else beyond this earth feel threatened by someone who has the spiritual and mental freedom that the Dalai Lama possesses. He is a man who is totally dedicated to liberating the mind and soul of mankind without bloodshed—not arguing, just asserting the truth as he knows it.

The Dalai Lama's Strategy in Continuing to Send a Trusted Confidante, Lodi Gyari, to Negotiate with the Chinese

For some years, Lodi Gyari, a long trusted confidante of the Dalai Lama based in Washington, D.C., has been traveling between there and Beijing in an effort to negotiate Tibet's, and the Dalai Lama's, future status. In the late summer of 2004, Mr. Gyari embarked on yet another mission to the People's Republic of China.

Representative Tom Lantos   He keeps working at problems more or less on a no-deadline basis. He believes that what he is trying to do—and I totally agree with him; it's the right thing—is to keep pounding away at a totalitarian regime in his own gentle and gracious and powerful way, as long as it is necessary, until he finally will persuade them to accept his position. So I would hope that this particular visit will be productive and that this is the end of the road. But I would be very pleasantly surprised if that were the case.

Paula J. Dobriansky   The fact that such dialogue has taken place is important in itself. It affords an opportunity to indicate the kinds of interest and also the very specific areas that are of concern to Tibetans. Secondly, in terms of where this is going, we don't know yet. This is only the beginning. We've indicated to both the Tibetans and the Chinese that we welcome such a dialogue. This has not happened, to my knowledge, heretofore. Secondly, in terms of the Chinese comments, there have been a variety of comments. Many times discussions are taking place, and then there are statements that are made across the board that might demonstrate questions as to where this will lead. So, at this point, we really don't know what will come out of these discussions. We have to wait and see what happens—or what *doesn't* happen—here.

Richard Gere   Near term, probably the biggest change is going to come inside of China, not about *Tibet*, specifically, but what China becomes. My own feeling is that as the business community becomes more politicized in China—becomes more part of the political structure—that there will be a rationality to their actions and behavior and policies, and that policy, that maturation, will have positive fall-down in Tibet.

I think that international pressure is desperately important; I think that the Chinese still care what people think, especially in a tricky moral area like this. His Holiness is an extraordinary head of a peaceful movement, which is known throughout the world now, and it's a very tricky situation for them, as they want to mature into a powerful country in the world—in terms of trade, in terms of culture, in terms of everything—and the Tibetan situation is something they have to deal with.

Is it something that they *want* to deal with? Not particularly. That's why it is so important for us, and for His Holiness, to keep talking about it and making it known. I think that the talks that Lodi is engaging now are still extremely preliminary. I think there will be a point very soon where the Chinese have to demonstrate that they're real and that they're not just taking up time until it's too late—and there probably *is* a moment where it could well become too late. Maybe another generation is that point, and that's why we're all working so hard now.

Professor Jonathan Mirsky   The Dalai Lama is a very optimistic person and he always hopes that some different kind of Chinese will emerge—the phrase he always uses is "more human"—and that they will realize that they could behave in a different way in Tibet. But the problem is that there are two—to use that phrase that Kissinger used to use—particularly neuralgic issues for Beijing: one is Taiwan and the other is Tibet. And they can't compromise on those; they can't do it. It's so deep-seated that after Tiananmen, a certain number of very high-ranking Chinese officials fled China and came to the West and formed what they call the Chinese

Democracy Party. And one of these men had been on the staff of the Central Committee. I had dinner with him and a number of Tibetan refugees in Paris at the end of 'eighty-nine and one of the Tibetans from Dharamsala asked him what he thought the Chinese should do with Tibet. He said, "Oh, if we democrats ever take over, we would give a great deal of autonomy to Tibet." And I said to him, "Why wouldn't you just give them independence?" And he said—we were still at the table—"Oh, if we lost Tibet, I would feel that my liver had been torn out!" And I asked him if he had ever met a Tibetan before and he said no, and I said, "Have you ever been to Tibet?" and he said no. And I said, "Tell me one thing—and I've asked many Chinese this question—that the Tibetans and the Chinese have in common, any custom, food, marriage, funerals, how they dress, *anything*." And, of course, they can't and then they always say, "But it's still part of China." It takes up an enormous part of what's called "Chinese territory," so they have this impression that somehow China would be very weak without Tibet.

Dr. Tenzin Tethong   I've been involved with a number of people in suggesting that the whole Tibet movement—the Tibetan struggle in exile—focus on highlighting the fundamental issues of the Tibetan problem and trying to focus it on the principles of a people's right to self-determination. At an earlier stage we did talk about a referendum, but a referendum in the context of how to ascertain the Tibetan people's wishes and right to self-determination. I've been trying to do this with this organization called The Committee of 100 for Tibet and a number of Tibetan community organizations and individual Tibetans who are involved in this issue, and I've been trying to say that we need to restate some of our fundamental goals, because in recent years we seem to be somewhat stuck on a treadmill and we're not making any real progress, or it doesn't seem to be that way.

Richard Blum   In terms of realpolitik, it is totally unreasonable for supporters of the Dalai Lama to expect a free Tibet. His Holiness, being a man of nonviolence in the Gandhian tradition, has made life easier for the Chinese. He has also kept a lot of Tibetans from being killed. The concept that, somehow, a group of Tibetans could last more than a very short period of time trying to take on one of the world's great military powers would just reach a level of insanity. The ideal outcome would be an autonomous region where the Tibetan people could protect their religion, culture, and language. My personal view is that Tibet can become more democratic and more autonomous only if China itself continues to change in a major way.

Orville Schell   From the practical, realpolitik, position, there is no reason for the Chinese to be conciliatory. This is where the Dalai Lama is so interesting and so estimable, for to him the tactical question of how you win is not the only concern. He factors into the equation: how do I have to be to win, and what does that model suggest to others and the future? China doesn't care about that. Their attitude is: how do we get to the bottom line? How do we prevail, not worrying about the methods used? So in this sense, we really have two different worlds colliding. You may say, "The Chinese will win; they are very powerful. Nobody recognizes Tibet. And the Dalai Lama is sort of irrelevant." From that perspective, China is winning and they know that when the Dalai Lama dies, that may be the end of it.

But from another perspective, of course, they lose. The Chinese will lose because they do not provide a model for making the world a more peaceful and happy place. That is what the Chinese simply do not understand because they don't have the corpus of spiritual, religious, and ethical considerations in their midst. The Chinese destroyed their version of Confucianism, which contained clear notions of how to behave in an ethical, moral way.

Richard Blum   If you go to Beijing, and especially to Shanghai, these places increasingly feel that they are in the First World. People talk about whatever they want to as long as their criticisms of the government are generic. In the TAR [Tibet Autonomous Region], particularly in what was eastern Tibet, the Tibetans and the Chinese actually get along reasonably well. In Lhasa, which is like an armed camp, conditions are quite restricted. The most important problem facing Tibetans today is that they are treated as second- or third-class citizens. At the American Himalayan Foundation in Katmandu, we see almost all of the young people escaping from Tibet, and it is less and less about religion and culture and more and more about the fact that these refugees lack a free education and decent employment opportunities. And modernity has played a role in all of this.

Dr. Ronald B. Sobel   I am reminded of an ancient story: An old man is planting an oak tree—putting an acorn into the ground. A much younger man comes walking by, sees what the man is doing, and sort of contemptuously asks him, "What are you doing? You're an old man; you're not going to live long enough to see this acorn become even a little oak, let alone a great oak." And the old man said, "You're absolutely right. But I'm not planting it for myself; I'm planting it for my children, my grandchildren, my great grandchildren, and *their* grandchildren and great grandchildren."

The Dalai Lama realizes very well the world of realpolitik and he knows that if in his lifetime the dream of redemption is not fulfilled, that nineteen centuries of Jewish leaders and Jewish people dreamt and dreamt and dreamt and dreamt, and finally, the dream was realized. The importance is keeping the hope alive because as long as the hope is alive, one day the realization will emerge.

Will it emerge in our lifetime? In all probability, it won't emerge in the lifetime of His Holiness. In 2005 he's going to celebrate his seventieth birthday. Well, the ancient psalmists said, "The days of our years are threescore years and ten, or by reason of strength, fourscore years." Strength has certainly been the hallmark of the Fourteenth Dalai Lama, and with all of the advances of modern medical research and medical practice, he can expect to live not only beyond seventy and to eighty, but probably beyond eighty. And by that strength—the strength of his purpose and character—God willing, he shall. He's lived a full lifetime, by years, but who of us sees all the dreams fulfilled in a lifetime?

China is not about to relent unless some radical events take place that we can't even imagine happening. Politically, socially, economically, it's unlikely. But like that old man who planted the acorn, so does the Dalai Lama continue to meet, and those are the seeds that continue to be planted. When he speaks at the UN, when he's awarded the Nobel Prize, when he meets with the president of the United States, when he meets with a foreign minister, it's seed-planting time.

Chapter Eight

PROMOTING THE DALAI LAMA'S
SPIRITUAL MESSAGE ABROAD

Richard Gere   The quality of the teachers has much to do with that. I came out of the Zen Buddhist tradition. It was the first one I was drawn to and it's been a very powerful tradition. It isn't as heart-oriented as the Tibetan is: there's something so *cuddly*, in the best sense of *cuddly*, meaning home, meaning nurturing, meaning compassion, meaning all the kinds of juicy things of being a living being, that people naturally go there for the warmth of it. Now, along with that is a very, very strict mind—the wisdom and compassion aspects working together is really what the Tibetan approach is. But within this very strict mind of looking at the mind itself— of scientifically looking at layers of consciousness, what consciousness is, where do problems arise from? What is the nature of the mind?—are very, very deep questions, and they have no fear of going in any direction in their exploration. It's very balanced, with this extraordinary compassion. It's very hard to get through a teaching with His Holiness that has anything to do with compassion, that has anything to do with *bodhichitta* [good heart, altruism], that one does not weep from the pure, heart-felt joy of compassion, of feeling love. And anyone who comes into contact with a real Tibetan teacher, that's the first thing they're going to feel, because they want nothing more than *your happiness*.

Dr. Alexander Berzin   He went into exile with some of the greatest living masters. How many of these great masters would have been accessible in the West beforehand? There were a few who came out in the fifties, but very, very few. I don't think that the popularity and understanding of Buddhism, which we see as a worldwide phenomenon, would have been as great if people didn't have access and exposure to the great teachers.

Tsering Shakya   In a way, Buddhism is a religion of very affluent people. It doesn't provide immediate solutions; it is much more contemplative. When you look at the origin of the religion, in the Buddhist scripture it's a very urban environment—they talk about cities, they talk about merchants. Whereas in the other religions, like Hinduism, the scripture is always rural; it's an agrarian society. So Buddhism, as they say, emerged out of urban conditions in India.

Also, when you look at the way Buddhism spreads to different parts of the world, it always spreads at the time when a society is at its peak of affluence. Buddhism was at its highest state of popularity in India in the reign of Asoka [king of Magadha, India, circa 273–232 B.C.], when the Indian empire was greatest; and in China during the T'ang Dynasty [founded by T'ang T'ai T'sung, A.D. 600–649], when China was at the peak of its imperial power. Similarly, Tibet in the seventh and eighth centuries was at the height of its imperial power. So Buddhism has always been attractive to the growing power of an urban society that is emerging out of affluence.

Similarly, Buddhism appeals to the West because of its affluence. Buddhism doesn't appeal to any Third World countries, such as those in Africa or in Latin America—poor countries—because to say to poor people: your salvation is in *you* if you meditate and contemplate, doesn't appeal. So it's not surprising that in America Buddhism is adopted, because after you have gained all that fame and material possessions, you say: what's next? Sometimes Buddhism answers that, so it's not surprising that wealthy people are now attracted to Buddhism and think about their spiritual condition and what they are doing.

Lama Surya Das   Western Buddhism is mostly white and middle class; of course there are reasons for that. It doesn't necessarily please us all, but that is kind of the karma of the situation. Buddhism came in from Europe and Asia on the East and West coasts, not in the South. It came to people who have leisure time to read or to study or to listen to lectures. This is of concern to many of us, and there are many efforts to do things in the inner cities that are service-oriented—to have retreats for people of color or in Spanish—but it is definitely a challenge. Also, Buddhism is somewhat reclusive and hermitic. It is not necessarily the most suited [religion] for the single mother with three or more children that we find in the revival-ist churches in America, especially in the South, where people can go with their families. There's music—it doesn't require silence or meditation or philosophical study and listening to lectures.

Ven. Lama Thubten Zopa Rinpoché, incarnation of Lawudo Lama; spiritual director, Foundation for the Preservation of the Mahayana Tradition   Exile has presented greater opportunity to spread dharma outside of Tibet, in Europe, the United States, and other Western coun-tries. Much of this is due to the deeds of His Holiness the Dalai Lama—his wisdom and his compassion. He has incredible skillfulness in his wisdom. The whole world has benefited. He has brought happiness to so many people in large and small Western countries—even poor people—and provided answers to their problems, peace and happiness, just by *see-ing* them.

Rabbi A. James Rudin   Secular Jews and what I would call secular Catholics, who give their church very light shrift—they don't go to confes-sion, don't go to novenas, don't send their kids to parochial school, and go very rarely to mass—but when they get to the Vatican, there's this *aura*. And the Jews, especially, get it: it's *The Pope* and they want to be touched by it or feel part of it because it's history. In the case of the Dalai Lama, he doesn't have a big palace and all that you have at the Vatican, but he is a celebrity—some people think he's a divinity—and that rubs off. There is a need of the secular and profane for something sacred, and this is sacred space and a sacred man, a holy man. I used to get it even as a rabbi—"Let me open the door for you, Rabbi"—and that's on a low level compared to the Dalai Lama. You also get this with the priest with the collar. And with the Dalai Lama, when you combine that with his personality and his his-tory, you have people who want to go out of their way to touch and be part of it. They can go back to their families and say, "I was with the Dalai Lama; he's a very holy man." You could write a book on the hunger, and he meets this hunger for some people.

Mickey Lemle   The Dalai Lama was giving a Kalachakra Initiation outside Benares. Approximately two hundred and fifty thousand people were in attendance, including many who had come from Tibet. When the

Chinese found out about the Kalachakra, they put a bounty on any Tibetans their border guards turned back. Some people crossed several mountain passes, and I saw people who had suffered frostbite just to see His Holiness. The meeting was a cross between a great spiritual experience and Woodstock. The rain came down and tents blew away. I asked people why they had endured the hardship of getting there—some had traveled for three months, walking across Tibet—and the answer was, invariably, "For just one time in our lives, we wanted to see His Holiness in person."

Professor Robert Thurman   I was always drawn that way. I always felt as a stranger in a strange land. I never believed in blind faith, which I thought was a stupid idea. I was interested in philosophy—I read everything from Plato to [Ludwig Josef Johan] Wittgenstein [1889–1951]—but I was not satisfied with Western philosophy. Then I discovered Buddhist philosophy, which I really liked. I liked the idea that you could *live* your philosophy. The minute I met the Tibetans, I knew that that was what I had been looking for. I learned the Tibetan language in ten weeks. Why did I become a Buddhist? A Tibetan would say it was "unconscious rebirth." But I don't know or remember that. I imagine it must have been.

Richard Gere   He's absolutely my teacher. I'm not a Tibetan so I don't see him in the same way they do. He's my spiritual teacher. I have utmost respect for him in all possible ways, but he's my personal teacher; he doesn't have the time to be what was traditionally thought of as one's personal teacher—there's no time in the world for him to do that for all of his students. That's the relationship I cherish the most with him. But I also have a relationship where we do talk about political strategies; we organize events and just day-to-day mechanical stuff that has to be done—discussion of how we're going to do this, making it clear to His Holiness what his program is going to be and how to approach it, and what is important and what is less important. I find it very difficult sometimes in bouncing from one of those roles to another.

Dr. Jeffrey Hopkins   I first met him in 1972. I was on a Fulbright to India and I happened to arrive in Dharamsala just before he began a series of lectures over sixteen days, four to six hours per day, on the Stages of the Path and at that point—my first contact with Tibetan Buddhism was at the end of 1962—I had moved to a Tibetan and Mongolian monastery in New Jersey. I lived there from 'sixty-three to 'sixty-eight and then went to graduate school, so by that point I had been involved with Tibetan Buddhism for some ten years and had studied with some really good people.

Frankly, I did not think, given that he was a governmentally appointed reincarnation, that he would be that well educated, or that his lectures would be that interesting, because a number of reincarnations are appointed for political, social, economic, geographic—you name it—reasons. But I went with my tape recorder—in fact, I think I was the first person to record his lectures—and I started with a negative impression, but that was not my impression upon having encountered him.

He spoke *quickly*—his Tibetan is in great contrast to his English—he's known for speaking very quickly and very clearly. At that time he also spoke very loudly in a very strong voice. Then gradually over the course of the sixteen days, I began to find points that were of particular interest to me and that reverberated in my mind. When I had an audience with him not too long after those sixteen lectures, I told him that I found some interesting things in his lectures and suddenly thought: Oh my! How arrogant that is! Anyway, he asked me what those were, I told him, and he was just *delighted*. So over the course of those lectures, I began to take interest in him as a profound scholar.

Dr. Alexander Berzin   I was coming from Harvard University, I had finished my Ph.D. oral exams, and had gotten a Fulbright fellowship to study in India to do my dissertation. After being in India about a month or so—this would be in November 1969—I went to Dharamsala to meet His Holiness. I had a private audience. I wanted to tell him about my project and see if there was any advice he could offer. I must say it was one of the most moving moments of my life because at Harvard in the sixties, the way that Buddhism—particularly Tibetan Buddhism—was presented was very similar to ancient Egyptian studies; it was as if it were a dead subject and all that one could hope to do was to try to decipher the texts and figure out what the way of thinking must have been, or might have been. Meeting with His Holiness really convinced me that it was a totally alive tradition. Here was somebody who actually knew what everything meant and who had put it into practice. This started a whole new phase of my attitude toward Buddhism. I had an idea that it was a living tradition, but my conversation opened it up as a living tradition.

Geshe Tsultim Gyaltsen   People were asking me if we had a center. They said it would be good because it would be so much better for students to study together, so I started my center. I asked His Holiness, through his office, for permission. His Holiness visited the center in 1979 and gave a teaching. The next day he was going to leave, so that night his bodyguards sent his message: "Tomorrow I am coming to the center to have lunch with the Tibetan people." They also said that the lunch would be given by His Holiness's office. When I got that message I didn't believe it. His Holiness did come from his hotel to have lunch with us, and everybody said he was very kind. At that time, there were not many Tibetan people in Los Angeles—maybe we had eight, that's all. The day before he gave the teaching, I made him a throne there, but he said he did not want to sit on a throne at the lunch. He said, "Put a cushion on the floor." We had a Tibetan lunch—some vegetables—almost like a family having lunch together. Then he left for the airport. We had a tremendous time.

Lama Surya Das   My first lama, Lama Yeshe, sent me to meet his Holiness the Dalai Lama in June of 'seventy-two. I was twenty-one, still pretty young and impressionable. I took the train across India. I had letters of introduction from Lama Yeshe and Lama Zopa. I met His Holiness one-on-one for about forty-five minutes in his interview room. That really was incredibly powerful and inspirational for me, especially that he was so free from protocol and so intimate—there wasn't that much bowing, and I sat next to him on the couch and he shook my hand at the door. Tenzin Geshe Tethong was the only other person in the room; he was partly translating, but His Holiness spoke English and I had my little pidgin Tibetan coming along. His Holiness was so impressive and in the most simple and humble way—I don't mean pomp and circumstance—really authentically, marvelously personal and beautiful and deep. And I'll never forget what he said after we had talked a while, toward the end of the audience—it was more like an interview but let's call it an audience—he said, "Thank you so much, you and all the young people like you who come from afar who are interested in the Buddha dharma, in this wonderful treasure, that you have time to practice it and learn it and realize it. I myself am too busy; I have a lot of things to do for the people of Tibet, and I hope one day, when I retire, I can go back to being a studious monk and meditator." That sneak! He really turned the tables on me. It was sort of like he was treating me [as being] in the driver's seat of dharma, saying he's too busy with his responsibilities—that it was people like me who were practicing the dharma that he was grateful to! It was the humblest thing and also the most empowering thing I'd ever heard from anybody in my whole life.

The Principles of Tibetan Buddhism

Ven. Bhikshuni Tenzin Kacho   In general, three—the Kagyu, Sakya, and Gelupa—all have the same root, with Atisha [Dipankara], an Indian master who came to Tibet around the tenth century. The Nyingma tradition, which means "the old school," actually started in the eighth century with Guru Rinpoché, or Padmasambhava [an Indian tantric adept]. The four traditions actually are similar in the fact that they are all from the later flowering of Buddhism in India. Buddhism came into Tibet really quite late, in the eighth and tenth centuries, while the Buddha lived in the sixth century B.C. Gelupa would be different more in the way of the lineage of teachings and styles. It was propagated by Lama [Je] Tsongkhapa. When you read stories of his life, it was so full. He was a prolific scholar, a very practiced meditater—he went into retreat for years—and a fantastic teacher as well, and he founded monasteries and built so much in his lifetime that it just seems improbable that one person could be so prolific in his life. Yet, he did this, and his writings and his works are very well recorded. Gelupa really stems from this particular teacher who lived in the fourteenth century.

Dr. Howard Cutler   You would think that at this point in his life His Holiness would act like an old, tenured professor who has offered the same courses for forty years. Yet even at this stage—as I have discovered in personal discussions—he is willing to reevaluate his beliefs, provided there is a basis for that. Someone once asked him what his reaction would be if something in the Buddhist canon could be proven wrong. He replied that if such a thing could be proven conclusively, then the text would have to be changed. Then he was asked, specifically, "What if it could be proven that reincarnation doesn't exist? Would you change your mind?" He replied, "First of all, I would like to see how you would design the experiment proving that it doesn't exist. Once you do that, we will take a look at it."

Tibet's Mystique in the West

Rinchen Dharlo   I don't think His Holiness thinks of it that way. He's very much practical; he's not superstitious at all and doesn't even believe much in prophecies and that kind of thing. And whenever he goes to teach people, he says, "Don't think of me as the Dalai Lama; don't think of me as someone from Tibet with special powers. I have no power at all; I'm just a simple human being and I'm here to share whatever I have learned—whatever I think would be helpful for mankind. That's all that I have." And he doesn't pretend to know much. I don't really think that he thinks Tibet is something very special.

Dr. Piet Hut   You have the idea of one of the last mysterious places—Shangri-La—and that this mysterious place plays the role of the "good guys" against the "bad guys," the Chinese who occupy their land. Add to that the fact that the major nations don't really help them and you have the ingredients for a good movie. And that setting for a good drama, combined with the unique personality of the Dalai Lama, contributes to this unique situation. It is interesting that it took so long for him to gain the media's attention since in the 1960s and the 1970s all the ingredients were already in place.

Lama Surya Das   Of course Tibet and Shangri-La were part of my consciousness, although it wasn't necessarily the only thing that spoke to me when I was fourteen years old. I read *The Razor's Edge* by [William] Somerset Maugham [1874–1965, English novelist and dramatist], which is about Tibet, when I was sixteen or seventeen, and *The Third Eye*, by [Dr. Tuesday] Lobsang Rampa—these were classic best-sellers—and *The Lost Horizon* was a paperback best-seller early on, in the forties or fifties. I read those books long before I ever thought about going to the other side of the world. Interestingly enough, I always had dreams when I was a kid of being on the other side of the world, and at first it scared me. I told my father and he said, "Oh Jeffrey, it's just a dream." When I told Lama Yeshe that, he said, "Well you probably lived here in your past life; your father may have been Jewish, but that was Buddhist wisdom he gave you."

Professor Jonathan Mirsky   [re the "mysterious" Tibet] That's bullshit! No person who is serious about Tibet can take that seriously. There are probably ten books now that say Tibet was never Shangri-La. Get over that! Of course there was that aspect of Tibet—the mystical, lost kingdom and all that—but that's just crap. Of course there are people who think that and it's not that it's wicked of them to think it, but they like to think that Tibet was and somehow could again be a great, good place—different from every other place that's ever been—and that the Dalai Lama is the personification of that great, good, innocent, spiritual Tibet.

Dr. Alexander Berzin People who come to Dharamsala break into three groups: those who come for basically spiritual teaching, either for big discourses by His Holiness or for going to study at the Tibetan Library in Dharamsala that His Holiness had built or at several retreat centers in Dharamsala. Another portion, the leftover hippies, are still coming for recreational drugs and that sort of thing that have always been almost everywhere in India over all these years; they are mostly quite young people. Then there are the Indian tourists who come primarily to get out of the heat of the Punjab, and they would come just to get what they would call in Hindi *darshan*, which is just the blessings of *seeing* His Holiness [or a relic] without necessarily attending any teaching. But hardly anybody would come up just because His Holiness is a world political figure, basically because unless you come for a very, very specific purpose, it's very difficult to get a private interview with His Holiness anymore. You can go to one of these public audiences where you file past and give a Tibetan scarf, or you can go to a teaching, which is always a Buddhist teaching, so people wouldn't have exposure to His Holiness as a political figure unless they came as a reporter or somebody like that.

Orville Schell In China there is not the same kind of fascination with Tibet that has existed in the West since the nineteenth century—the idea of Shangri-La, the myth of the Kingdom Behind the Mountains and its spiritual isolation and perfection. But there is another curious version of this: even during the Cultural Revolution, in opera and ballet, a colorful and exciting sense of the exotic, the idea of Tibet being free, a certain sexual liberty unfettered by the confines of the Party strictures. All of this had a certain allure. On the other hand, China has long viewed Tibet as a cold, high-altitude, inhospitable place-in-exile outside the embrace of true civilization in Central China.

In the last ten to fifteen years, a new element has been added as the cities have grown and urban life has become more intense. There has been a greater tendency to romanticize life in Tibet as nomadic, free, colorful, sexually liberated, and spiritual. Since Tibet is accessible to Chinese tourists, there is now a much greater fascination, somewhat akin to the West's fascination. You see this represented in oil paintings and in fiction, the idea that this is where you go when you want to break away from the strictures, the pollution, the mercenary, godless life of the lowlands in Central China, to the more spiritual, free life up in the mountains. Our ability to mystify and believe in the mythology of Tibet is in no small measure due to the Chinese occupation and the destruction of Tibetan and Buddhist culture. On the other hand, China is now heading into the industrial and post-industrial syndrome, where it is looking for the same kind of escape the West was looking for in the late nineteenth century—to break out of those Dickensian, dark, polluted, soulless cities. Whereas before, China was poor, rural, and simple, it is becoming ripe for the syndrome of escape. The wheel of life keeps on turning.

The Dalai Lama as Spiritual Mentor

Ven. Lama Thubten Zopa Rinpoché   The Dalai Lama is the model of Buddhism. He has compassion and wisdom and he's so down-to-earth and so humble to everybody. So people see in him a true leader. People in the Western world with problems see that Buddhism has something good to offer in their lives. It's basically a mental discipline—to keep away from that which harms you and harms others.

Tsunma Jampa Dolkar   What His Holiness teaches is universal in terms of love, compassion, and being kind. He says, "My religion is kindness." And no matter what the situation is, that is an appropriate way to be—just be *kind*. I would hope that he would be able to return to Tibet for the benefit he would have for people in the country there. His Holiness benefits everybody, no matter where he is, or what he does.

Rt. Rev. William E. Swing   When I presented my thoughts on the United Religions Initiative [an effort to create a United Nations–like organization composed of the world's religions], he was very effusive concerning the possibilities. We were with him in Jerusalem, at a meeting where he displayed a great capacity to listen, long and hard, to others; I was impressed by his willingness to spend a whole day listening to people.

Father Laurence Freeman   He operates on many levels, actually, intellectually and philosophically, so he can speak at a level that is Buddhist but is very easily understood and received by anyone, really, and that is where he has his universal appeal. There are times where that could seem banal—that what he is saying is very simple—but when I was teaching at Georgetown last semester the Dalai Lama had come to Washington and was speaking at the National Cathedral, and I took a group of students to hear him. He spoke for about twenty minutes and my thought was with these students who had never heard him speak before. What did they think? Was it worthwhile for them to queue up for such a long time? But every one of them was very touched and inspired and enthused about his presence because, they said, he spoke with honesty and humor in a way that religious leaders normally don't.

Tsering Shakya People believe in his wisdom and that fundamentally what he says comes from a very deep understanding of Buddhism and Buddhist philosophy. Coupled with that are his experience and authority. That is why people follow him, not simply because he's elected, or put in power, but that he has a deep understanding of human nature, of the fundamental problems, and that his training and education have provided him with that deep understanding. When he is talking and preaching in a Tibetan community, you'll see the profundity of his knowledge.

Sometimes in the West we don't see that because he talks for about an hour, or two hours, at most. When he's doing religious teaching for Tibetans it's eighteen to twenty days; people have to sit there and listen to that teaching. And he goes real deeply into very profound thinking attached to Buddhist teaching. When Westerners engage the Dalai Lama, they tend to engage with a very immediate, practical problem—such as what to do about ecology—whereas Tibetans tend to approach the Dalai Lama and his teachings in a very existential way: what is the purpose of human existence? So they tend not to go to one particular set of problems in asking the questions and one solution for that particular problem. Tibetans tend to think about what it's like to be human, what it is to *exist*. In the West, it's whether a tree is cut down here, or there's going to be a dam there. These are small problems. Tibetans don't go to the Dalai Lama and say: What is Buddhist marriage? What shall I do about my problem with my marriage? They tend to have a wider vision.

Ven. Nicholas Vreeland It is very interesting to see His Holiness seated on a throne before more than ten thousand monks. It is not like what happened in Toronto. He will sit for many hours a day, teaching a text word by word with total authority. These are his people: monks who came with him into exile in 1959; monks who have come to India in the last twenty years, escaping over mountains; and monks who were born to the Tibetan refugee community, an extraordinary array of monks. His Holiness will be teaching with force, mastery, and authority, both intellectual and spiritual. With them he is the Dalai Lama, assuming that role as he sits there before his people.

Patrick French   He's different from other religious figures—Billy Graham or the Pope or even the inspirational Muslim leaders. Normally the reason why religious figures become important is because they've got a very specific, intense message. Often that message requires you to change your life. In the evangelical Christianity movement—and how enormous that is, particularly in the United States—a religious leader is saying you have to change your life, which elevates that leader. But I don't think the Dalai Lama is like that. He's often flippant in his public talks. I remember, in one of the London talks, somebody stood up and asked a most earnest and sensible question. The Dalai Lama thought about it for ten seconds and then went [Patrick French imitating the Dalai Lama's clipped delivery], "I dunno." You could never imagine the Pope doing something like that!

Rabbi A. James Rudin   This man has a sweetness about him, a kindness that radiates. But if you took him out of his robes, put the glasses on, and put him in a suit and tie, and put him on the street in New York, you'd say, "This is a nice Asian—probably a lawyer or an accountant—walking down the street." So the mystery is: why does he personally appeal to Western-ers? Is it his religion or his biography or is it *him*? Or is it a combination? Put him in another setting—in a Rotary club, in a coat and a tie—and you'd have, as a representative of Buddhism, a very nice introduction to Buddhism. Maybe when he's with his own folks, in a more religious, spir-itual setting, he's slightly more assertive, but he's not a *commanding* figure. He was a commanding figure to the press that day [November 11, 1999] because everybody knew he was the Dalai Lama—he was a celebrity.

A Memorable Encounter with Jewish Tradition

In the spring of 1998, on the eve of President Bill Clinton's controversial visit to the People's Republic of China, His Holiness the Dalai Lama spent fifteen days in the United States to appeal for public support for the cam-paign to free Tibet, then in its fiftieth year of Chinese occupation. On Thursday, April 30, in his first public appearance of that tour—he would continue on to New Jersey, Boston, Atlanta, and Wisconsin—the Dalai Lama addressed the Washington, D.C.–based International Campaign for Tibet's annual Light of Truth Award ceremony, held at Congregation Tem-ple Emanu-El in Manhattan and sponsored jointly by Tibet House, the Tibet Fund, and Temple Emanu-El. The honorees were Martin Scorsese and Melissa Mathison, the director and screenwriter, respectively, of the film, *Kundun*, which chronicles the life of the Fourteenth Dalai Lama from 1937 through the late 1990s. His Holiness and the honorees were joined on the sanctuary stage that evening by John Ackerly, president of the International Campaign for Tibet, who made introductory remarks; Professor Robert Thurman, who offered greetings; Lodi Gyari, a close associate of the Dalai Lama, who presented the award to Ms. Mathison; film star and Tibetan freedom activist Richard Gere, who presented the award to Mr. Scorsese; and [United States Ambassador to the United Nations] Richard Holbrooke, who introduced His Holiness.

Dr. Ronald Sobel   A request was made of us: would we make available the main sanctuary of Temple Emanu-El for an address? Now, the temple is the largest Jewish house of worship in the world, and in New York City, it is the third-largest house of worship after the Cathedral of St. John the Divine and St. Patrick's Cathedral. There was really no question about our response at the moment that the request was made; it was just a matter of working out the logistics of his visit, but we welcomed that request warmly and affectionately.

Establishing Teaching Centers in the West

Geshe Tsultim Gyaltsen   It started in the 1950s. In 1979, when His Holiness came, there were one hundred at my center. Then I invited His Holiness to come in 1984. At that time, eighteen hundred people came to his teachings. In 1989, I also requested that he come to the Kalachakra Initiation in Los Angeles. At that time, there were five thousand and it's increasing every year. After that, in 1996, I requested that he come, and there were almost seven thousand. And in 2000, there were six thousand people every day for five days at the serious teachings. They come because they want to be free from suffering. They are having problems with society or within the family. Also, even if they don't have problems, they can see that there are tremendous problems in the world—people killing each other—and they want escape from that.

Tenzin Gephel   The Namgyal Monastery in India sent me to Ithaca. One of our monks came up, and some of our friends who lived in Ithaca discussed founding a new branch monastery of Namgyal in the West. They consulted with the Dalai Lama when he came to Ithaca in 1992, as well as when they went to Dharamsala to discuss it with him there. Then the Dalai Lama said it should be a very important project, a place for people learning about Tibetan Buddhism. So that's how the Namgyal Monastery came into being in 1992. This is the only branch of the private monastery of the Dalai Lama in the West.

Dr. Alexander Berzin   The kinds of people I teach differ in different places. In Latvia the people don't have a great deal of exposure to the Buddhist teachings. There's a great interest, a great enthusiasm, and I've cultivated the custom of going to these areas where people don't have so much access to teachers—the former communist countries, Latin America, and so on—and so there, it's pretty much on an introductory level. But here in Berlin, where I live, I teach a more general course as well as an advanced course, which is actually pretty advanced. We've been working for many years now on the Buddhist teachings about reality—what is called "voidness" in Buddhism—and doing it in tremendous depth and detail. So I teach many different levels.

Ven. Bhikshuni Tenzin Kacho   I am the Buddhist chaplain at the Air Force Academy. That came about because one of the new incoming cadets requested a Buddhist chaplain, or someone to work with, because—particularly in the first year of the academy—the schedules of the cadets are very regimented and they really don't have that much opportunity to go off the premises. One thing the academy tries to provide is access to a spiritual mentor. That cadet found me on the Internet. So I went and met the Jewish rabbi who was a chaplain there, who took us under his wing to make sure that we could establish an opportunity to meet there regularly, to have services, and to set up a regular program for us. I worked with that cadet for four years, and he graduated two years ago. I've just continued on. It's a very small group, but they continue to come every year. I'm hoping that it continues even when I'm gone. Many of the cadets whom I work with are not Buddhists, but they come with an inquiry because they have a curiosity about Buddhism as being something that is fresh and open-minded. Some people have felt that a theist view of religion and faith is not for them, and so they come to my gatherings with a lot of questions.

Ven. Lama Thubten Zopa Rinpoché   One very important thing we are trying to develop now is universal education. To solve the problems in the world—the problems come from the mind: unsatisfied desire and all that—we have to have a good mind and a good heart. We have the school already in India and Bukhara, and we want to start more in remote, poor villages. We have one small school in California.

The Appeal to So Many Westerners of the Serious Study of Tibetan Buddhism

Ven. Bhikshuni Tenzin Kacho   I began definitely in 1973, and the reasons were I was already exploring different spiritual paths. And then I started reading about the *lam rim*, or the Buddhist teachings and the presentation that the Tibetan Buddhist style does. It was so impactful for me and just rang very clearly, so I actually immediately moved to a Buddhist center and started studying every day.

Ven. Thubten Chodron, Buddhist nun, formerly Jewish; observer, Dharamsala dialogue, October 1990; founder, Sravasti Abbey, Newport, Washington   I've got to put this in perspective because I met the dharma in 1975 and even though I went afterward from America to India to live there and I was living in the Tibetan community, I focused very much on my own practice. So for a long time I didn't even know who His Holiness *was*. I mean I didn't know anything about the structure of Tibetan religious hierarchy, or anything about Tibetan culture in that way. But my teachers had directed me to go to one of His Holiness's teachings—this must have been in 1977—but it was all in Tibetan. There wasn't even an English translation because this was so early on, but I just knew that my teachers instructed me to go and that this was something beneficial. And so I sat out in the hot sun for ten days, getting the whole transmission of the text in Tibetan without understanding a word! That was the first time I met His Holiness in the sense of being in his presence, even though it was a large crowd. What impressed me most about His Holiness were his teachings; the thing that has always gone straight into my heart is his whole approach to life that comes through when he teaches. And that's what really attracted me to him because what he said made sense and it was beneficial in life.

Then, when I met him and had a chance to interact with him in a smaller group on a one-on-one level, what really struck me was that he practices and lives according to what he teaches. The way I've seen him interact with other people has continuously been with compassion, even in situations where I think it would have been very difficult. For example, when he talks to the Tibetans about the situation in Tibet, for years, ever since I first started going, he continually talks about: "Do not hate the Chinese; people may have destroyed our country, they may have tortured us, but do not hate them. And don't get violent." And he's consistently giving that message, even though many of the young Tibetans don't like to hear it.

Does One Need to Be a Buddhist to Follow the Dalai Lama to the Fullest Extent Possible?

Dr. Jeffrey Hopkins   That's a difficult question. He definitely is a Buddhist; he definitely feels that the Buddhist views on reality are the best; and he definitely in some of his books presents the Buddhist paths to enlightenment. And yet, I think if you asked him: if somebody wanted to follow what you're teaching fully, would they have to become a Buddhist? He would probably say: it's sufficient that they be compassionate; it's not necessary to become a Buddhist. This is a very long-range view on how long it takes to get enlightenment. Following his system, so to speak, to the fullest, means following it to the fullest in this lifetime in terms of what you can accomplish in this lifetime. What you can accomplish in terms of betterment may be more as a Christian, Muslim, Jew, and so forth, maybe even as a nonbeliever, than it would be otherwise. So I think it would turn into a trap to set up the thesis that if one were going to follow him to the fullest, one would have to become a Buddhist.

Dr. Alexander Berzin   There are many levels at which somebody could benefit from the Buddhist teachings. There are general methods that His Holiness says anybody around the world can benefit from, no matter what their basic belief system is. And His Holiness is very happy to share with the world—he feels that it's very important for all cultures and religions and philosophies and disciplines in the world to share their knowledge and their experience. So on that level, training and such methods are not as demanding as the deeper teachings of Buddhism.

Buddhism is basically concerned with working on ridding ourselves of negative, destructive habits, whether they're destructive to others or self-destructive, recognizing our own weaknesses, our shortcomings, and training to develop more positive qualities, not only in the sense of being more kind, considerate, sensitive, and compassionate in a balanced way, but also in being disciplined, not to act in destructive ways, to have concentration, not to be distracted, not to let your mind become dull, or come under the influence of disturbing emotions, like greed, anger, jealousy, hatred, pride, naïveté—all of these things. Buddhism requires a tremendous amount of work—it's an extremely difficult task. It also requires us to recognize our projections of fantasy, where we tend to react to them rather than to the actual situation that's going on, as an example, paranoia, to dispel these projections and see what actually is going on in the world and what actually is going on with ourselves. So if one wants to follow the Buddhist path seriously, it requires a tremendous amount of discipline and effort, and His Holiness doesn't try to hide that, or water it down. He's not trying to show people, to pretend, that Buddhism is an easy path; it's not, by any means. But one can benefit from many of the Buddhist teachings on a more superficial level, let's say—what I tend to call "dharma lite" as opposed to the real thing, dharma, if we can use the analogy from Coca-Cola—those are two different levels of commitment.

Can a Westerner Become a Practicing Buddhist without Prolonged Study?

Richard Gere   It's a continual study. One of the big problems is that it's not that hard to get to a state where basically you feel pretty good—there are techniques that are very skillful and powerful. With time, you can learn those techniques and, using them, you can feel pretty darn good and blissful. The mind itself starts to change and, just in general, everything is not such a big deal. And life is *good*. But that's not what Buddhism is about; Buddhism is about total *transformation*, and that's a radical expectation of yourself. You can't stop anywhere short of that.

Professor Jonathan Mirsky   The thing that has made Tibetan Buddhism special has already changed to a considerable degree in the West. What many people now regard and take seriously as Tibetan Buddhism is no longer very much like the Buddhism of Tibet fifty or a hundred years ago. I've read quite a lot about this and, as I understand it, what has been created in the West—in part through the efforts of Dharamsala—is a kind of Tibetan Buddhism that has been made palatable and understandable in the West because there are a lot of things in Tibetan Buddhism that a lot of Westerners would find either very difficult to comprehend or maybe wouldn't even like if they understood it. So what's been created in the West is something that is for *us* and not necessarily for Tibetans. I've gone sometimes to these lectures of the Dalai Lama about things that are important to him spiritually. It's very tough; I don't get it at all. So it's hard, and a lot of the things that people think they believe about Tibetan Buddhism are actually not it.

Tsunma Jampa Dolkar   I know what it's like to have a calling. I'm very fortunate because I have an authentic teacher who follows the teachings of His Holiness the Dalai Lama, and the whole focus of my life changed because I decided that I wanted to be like my teacher. He really embodied and put into practice on a daily basis the Buddhist teachings of being kind and compassionate, practicing humility, and having a good heart. I'm really fortunate because my teacher teaches me the same as his other students. I don't really feel so much that I'm a girl; I feel like I'm one of his students—there's that level of equanimity there—and the same is expected of me as from his other students and those at the monastery in India.

With regard to His Holiness the Dalai Lama, I've been very fortunate to be able to attend his teachings both in India and in the United States. In fact, the last picture of me with hair was taken about five days before I was ordained. My teacher and I were in Southern India at a monastery. My teacher and I and another one of his students had gone there, and my teacher specially requested to His Holiness that he come and bless our center, and so I was with him. His Holiness was very kind and had a group picture taken. That was very special for me because I knew that within a few days I was going to be ordained, and to be in his presence, in his quarters, was just amazing to me, and very profound. Then he came to our center in September and blessed it, and it was really a very special experience.

Is There a Need to Be Fluent in the Tibetan Language to Really Grasp These Principles?

Richard Gere   I wouldn't know because I can't tell the difference. Look, in my lifetime, I've seen this enormous change. Thubten Jinpa [Langri] is His Holiness's prime translator. I remember, back in India, when he was a monk, very young, and just beginning to translate into English for His Holiness. The first thought I had was: we're still in the beginning stages, the pioneering stages of translation of Tibetan Buddhist material into Western languages. When I started with the Tibetan path in the early 1980s, there was only a handful of people, and they were coming out of several institutions. Jeffrey Hopkins, at Virginia University, was the main one, and there was a core group of people who had come out of Geshe Wangyal, in New Jersey, and Jeffrey and Robert Thurman and several others were part of that. So it's pretty recent, having translators really grapple with how you translate this to Westerners, especially in English.

I had funded a translation of the masterpiece of Lama Tsongkhapa, who started the Gelupa sect, that was translated into Russian before it was translated into English. That was fifteen years ago, and there was not an English translation until two years ago. So it's really the beginning. Hundreds of years from now, they'll probably talk about this period when these translations just started to emerge and words were starting to be accepted from one translator to another: How do we translate this term, this idea? Do we have great translators now? Absolutely! And there's real poetry. Thubten Jinpa is doing real genius work.

Dr. Alexander Berzin   It all depends on their level of interest and their language ability. I never encourage people to put all their emphasis on the language to the detriment of their study of the Buddhist teachings and their practice of it in meditation. If someone has a facility with languages, I certainly don't deceive them by saying that the Tibetan language is an easy language—it's *not* an easy language—but if you want to study Tibetan Buddhism really seriously, then at this historical moment you still have to learn Tibetan, primarily because not that much is available in translation into European languages, and what is available in translation often is very confusing because the translators don't agree at all on their terminology. And so if you read something in one book, it's very hard to put it together with what you read in another book because the translation terms are different for the same Tibetan word. What I try to do on my Web site, berzinarchives.com, is to give the Tibetan terminology for all the technical terms so that if people are studying seriously, even if they don't learn the Tibetan language, they are able to read. Nevertheless, if they learn at least the basic technical words in Tibetan, and if other translators and authors likewise put the terms in parentheses so they're translating the original Tibetan term, then people can put the material together.

You're never going to get the translators to agree on their translation terms. This, I think, helps to minimize that confusion. But my teacher, Serkong Rinpoché , said to me very clearly and strongly—mind you, I had already studied the basic languages and was already an interpreter— "You're never going to find any teacher who has the time to be able to teach you everything you want to study. The only way to really go further, more deeply, is to be able to read the original texts yourself. Then you can always find more easily teachers who will answer your questions about your reading, but not somebody who's going to explain every single word of these huge texts."

Ven. Nicholas Vreeland   I went to the monastery in India as a layman, not speaking Tibetan. My monastery had recently been reestablished; in Tibet it had been a rather important monastery, with about three hundred fifty monks. In India, the monks were incredibly supportive. My studies there were greatly helped by the degree to which they assisted me. My Tibetan language skills were developed through debate. It was sort of like being pushed into the deep end of a swimming pool to learn how to swim. Life was pretty simple—food was simple, water scarce. Life revolved around studying; you would get up around 5:30 A.M. and sit in your room, memorizing texts, repeating each line over and over. Some of my fellow monks could memorize a hundred pages or more, whereas fifteen to twenty pages were very difficult for me. Later in the day, we would debate the subject of our memorization.

Conversion to Buddhism

Ven. Thubten Chodron   From the Buddhist side nobody cares whether you call yourself a Buddhist. It's more in terms of an individual's personal practice. When people first come there's a lot that they can benefit from in the Buddhist teachings, even if they are religious in another faith, because a lot of our meditations—on how to develop love, how to develop compassion, how to handle anger, how to work with jealousy, how to concentrate, how to calm the mind—all of these kinds of meditations and teachings have nothing about theology in them at all. They're just practical advice, and so people from other religions can listen to them and then practice them in the context of whatever their own theological view is. If somebody wants to go to the end of the Buddhist path, then I don't think it's so necessary whether you call yourself a Buddhist. But one would have to get very clear in one's own mind what one's own views were. It's like you can practice some things that are universally applicable to people of all religions and that benefit you just as a human being. For example, in Buddhism our spiritual goal is enlightenment. Well, if somebody doesn't believe that enlightenment is possible, they're not going to aim for it. At some point, if people are thinking about what their spiritual goal is and they've heard Buddhist teachings, they've got to think: Do I believe in enlightenment? Is this possible? Can I attain it? What's the method to attain it? And then they have to check this out. It's only if they conclude that, yes, this is a feasible goal, that they will then decide to follow it.

Rt. Rev. William E. Swing   There is a bit of mystique around the Dalai Lama, so some people temporarily try on the Buddhist clothes. The Dalai Lama will very clearly respond: Don't be a second-rate Buddhist; be a first-rate Jew or a first-rate Christian. Whatever you learn from Buddhism, go back and take it where you came from. His message is not one of missionary zeal; it is a matter of great respect for the other religious traditions.

Patrick French   He says that he doesn't think that Westerners converting to Buddhism is necessarily a good thing because they don't have the social infrastructure that will enable them to maintain their religious practice. Why go through the excitement of conversion and then, in fact, find that they don't have the community that enables them to sustain that religious tradition? So if you're a follower of the Gelupa school of Tibetan Buddhism, yes, it is a very rigorous religious system in terms of the religious practice you have to undergo, and it's also quite morally rigorous. And that's something that often gets forgotten. I give the example in my book that the Dalai Lama is quite strict in his teaching on sexual ethics, against homosexuality, for example, and yet that is simply excised from editions of his works in countries that aren't going to like that particular stand. So you do have this odd process where different versions of the Dalai Lama are invented and promoted in order to sustain a particular market. He's partially aware of it. It's something I've talked about with him and with people around him. And I think that he's not particularly interested if people put out phony or partially phony books, which are purported to be by the Dalai Lama, but in fact are rehashes of public lectures he's given or whatever. He's not particularly concerned; it's strange, but that's how he is. It ought to concern him more; maybe it ought to concern the people around him more.

Rinchen Dharlo   When he travels in the West, he doesn't promote Buddhism. But then, for a country like Mongolia—it's a Buddhist country—he sees that for them it's important to continue with their Buddhist tradition, so he is helping them. Whenever he is asked to give a religious teaching, the first thing that he says if they are non-Buddhists is, "You should remain with your own religious tradition." He always tells them not to change unless it is absolutely necessary.

Father Laurence Freeman   He's very sincere about that, for a number of reasons. One reason is that he realizes it's not as easy as a lot of Western-ers think to become a Buddhist; the Noble Truth is easy to accept, but becoming a Buddhist is not so easy. The Dalai Lama says, "People have the right to choose their own religion and the right to change. And people can choose the religion that is temperamentally or culturally best suited for them." You wouldn't hear many bishops putting it that way.

There has not been a tension in the dialogues I have had with him. They took off from the end of the Good Heart seminar; we produced a book called *Good Heart*—it was very popular—and then when I met with him about a year or two after that, he said he had got so many letters from Christians who thanked him for the book, and I by that time had thou-sands of contacts from people around the world who had found the book very powerful and very encouraging; it gave many Christians an opportu-nity to make contact again with the Christian tradition in a way they felt comfortable with. And he was very pleased with that.

We invited him to Italy, to one of our monasteries, and we had a retreat together there, and we spoke about image and word in language in the spiritual quest. We had a couple of public events and one was attended by about two or three thousand young people, Italians, and he began by say-ing—and these are all Italian Catholics, or ex-Catholics—"I must say, I really advise you to stay in your own tradition; discover what Christianity really means."

The "Jubus"

The Dalai Lama's spiritual message has attracted many converts to Bud-dhism in the West, among them a significant number of Jews—"Jubus" as they are known in certain circles.

———————

Dr. Alexander Berzin   I must say I haven't given that term any thought whatsoever; I don't react to it one way or another. It's just a *word*. I don't particularly come across it in my own travels.

Lama Surya Das   I hate that graceless term! I'm not a Jubu; I'm a Buddhist—I'm a Jew on my parents' side. I would never say, "I'm not Jew-ish." I had a Passover Seder at my house last spring with my five-year-old niece at my brother's request. My mother is real proud of me. Unfortunately, my father is gone, but he only died seven years ago, so he got a little *naches* [joy, gratification] out of it, too, before he went.

According to Rodger Kamenetz, author of *The Jew in the Lotus: A Poet's Rediscovery of Jewish Identity in Buddhist India*, surveys show that between 6 percent and 30 percent of American Jews participate in Buddhist groups.

Rabbi Irving Greenberg   I don't know that there's any way of measuring it. We were struck in walking around Dharamsala at the people who came and hung around the various activities around the area, that there was a disproportionate number, it seemed to us, of Jews and Israelis. But it was not a scientific study. It's entirely plausible. He [the Dalai Lama] noticed it in terms of where he was getting help from. Kamenetz claims the Dalai Lama does send the Jubus back to us first, or encourages them to come back to us.

Dr. Chaim Peri   I met many Israelis who turned to Dharamsala for spirituality, to find some meaning after [having served in] the army. That is the regular Israeli track: you finish the army, you go to India—or South America—in the final ritual of maturity here.

I teach my kids that Buddha was a great teacher at the time of Abraham and, just as there is alternative medicine and regular medicine, one is not inferior or superior to the other. They are great teachers of humanity; that's what Buddha is. What one calls idol worshipping is a means, and that is not allowed in our religion. That's us; I wear a yarmulke—this is my culture and this is what my forefathers did. I can understand the Jubus, but not when it gets to the point where it becomes a totality and erases your other identity. The Dalai Lama adores Judaism; he is not encouraging anyone who is getting close to Buddhism to abandon Judaism. He sees it as a very rich foundation for something that is added to it.

At the same time—and you cannot expect it from large numbers of people—as individuals who have the intellectual inclination and the emotional ability to build on their Judaism with something that is, in a way, purifying for Judaism, it is an upgrading of Judaism in many ways because when you come into a synagogue you cannot daven [pray] unless you have a minyan [ten male worshippers present in the Orthodox tradition]. We have forgotten something about meditation. I see here in Jerusalem wonderful people who use meditation to find the deeper facets of their Jewishness, and they don't consider this anything foreign to Judaism because we've been a community under siege and we stick to each other—sometimes sweat touches sweat.

Dr. Blu Greenberg   The Dalai Lama did speak about that, but he spoke about it more in terms of stages. He encourages people in the first stage to go back and discover their own tradition. But then he did add that if they can't find satisfaction and spiritual fulfillment in their own, then he welcomes them. So there was that implicit statement that they do have to cross over. Whatever they call themselves, they've actually crossed over into Buddhism. They're *halakhically* [Halakhah is the body of Jewish law] Jewish but they're totally Buddhist.

Dr. Ronald B. Sobel   I don't know what 30 percent of his followers are Jewish, but let's assume that the figure is approximately accurate. There may well be a visceral sympathy, even among the American Jews who aren't really all that fully conscious of the historic exile experience of their own people. It's in their bloodstream, their cultural, spiritual bloodstream, and so there's a simpatico there.

Then you have to also understand that at the end of the twentieth century, at the beginning of the twenty-first century, there is a worldwide renewal of a search for what is called "spirituality," a very elusive kind of thing. And very frequently it's easier for people to find what they think is spirituality in a tradition other than the tradition in which they were nurtured, born into, grew up with, because spirituality seems to be something other than the familiar. What you grew up with is familiar; what you have never previously experienced, obviously, is nonfamiliar, and so the spirituality of "other" can be very enticing.

Lama Surya Das   My nineteen-year-old friend [also named Jeffrey Miller] was shot and killed at Kent State in 1971 and that turned my head around. But I had already met Buddhism in 'sixty-eight, in college at SUNY Buffalo, and I had those kinds of interests, like psychology, philosophy, and Eastern thought. I went to my first Zen [a Japanese Buddhist branch teaching self-discipline, meditation, and attainment of enlightenment through intuitive insight] retreat at the Rochester [New York] Zen Center, as I was a little interested in Buddhism, but not Buddhism per se—more like Eastern thought, or the big questions of life. I was seeking and hadn't found what I was looking for in the churches and synagogues of my youth, so I sought it elsewhere. I started trying to meditate, I heard various people speak, chanted with the Hare Krishnas, heard Baba Ram Das and Joseph Campbell and other people like that speak at that time, and was thinking and reading about those things. When my friend got killed, it really turned my head around. I thought that rather than fighting and demonstrating for peace in the streets, I really had to seek peace in some other way, and meditation and yoga and Eastern thought seemed to specialize in that. So when I graduated from college in 'seventy-one, I went to India and stayed there a long time.

Ven. Thubten Chodron   As a young person, I was asking a lot of questions: Why am I alive? What's the meaning of life? I grew up during the time of the Vietnam War and saw some of my friends going to 'Nam, and some came back in body bags. We say we want to live in peace but here we are killing each other, and how come human beings can't get along? So I had all these kinds of doubts and questions. When I explored the religions that were available to me in the community I grew up in, which was basically Judaism and Christianity, I couldn't find any answers that made sense to me; I couldn't believe that kind of worldview. And so by the time I got to college I had pretty much dismissed religion. In college I majored in history and found that in every generation, people were killing each other in the name of God—even nowadays, you see people killing each other in the name of God—so I got quite cynical and decided that religion really is not a good thing. I wasn't in a good state of mind, but that's where I was in my development, and what really struck me when I finally encountered the dharma, the Buddhist teachings, was the open-mindedness. First of all, my teachers—the first teachers I met—said, "You don't have to believe what we say. You listen. You're intelligent. You think about it, you test it out logically, you check it out from your own experience, and you make up your mind what you're going to believe and what you're going to practice." I liked that attitude very much and that enabled me to continue to learn. And then when I did start checking things out logically, it made sense, as far as I could understand, and when I started practicing the techniques for working with the mind and with the emotions, I found that they worked. Not instantly—His Holiness always says it takes time; be willing to undergo hardship and put in time and energy—but I've really found that to be true. By putting in the energy, because cause and effect work, it's possible to retrain our mind and let go of a lot of things that cause unhappiness to oneself and others. And so, just the fact that it made sense and that it worked is what drew me into Buddhism.

Dr. Blu Greenberg   When we made Shabbat we invited the former Jewish monks and nuns. One of our colleagues, Moshe Waldoks, led the service, and when we got to Aleinu [the prayer of divine sovereignty], and Adon Olam, the last prayer, and at various other points he sang a different melody other than the traditional melody that everybody sings. I had the urge to go up, take him by the buttonholes and shake him and say, "Moshe, sing the old melodies!" because I had this fantasy that it was going to awaken their Jewish souls and they'd be filled with nostalgia and they'd come running home. There's a joke about this woman who travels for three months and she gets to the top of the mountain to meet this guru where she waits days and days. She finally gets an audience with him, and they tell her that she only has thirty seconds. So, after having traveled for over three months and waiting for days to get this audience with this famous guru, she finally gets her thirty seconds with him and she comes in and says, "Moshe, come home!"

Ven. Thubten Chodron   The Jews had invited these Tibetan lamas to come for Shabbat dinner on Friday night. Mind you, the Tibetan lamas don't know English and they don't know anything about Judaism. They arrive there just before the sun goes down, so all the Jews are in the garden facing toward Jerusalem, which was west, toward the setting sun. They started doing their prayers, still facing Jerusalem, and then they did some singing and dancing, and then we all went inside and had dinner. Some of the Tibetans afterward asked, "Are these people worshipping the sun?" They thought that because they were standing outside doing their prayers facing the West that they were sun-worshippers! So we started off the dialogue on a very basic, rudimentary level. It was good for everybody.

Is Conversion to Buddhism Somehow More Acceptable Than to Christianity or Islam?

Dr. Blu Greenberg   Personally, I don't think it happens to be true. One of the things I felt was that for us the Dalai Lama was so pleasant and pleasurable because there isn't that history, all that angst and all that stuff that went between us—we've been involved in Jewish-Christian dialogue and Jewish-Palestinian dialogue—and all that baggage that we all carry.

Here it's just pure friendship. But I don't think that's what's operating; I don't think they become Buddhists because it's more acceptable. I think they become Buddhists because it is this emphasis on otherworldliness and spirituality and the mystical qualities of Buddhism that they're seeking.

Rabbi A. James Rudin   We found out in our cult work [Rabbi Rudin and his wife, author and playwright Marcia Rudin, are experts on cults and have written and lectured extensively on the subject] that Jewish parents—all parents—were always less upset with their kids, except for the Unification Church, who became Eastern devotees, even of Hare Krishna, than they were if a kid became a Jew for Jesus. In other words, the East was always well-liked—it's not as lasting or deep and doesn't demand as much. Obviously, for historical reasons, when a kid becomes a Jew for Jesus, it's much more in the gut than someone who goes to India and becomes a Buddhist follower or devotee; it always seems a little softer. And the Dalai Lama is a phenomenon. I can't explain it, except that it's *him*.

Dr. Chaim Peri   I am an Orthodox Jew, as liberal as I am, and I believe that Judaism's mission is universal. I was standing in a Buddhist monastery, speaking to about two hundred monks, and at a certain point I took out my tsitsit, which I wear underneath, and I told them about our mantra, the Shema, the unity of the Lord. I said, "Our mantra is very real. Unlike the Arabs, we don't say Allah Akhbar! God is Great! We just say Shema Israel!" It's about communication: "Listen O Israel!" Every Israeli, every Jew, should listen to each other, because God, as [Martin] Buber [1878–1965, Austrian-born Israeli philosopher] says, resides between two human beings. And before we reach the climax of our daily prayer, we take out these fringes, which have knots and strings, we put them all together, and in unison—this is our little secret—we say: "Bring us together from the four corners of the world." I elaborated about this yearning of Jews to go back to Zion, and some Israelis who came there for their spiritual search said to me, "*This* is what tsitsit is for?" They had to come to Dharamsala to find out!

Christian Converts to Buddhism

Tsunma Jampa Dolkar   I was an investigative reporter many years ago; then I was in financial marketing for several of the large mutual fund companies in the Boston area, in retirement marketing and strategy. I was studying meditation in Chegong about six and a half years ago and my teacher, who was an old North Korean Taoist who had escaped from North Korea to South Korea, looked at me and said, "You need to go to Tibet; you need to meditate; you need to find a teacher, and you need to learn the language."

So I went to Tibet Arts, a store in Cambridge, asked them if they knew of a Tibetan language teacher, and they gave me a name. I was an atheist— I didn't have a religious background; I knew nothing about Buddhism. I had lived in Boulder [Colorado] so I knew about His Holiness the Dalai Lama because of the Buddhist community there, and so I wrote down this name, Geshe Tsulga. I thought it was a name like "Sue Macy": I didn't know that he was a Tibetan lama—I knew nothing about him—so I called the number and left a message saying that I wanted to learn Tibetan. I got the call to come to his house on a Sunday night and I went there. I took just one look at him and I knew that my life was going to change. My teacher made it very easy for me. No matter what had been in my life, at the time when I met my teacher, I knew that that was what I was here to do. I studied Tibetan with him for several months and then I went to my first Buddhism class. I was just sitting there the whole time, sighing, "My Gosh! I'm going to be a nun!"

Richard Gere   Most Tibetan teachers would say that Westerners are better students because it's new to them—it hasn't become habituated—and the excitement that a Westerner brings to his studentship is pretty powerful. And Westerners take a lot of notes, ask a lot of questions; we get very excited about things and sometimes they have to calm us down. I remember, a friend of mine, Nicky Vreeland who was a Western monk. When he went to his monastery in India, he had his robes on and had been ordained by His Holiness. There he began his studies as a celibate monk. He said that when he was taking his classes he would just get so filled with joy and emotion, but his teachers kept taking him aside and they would make these gestures—kind of like, take it slowly, slowly—to *calm down*, because he was so into it. But I think the Tibetans are impressed, in general, with the Western curiosity. And, also, the kind of education that we have is a good matrix of mind for exploring the nature of reality.

Ven. Nicholas Vreeland   I don't honestly know what pulled me toward a spiritual path. But I *was* pulled. I felt a profound desire to learn about Buddhism. I only became satisfied once I made my way to the Tibet Center in New York and began studying. I had a taste of the fact that life is not all that it's drummed up to be—that life ultimately has a quality of suffering—and the most profound or responsible way that I could live my life would be to devote myself to my spiritual practice. The scary part was that I realized that I had the freedom and opportunity to do so as a monk: I wasn't involved with someone; it was one of the moments in my life when I had that freedom. However, I refrained from making any serious commitment to becoming a monk. After a few years, I consulted with His Holiness, and his advice was that I become a monk, so I did. I don't consider that what I did was to convert. Although I was baptized at age fourteen in the religion I was brought up in, while attending an Episcopal boarding school, I don't consider that I ever took a step away from any spiritual commitment to a different tradition. I simply kept on going.

The Lure of Buddhism for Celebrities

Dr. Blu Greenberg   Richard Gere is political; his interest is political. On the other hand, he did spend those days in Dharamsala just sort of soaking up the atmosphere, and it *was* spiritual; he wasn't out there politicking.

Rinchen Dharlo   Richard doesn't pretend to know a lot about Buddhism, but he has received [teachings] and he knows as much about Buddhism as many religion professors know. He's a very serious practitioner.

Richard Gere   Kindness, on the very surface level, is just *kindness*. But as you start to really go into kindness, it's a vast area and implies so many radical concepts, such as interconnection. His Holiness, because he's so skillful and is such a giant, can say extremely difficult things in very simple ways. I remember a discussion about knowing if someone was enlightened—I think it was a comment from the Buddha—that if you can't explain emptiness to a fisherman, then you don't *have* it.

Sister Mary Margaret Funk   I've seen Richard more than Steven Seagal. Richard seems to be a good guy in all of this—very respectful—and he does his part. And he is also pretty sincere as a practitioner. His lifestyle and all that, I can't vouch for that, but I had a wonderful lunch with him down here. We were the only two that didn't speak Tibetan, so we had a wonderful visit. I think he's searching to reconnect with his Christian roots—he definitely was a Christian before he became a Buddhist and he's integrating that—and he has a sincere, genuine straight-up relationship with the Dalai Lama's family. He's doing good things with his foundation, and it's much appreciated. He's very single-minded, very focused. He's their best champion.

Professor Jonathan Mirsky   He definitely needs these rich people because they raise a lot of money for him. A lot of them are really morons, like that night he was being interviewed by Larry King as "a leader of the Muslim world," or Sharon Stone, who said, "Please, please, please welcome the Dalai Lama, Mr. China." There is a certain amount of that stupidity, but when you see him in Dharamsala, every day receiving Tibetans who have walked hundreds of miles across very, very difficult terrain to come to Dharamsala to see the Dalai Lama and then walk back into Tibet, and they come up to him weeping. And the way he treats each one of those people as he puts his hands on their faces and their hands, that's all *real*. I don't think he treats them with any less respect than he does all the famous groupies around him. People are always trying to get a piece of him because he is very accessible once you're actually in his presence. One of the things people say about him is that he seems very open and friendly. And he *is* open and friendly.

Ordination by the Dalai Lama

Ven. Nicholas Vreeland   The ordination ceremony is elaborate. His Holiness, accompanied by many attendants, sits on his throne, overseeing the procedure and performing the rite of ordination. The powerful aspect of the ceremony which is conducted in Tibetan is that the commitment is acknowledged and given the force of that acknowledgement by this extraordinary Being—the greatest Buddhist spiritual master of our time. It is very inspiring to feel that you have his blessing as you are taking this vow—that he is bestowing this vow, that he is actually accepting you.

Ven. Bhikshuni Tenzin Kacho   The idea [of becoming a Buddhist nun] started in 1975, when I was in India. My main teacher suggested that I become a nun. But I waited ten years, to raise my daughter and also to grow up a little bit, myself. I feel that if I had just gone ahead and done it immediately, I wouldn't have lasted because I didn't have any maturity to do that. Also, in 1975, the Dalai Lama was not ordaining Westerners. Then the consideration to do it came up again, very strongly, in 1984, and I wrote a letter to His Holiness, asking him if he would ordain me. And I particularly wanted to be ordained by *him*, partly because of my growing confidence in him, and I felt that if I did my ordination with someone whom I trusted and had faith in very deeply, that my own personal commitment would also be strong. So in 1985, I moved to India and I was ordained in a very small ceremony in the private quarters of His Holiness—there are some interior meeting rooms and a smaller shrine room, and we were in there. There have to be six fully ordained monastics there, and I took my novice ordination because they do not have the full ordination for nuns in the Tibetan tradition. There were only six of us ordained: three monks and three nuns. Fortunately, one of the monks that was being ordained is a translator as well, so he translated almost the entire event for me, just whispering what was going on as they went through the ceremony. That was extremely helpful and wonderful. I was a bit dazed because I had just arrived in India and the jet lag was catching up with me. But the ceremony itself was very beautiful, very profound. When I exited several people came rushing up with offerings and blessings, and one of them jokingly said, "Well, they say that the best time to make offerings is right away, when you haven't transgressed any of your vows!"

The Dalai Lama was very curious as to who we were and he was looking at us quite intently. He didn't speak very much because it was a very formal service. But what did come through was his curiosity—a real looking to see who was there. He gives you a name when you take the ordination, and he was very careful about the names he gave people.

Dr. Alexander Berzin   The lineage of fully ordained nuns did not make it to Tibet, and in many of the other traditional Asian Buddhist countries it also was broken. But it does survive in Taiwan, Hong Kong, and South Korea, and so the impetus came from Western novice nuns who wanted to revive the full nuns' ordination. For that a number of them went to Taiwan, particularly, and some went to Hong Kong. His Holiness was very encouraging of that and has sponsored a number of studies to see how it could be integrated in terms of the slightly different lineage from the Tibetan tradition and to do more of a scholarly study of it. A number of Tibetan nuns have taken this ordination now, and there's a much greater official status of nuns within the monastic structure because of this renewed ordination. Still, not that many take it, but it's on its way.

His Holiness is also very alert to, and interested in, the various aspects of the ordination ritual. The position of women is not as nice as that among men, to put it just very simply, and he is looking to see what would be the means of revising this within the traditional structure of how revisions are made in Buddhism. So in general, the situation of nuns has improved greatly. There are a number of Western nuns who have begun to establish nunneries in the West, and there's certainly an increasing interest in it among the Chinese community—I'm speaking about Singapore, Malaysia, and Taiwan—and many of them are following Tibetan Buddhism. There are more than two hundred Tibetan Buddhist centers in Taiwan. That is an indication of how much it's growing, not just among Westerners, but in many of the Asian countries as well. I think this interest is primarily because of the fuller explanations that you get in Tibetan Buddhism and, probably, a lot from the personality and the influence of His Holiness. People are very inspired; he's an extremely inspiring person.

The Dalai Lama's Motivation to Continue His Mission in the West

Dr. Tenzin Tethong   In the early years of exile I think it might have been quite difficult—this is just looking back now, I hardly thought of those things in the early years of exile—because His Holiness was only about twenty-five or twenty-six. All the spiritual infrastructure of Tibet— everything from the great monasteries to the ancient temples and all the monastic ceremonies and rituals, many of which were very elaborate— none of that followed him into exile. Basically, he was in Dharamsala. His tutors were nearby but they were also living under very modest circumstances, and all the monks and monastic structures were no longer in India. In fact, the small number of monks who had escaped were physically in very poor shape, and there were no great assemblies, great rituals, or ceremonies taking place in the early years. Naturally, it looked like the institution of the Dalai Lama was now in the hands of a young man who was in exile, who was a refugee with none of the trappings of the institution. So in those early years, among the Tibetans and other Buddhists from the Himalayas who encountered the young Dalai Lama, I'm sure they felt that because there was very little of the grandeur of the institution of the Dalai Lama.

Geshe Tsultim Gyaltsen   In India, study and practice in the monasteries is much better than in Tibet because we have a lot of big monasteries in South India, Nepal, and Sikkim, and in the monasteries, thousands of men—my college has five hundred and other colleges have maybe two thousand monks—and they are studying and practicing now just like [they once did] in Tibet.

Ven. Nicholas Vreeland   It surely has been difficult for the Dalai Lama to lead the Tibetan people in maintaining their spiritual enthusiasm during all the years that he has been living in exile in India. There were many years when there was no communication, and during those years Buddhist practice was absolutely not tolerated by the Chinese authorities in Tibet. What is interesting is that almost fifty years after His Holiness left Tibet, the people of Tibet continue to attribute spiritual authority to him. Spiritual authority is not something you can ever impose; as soon as you impose it, you've lost it. His Holiness's authority is the reflection of his extraordinary spiritual qualities and mastery. I believe the purity of the role he plays spiritually with respect to his people has been tremendously enhanced by the challenges imposed upon him by the Chinese occupation.

The Lack of Profundity of His Message

Rabbi A. James Rudin   When the Dalai Lama got up to speak [at an interreligious dialogue at Seton Hill College in Greensburg, Pennsylvania on November 11, 1999], I've got to tell you that I was very disappointed, not in his English, not in his style, but I didn't think the message was that deep. It was very simple. Maybe that's the strength of the Dalai Lama; maybe it's the man himself. He didn't criticize China. I was waiting for that. He didn't talk about the government at all; he didn't talk about politics; he didn't even talk about *Tibet*. He talked about interpersonal relationships, compassion, mercy, kindness—he used a lot of these words; I guess those are in his stock vocabulary. He did go on a while and he was very good, and very charming. But I said to myself: if this man were a rabbi or a Christian minister, it would be, to me, just a very routine speech. But, of course, what I was encountering was the charisma of the man, the personal history of the man, what Buddhism means to a lot of Americans, and the celebrity quality. I was just struck by the simplicity of his message. I wouldn't say it was *shallow*; that's not fair. It wasn't shallow, but it was just that I was looking for something more profound and as I was listening to him—he went on for about thirty minutes, in English; he was very sweet, very kindly—I wondered: outside of his immediate followers, what is his attraction?

Dr. Howard Cutler   When he speaks to large audiences, he directs his words to their level. The fact of the matter is that he is one of the most intelligent and intellectual people, with an incredibly sharp mind. The audiences who come to his public talks don't see the intricacies of the visualization techniques involved in the Kalachakra Initiation. They don't see him when he talks on Buddhist psychology to a group of Ph.D.s: the Buddhist system of mind is so sophisticated that it has identified eighty-one thousand different mental states. He can talk about this from memory and make his listeners dizzy because he was trained in logic, debate, and analysis using human reason, of which he is a huge believer.

Rt. Rev. William E. Swing   If I made the same speech, word for word, that *he* made, people would walk out of the building. In America, people are ready for rat-a-tat speech with thirteen dimensions. The Dalai Lama begins to speak and it's so simple that you think: this is Spirituality 101. But when you listen for half an hour, you discover that he has taken a very complex situation and reduced and reduced it to its smallest, distilled moral clarity. He locks into the one moral point. It might sound trite if you have a glib ear. But if you stay with it, he is reducing the point down to the childlike morality and ethics of a complex situation. People respond to him; they check their sophistication at the door and go with him on a journey. The game is played by *his* rules, on *his* turf, and, ultimately, what he says is quite profound.

Dr. Ronald B. Sobel   There are libraries all over the world filled with great texts that reflect intellectual grandeur, depth of learning, and breadth of understanding that can take one's breath away. But how many persons' breaths are taken away? For is it not the fact that most of those great, scholarly works of profound thought and scholarship remain on the bookshelves, collecting dust? Thank God that they're there because that adds significantly to the reservoir of human wisdom and learning. Someone once jokingly—but maybe *not* so jokingly—said that theologians are the worst enemies of religion. On the one hand, you're startled. But on the other hand, then you think: you know, possibly, if the theological message becomes so overly scholarly, human beings don't get it at all. What makes all religions the same, and what makes all religions different? It seems to me that what makes all religions essentially the same are the fundamental questions that they ask: Where did we come from? Where are we going? Why are we here? How ought we to behave while we are here? And what is the significance and meaning—if any—of our being here? Those fundamental questions are the fundamental inquiries of all religions—ancient, modern, medieval, Eastern, Western, Northern, Southern; the most sophisticated twenty-first century religious thought as well as the most primitive religious thought—those are the fundamental questions.

How the different religions answer those questions in different ways is what makes religions different, but those are the questions—that most human beings are simple. By that I am not being dismissive, not at all; they're simple in their needs, they're simple in their wants; they are simple in their sophistication because they haven't really had the opportunities for really advanced kind of learning, even here, in America. Just because a person has a bachelor's degree and has matriculated even from one of the better of our colleges and universities, can we automatically say that they are intellectually profound? But what do all human beings have, whether they have a third grade education or a graduate degree? They want to know the answers to those fundamental questions.

And those are the questions that in his inimitable way the Dalai Lama, with his fundamental goodness, is able to address. Profound? Love and compassion; when he spoke here at the temple, that was his theme—love and compassion for the twenty-first century. It was elementary. But, by God, we need to hear again and again and again the reaffirmation of those fundamental simplicities that too many people—both in their personal and corporate lives—just seem to have set aside.

PART IV

Confronting Challenges and Uncertainties

Chapter Nine

THE DALAI LAMA AND THE EXILE COMMUNITY TODAY

Lama Surya Das   In 1972 the international aid organizations were just starting to help. It was pretty quiet. And, of course, the Dalai Lama had not yet been discovered by the celebrities and the Western media. When he escaped from Tibet in 1959, he was on the cover of *Time* magazine, but he hadn't traveled that much and he wasn't the media celebrity he is now, so it was easier to get an interview with him and to see him. It was also very peaceful there, in a sort of chaotic refugee way. But if you were a Buddhist, it was a beautiful place to be, to go to the Dalai Lama's residence and hang around his monastery.

The Evolution of Dharamsala

Dr. Alexander Berzin   It has changed tremendously over the nearly three decades that I lived there, and it has continued to change. In the early days, Tibetans were still working on road gangs. Not so many had moved down to the settlement camps of South India—those were just getting started—and that was very difficult; the Tibetans had to clear jungles, make fields, and get used to a radically different climate in south India from what they had experienced in Tibet, or even in the Himalayas in India. And then, over time, things changed very much: transportation became much easier whereas before you had to walk everywhere; the dirt roads got paved; taxis came in; telephones came in; eventually Internet cafes came in.

In terms of the Tibetans themselves, it was sometime in the early eighties that the Chinese relaxed the border situation, and so you had a whole new wave of people coming from Tibet—Tibetans refer to them as "newcomers" as opposed to the people who came out in 'fifty-nine. That changed the social situation very much, because they had to help settle these people in. There was a much larger influx of aid and volunteers from the West to help with resettlement and adjustment. These people added a new blood—a new vigor—especially to the monasteries because they were deprived so much in Tibet of religious education, spiritual education, that they were very, very enthusiastic to study, much more than the ones who had grown up in India. This was inspiring for everybody.

From the point of view of the Westerners living there, the situation changed over time because up until around the late seventies or early eighties people from the Commonwealth countries could stay in India without a visa, and so you had many long-term residents who were studying there. I was staying mostly with the community of Westerners who were studying at the library in Dharamsala. There were long-term courses, long-term training, which afterward, when everybody needed a visa and it was more difficult to stay for long periods in India, the courses and trainings were much shorter, and so that changed very much the situation.

As Dharamsala developed, it became a bit of a tourist place, particularly for Indians, and a huge amount of tourist hotels went up. Also, as the Tibetans got more and more sponsors and were more successful in India, a tremendous amount of building was going on—when I first went there, in 'sixty-nine, hardly anything was there—and nowadays it's very, very built up. It's a common phenomenon that young people come to India for the so-called hippie scene that's been going on for decades, but once they're there, many of them become intrigued by spiritual things and turn to that rather than their original purpose. And so it organically works like that. I can't recall His Holiness making any specific statement to that movement, but an awful lot of them will be coming to His Holiness's general Buddhist talks and teachings, so many of them turn to it and turn away from the drugs.

Ven. Bhikshuni Tenzin Kacho   In 1985, Dharamsala was going through a big transition. I had lived there in 1975 and it was very poor then, very impoverished, with very little water or electricity and no latrines. People were using almost anywhere they could as a public toilet, often the bushes, sometimes right near the few water taps because there were bushes around there, so it was quite precarious. I didn't go back again until 1985 and the shift was quite huge. By this time there was an increase in attention and interest, a much greater interest, and growth in the way of buildings and more facilities for people; the hospitals and other services were growing. But even in 'eighty-five it was rustic. I entered the Tibetan nunnery there in Dharamsala. I took one of the nuns to the dentist and there was no preventative care, really; if people had sore teeth, they just lined people up, they got a shot, and their teeth were pulled. As I waited for her, I could hear teeth dropping into a tin bucket.

Tsunma Jampa Dolkar   The first time I went there, it was very special for me because I was with my teacher and he hadn't been there for several years and everybody was so excited to see him—he was so welcomed there. That was the first time that I met His Holiness and could shake his hand. It was a very profound experience for me. It was also during monsoon season; sometimes it would rain so hard that you physically couldn't even go out the door—you couldn't *open* the door; it was like a fire hose was shooting down.

Dr. Blu Greenberg   I thought it was pretty. It was quaint but some of it was pretty modern and a lot of it was very poor. But the scenery—we stayed in Kashmir Cottage, which overlooked the mountains—is breathtaking with the mist and the colors and the sky and the steepness. There are many points of beauty. The colorfulness of the places of worship and the temples were gorgeous, and the robes—the combination of orange and saffron and burgundy—it was a very colorful experience.

Professor Jonathan Mirsky   It [Dharamsala] has had two existences: long ago it was a British hill station and some of that remains, up in the woods, behind it. Right now it's kind of a hippie-and-backpacker haven, a center for people who are interested in Buddhism and want to be near the Dalai Lama. The weather is very good. The only unfortunate thing about it is that it's now become a rather kitsch tourist trap. But it's a nice place and the Dalai Lama lives in a large but very simple bungalow. What's odd about it is that it is guarded by Indian soldiers with machine guns in their hands. At one point on one of my visits there, I went outside with him. We went out the back door, and the soldiers hadn't been told he was coming out that way. All they knew was that a door was opening. They sprang around and pointed their weapons at us. And I said to him then, "Here you are, the great apostle of nonviolence, and you're being guarded by these soldiers." But, of course, you have to understand that the Indian government is in a very tricky position with the Dalai Lama: they can't let anything happen to him but they also are very eager to control his movements because they have the angry Chinese on their necks all the time, so they have to be quite careful with him.

Transferring the Dalai Lama's Authority from Lhasa to Dharamsala

Dr. Alexander Berzin   For His Holiness, that doesn't seem to be at all a problem. It has nothing to do with where he physically *is*; it has to do with his personality, his personal development, and his strong involvement in the social welfare of his people. He feels the closest with the Fifth Dalai Lama and the Thirteenth Dalai Lama, both of whom put a great deal of effort into trying to take care of the general social and political situation of the Tibetans and not exclusively working toward their spiritual welfare. And so I don't think it comes so much from the institution. Other Dalai Lamas have been more retired; some of them didn't live very long—died in their early twenties—but it's just from His Holiness's way of being.

For the people in Tibet, His Holiness is a symbol of Tibet, a symbol of hope, and so this is something that is very noticeable in terms of a difference between the Tibetan situation, in which the country was very much devastated by the takeover, and other Buddhist countries such as Cambodia. Tibetans who have spent years and years in concentration camps as a whole were far less traumatized and have dealt with that trauma far better than Cambodians who suffered similar types of difficulties. Both of those societies have Buddhism, so you can't ascribe it simply to Buddhism. The only explanation that makes any sense is the figure of His Holiness and the hope that he symbolizes for the Tibetans.

Professor Robert Thurman   When I first met him, he was not as happy as he is today. I began to notice a major change in him in the 1970s. In fact, every time I've seen him, I have noticed changes. There was an important change from 1964, when I first met him, to 1970, when I spent about a year with him. During that period of time, he matured considerably and became much more philosophically and doctrinally fluent; his command of material was really tremendous. Then, when I saw him in the late 1970s, after an eight-year hiatus, I recognized a significant jump: he had this *power*.

The Evolution of the Dalai Lama's
Government and Administrative Style

Dr. Tenzin Tethong   Until 1990, the exile government had had an elected parliament, but the executive was nominated by His Holiness and approved by the parliament. So in 1990, for a complicated set of reasons, but mainly to advance the democratic structures in exile, a larger, extraordinary congress was called together, and His Holiness suggested that the ministers of the Tibetan Government-in-Exile be elected. To insure that, the people had more than the average amount of support, a threshold of 70 percent approval was suggested. So this congress took place in 1990; three people were elected in that first election, and I was one of them. So I spent the next five years in Dharamsala, responsible for several portfolios, including for a short while serving as the chairman of the cabinet of His Holiness.

Richard Blum   His Holiness has tried to find a balance. He has made the Government-in-Exile much more democratic. The people elect the members of the Kashag and the assembly. I always say to the Chinese, "If you want to understand how the Tibetans today are treated by the Dalai Lama, look at the Government-in-Exile."

Dr. Tenzin Tethong   During the period I served in the Kashag, basically the members in the cabinet ranged from three to six, and so we functioned very much like a committee. Even as chairman it didn't mean that you had a complete say over how everything went. We functioned very much by consensus, so the role of a chairman would often be to bring up issues that needed to be tackled, decisions to be made, and to try and bring some kind of consensus. So it involved being not dictatorial by any means, but trying to persuade people to come to a certain viewpoint. Even as a member of the Kashag, you had to play that role—you were one of many always trying to bring consensus; we didn't function in a way whereby we simply went for a quick majority decision on any issue. So that was the primary role of the chairmanship and, of course, being chairman of His Holiness's cabinet also meant on any key discussions that we were initiating, or any initiative we were going to take, or were taking, the chairman had the formal responsibility of keeping His Holiness abreast of developments.

Generally His Holiness is not involved in the minute-to-minute situation. He is usually involved in the more, shall we say, important, or bigger issues that we occasionally have to deal with. Once in a while there may be an issue where he may be more specifically involved.

Tsering Shakya   In the early period, when he was in his twenties and thirties, of course he needed these confidantes and advisers much more. Now the situation is reversed; he is much older and surrounded by much younger people, and all his old teachers, from whom he sought guidance, have passed away. I think he is very isolated in terms of personal connection with individuals. There aren't many high lamas he is close to, who are older and have the same wisdom and learning, to whom he can go.

T. C. Tethong   He always says that he needs more people in his administration who could serve as links between the older and younger generations. When he was in California in the mid-1990s, I informed him that I could go back to Dharamsala and serve him for a few years, since my children had grown up and had finished their college education. After about six months, I received a letter [saying] that I should serve as his representative in India. While there, I was elected as a member of the cabinet and received the portfolio for Information and International Relations, a post I held from 1997 to 2001. I have worked very closely with him and have never seen such a disciplined man. After a long day, while I might take off my glasses and throw them on the table, *he* will very carefully wrap his glasses in his handkerchief. He does not like people to make him idle or to spend time speaking about nothing. It is wonderful to watch him, but hard to keep up with him.

Dr. Thubten Jinpa Langri   When traveling with him, one often gets exhausted while *he* appears to be almost always quite fresh. Last summer, for example, after a break of three weeks following the Toronto Kalachakra, I had to join him in England, Scotland, and Rome. I came back to Canada completely exhausted—it took me two to three days to recover. But His Holiness keeps a high level of energy.

T. C. Tethong   He doesn't like to be idle; he is doing something *all* the time. In the early years in India, he would play badminton and table tennis and go for walks. It was fun to see the security officers trying to keep up with him. Occasionally he will sit around with friends and talk, but he is busy most of the time.

Delegating Responsibility

Dr. Tenzin Tethong   It varied a bit. In most regular, normal affairs that needed some attention, decisions or his recommendations would be forthcoming very quickly. And he would probably encourage us to make the decisions quickly also. But then, on some more difficult or complicated issues, he would probably take time, ask us to reconsider or think of making a decision down the line. He would also consult other sources and individuals on the issue—not necessarily in a formal way, but he would consult other people at various times.

Tsering Shakya   His Holiness doesn't watch over everything, although he's kept informed. He has always wanted them to relegate some of this. This is a problem. Politicians and people who are born into their positions—if a politician has acquired power he will be watchful all the time about what is going on, otherwise he will lose that power—but the Dalai Lama has never had to fear that he will lose his power because he's born into it. So he can always relegate and delegate his duties and tasks; he doesn't always have to be consciously watching. So, in a way, the Dalai Lama doesn't govern through absolute involvement in every practicality.

Another problem with the Tibetan situation is that sometimes Tibetan politicians are totally incapable of making decisions; they go to the Dalai Lama for his guidance for the smallest problems. When the Dalai Lama meets with the Tibetan politicians and administrators, he is always saying, "Please don't come to me; make the decision. You know you have elected people; use your authority." What he means is that by being elected, you have been given the authority to make decisions. He, in fact, wants to relegate so much of his responsibility.

Dr. Alexander Berzin   He seems to certainly stay on top of everything. He does delegate responsibility; he doesn't want to be in a position of the one who's always making all the decisions and having everybody being dependent on him. But that's difficult to actually implement because Tibetans all do, most of them, look up to him. But he certainly delegates; he's not personally choosing all the little details. I've noticed it in my own case; once he has confidence in somebody, he says, "You know. Use your own judgment" in terms of how to deal with a situation. And you report back, of course.

Dr. Thubten Jinpa Langri   Before I began interpreting for him, His Holiness knew me as a scholar in the monastic universities. He used to visit these universities and attend debate sessions. Although he did not know me personally then, he was familiar with my face from seeing me as one of the young students who participated in debates. In the autumn of 1985, I went to Dharamsala and attended teachings His Holiness gave to a group that had been organized in Los Angeles. It happened that the regular interpreter could not be present on the first day. The word got around that I spoke English, and I was asked to fill in. I replied that I had never really, formally, done any translation work and, in any case, I wouldn't really dare to interpret His Holiness's teachings. But finally I was plucked out of my seat and I started interpreting. The next day, the person who was supposed to translate showed up, and I shared the microphone with him as we translated alternate portions. It turned out, however, that I was more familiar with the text His Holiness was teaching. During that week, I had a personal chat with His Holiness and he said, "Oh, I never associated your face with someone who spoke English." He had evidently remembered me from my student days in South India. Then he asked if I would be able to travel and interpret for him.

Rinchen Dharlo   If he gets a piece of information he never forgets it. And sometimes when you are in his presence if you don't remember things you have reported to him the previous year and happen to repeat it, he'll say, "Oh, you told me this *last* year!" I always have this problem—you prepare yourself for what to report to him and when you are in his presence, you forget what you wanted to tell him and end up telling him something else. And sometimes before you speak to him he keeps on asking questions, and then you're lost again. That happens to me very often, although I've traveled with him so many times here in the States. Actually, he's very open and very informal. But still, we find it difficult, maybe because we have always treated him as the human embodiment of the Lord of Compassion.

Dr. Jeffrey Hopkins   In terms of interpreting in public, it was a great both thrill and challenge, and part of the thrill was the challenge. I'm a very conservative translator: I try not to add in things from myself to soften the way things are said, and yet you want to speak in ways that people can understand. And so, seeking that simplicity and directness, the appearance of my merely being a window through which people could see *him*, these all brought a tremendous amount of attention to what I was doing. I enjoyed it immensely. I also enjoyed the suspense about wondering when I was going to mess up something. One reason why I could enjoy it is that he can speak for a lengthy period of time—probably longer than anyone else does in the world—before the translator gets the chance to translate. And why I could enjoy it was that he would listen to the English most of the time and then fill in and say again what I had left out. In terms of collaborating on books, in some cases he sat down with me and taught me books with the specific intent—though I would record what he was teaching—that I make a book out of it. In other cases, I'm taking teachings that he has given in public, putting them together, and then going back and asking him about his own experiences.

Rinchen Dharlo   In 'eighty-eight I was on the board of the Global Forum for Spiritual and Parliamentary Leaders. There was a big conference in Oxford, His Holiness was in London, and he was coming to address that conference. I was not coordinating his visit; I was simply part of the conference organizers, so from the organizers' side I was there to help receive him. We were forming a line at the time when he was about to arrive, and a rabbi from Holland walked up to me and said, "I know the Dalai Lama; I met him once in a conference in Holland." Then, as we went down to seat His Holiness, the rabbi walked up to him to shake hands and said, "Your Holiness, I met you . . ." and the Dalai Lama said, "Yes, in Holland!" The rabbi was so shocked. "That was just one meeting," he said, and he had been with a group of people.

Pema Chhinjor   My brother, who was a freedom fighter, was on hand to receive His Holiness as he crossed a river on his way from the Norbulingka to exile. We escorted the Dalai Lama to the Indian border, and then he turned back and resumed fighting. Later, in the 1960s, when my brother came to India, he met His Holiness in Dharamsala. In 2002, he returned to Dharamsala. By this time, my brother had completely changed: he was an old man. He was standing in a queue with thousands of people when His Holiness saw him and went directly to him, saying, "You look *older*." It was amazing that he recognized my brother. This gives you the impression that His Holiness is not an ordinary man.

Tolerance of the Mistakes of Staff Members

Rinchen Dharlo   He would definitely show his unhappiness. He's someone who is so *direct*; if he feels that something is wrong, he won't pretend not to know. He will gently point out that it was not right.

Richard Gere   I have to say that I've seen him when he can be quite wrathful, in a skillful way, with me and with other people. I don't think that he is this laughing, smiling Buddha all the time. He's skillful about what's required at the moment and if he *is* wrathful, it's certainly not personal; it's because something needs to be done. But is that easy laugh always there? Of course it is.

Mickey Lemle   I once heard him say, "When I was a young man, I had a temper; I used to get angry. I have been doing Buddhist practice for many, many years and have really worked on my anger and in the last few years I have been able to reduce it a little bit." I thought: there are people who do a workshop in California for the weekend and say "I've gotten rid of anger."

Dr. Howard Cutler   He has worked very hard for decades and decades to develop a certain outlook and perception of life. At this stage of his life, he never gets intensely angry. I have observed him under stressful situations and have noted that his actions correspond well with his words. Certainly he has his frustrations, and some disappointments. But it is more like the surface of the ocean—surface waves rather than deep feelings of anger.

Professor Robert Thurman   He doesn't like it when a kind of gaga devotee is talking with him about how to help the Tibetans and instead of coming up with some new idea will declare, "Whatever *you* say, Your Holiness." He becomes impatient with people who think he knows everything and will know what to do in every situation. He wouldn't want a driver to ask him, "Should I go right or left? Should I run the light?" Yet that same person will go to a teaching and see him as their *Dalai Lama*.

The Dalai Lama's Policy on Financial Matters

Pema Chhinjor   When I served in the cabinet, His Holiness had two quite old vehicles. The drivers told me that they worried about mechanical failure and that they also felt it was quite risky driving these cars from Dharamsala to other Indian towns and cities. As a result, I went to Delhi and purchased a new car. One day, His Holiness was leaving on a trip and needed to go to the airport. His driver asked, "Which car would you like to take? Would you like the new one?" His Holiness asked, "Whose car is *that*?" The driver replied, "The security minister bought this car for *your* use." His Holiness said, "No, I don't need it; the old cars are okay." So we sold the new car.

Dr. Jeffrey Hopkins   I was asking him to write a letter of support for a group in Germany that wanted to help a Tibetan group that had settled in South India to build a temple, and he said in English, "Corruption!"—that they don't need a temple; they can meditate in the woods. So I was put in the position of arguing with him that not everything that went on in temples and institutions was corruption—in other words, I was taking the opposite of what was usually my own argument—and we discussed this for a time. I was tremendously impressed by his frankness and the need to be fully honest in his presence.

Rinchen Dharlo   His Holiness is very generous with his time when he teaches, and generous with money. Whatever he gets offered he gives back to the people. As a result, his office sometimes finds it very difficult to manage with the funding because he gives away so much. In India, sometimes, when abbots of monasteries come, or lamas meet him and some of them put forward some of their difficulties—financial conditions of the monasteries—he says, "Okay, I would like to make a contribution and I would give this much," without even checking how much money is left. He gives away *a lot*. He does not have any attachment to wealth. And not only for himself, but also whatever he has he does not even give to his relatives; he thinks that it's not appropriate for him to spend the money he is offered to benefit his relatives. For example, his older brother's son, a bright, very intelligent young man, came to the United States to study, and some of his mother's friends agreed to help with the tuition to Georgetown University. He was doing his master's and had finished one year by getting help from here and there. Then, after one year, he could not continue because there was not enough funding for him and he stopped. And His Holiness did not help; maybe either he did not approach him or His Holiness thought it was inappropriate to spend the money for the scholarship for his nephew. Then his younger brother has two children—a daughter and a son. When they graduated from high school, their parents wanted them to study in the States. They haven't received a single dime from His Holiness, and their parents don't have the means to support their education in the States. They could support tuition in India, but the children wanted to be in the States. They had a very hard time and their daughter barely managed the funding and got a graduate degree; the son did not complete his college education on time, mainly because of funding. This is the way he is.

In Dharamsala, sometimes his mother would prepare cookies—he loved eating cookies made by his mother. Sometimes she would go to the

Indian grocery shop and buy apples and take them to His Holiness. One of his attendants, a senior Tibetan officer, said that one day his mother brought a lot of apples and he said, "Mother, why have you brought so many apples? You could have brought just three; I would have very happily taken one apple as my mother's gift, but you have bought so much and you don't have the means to buy, and I can't even help you." That doesn't mean he has a lack of cash; he has money, but he doesn't spend a single dime to help his relatives or spend it on himself. He always thinks of others and whatever he has, he thinks that it belongs to the Tibetan people.

He really doesn't want much for himself and sometimes when he goes to teach, people who buy the tickets think that the proceeds go to him. Nothing goes to him. Organizers very often make donations to him, but he doesn't accept them. When he received his Nobel Prize for Peace, he divided it among different causes: he gave a large sum to Mother Teresa to treat lepers; he sent huge funding to Africa to feed the hungry; and he even gave money to the University for Peace, in Costa Rica. Also, the Tibetan administration received some part of it after some American friends told him, "You should keep some of it for the Tibetan cause." He always, always thinks of others. When he was asked how he was going to use his Nobel Prize, he said, "Tibetans are poor—the Tibetans are refugees—but they are not dying of hunger; I want to feed the hungry and send my money to Africa to feed the hungry." Later on, people came with all kinds of proposals and it was divided into several portions.

Pema Chhinjor   Dharamsala is a hill station with few good roads. When I was minister of security, I was concerned over how long it would take to transport His Holiness to a good hospital should he suddenly become ill. I was in touch with the Indian government for two years, asking them to provide a life-saving vehicle. Finally they sent one that was fully outfitted with life-saving equipment. When I reported to His Holiness that this very expensive vehicle had arrived and would be kept at the palace, he completely disagreed. He asked why such an expensive car was to be provided for *him* and not be used by all the people. He told me, "Just give it back to the government of India." And the government officials were shocked.

Mechanics of the Dalai Lama's Ever-Increasing World Travel

Rinchen Dharlo   All the details of schedules are prepared by the local organizers. For his visit to Miami [in September 2004], the local organizers put together a schedule and sent it to the Office of Tibet [in New York]. The representative would go through it and he would send it back with some changes. When he felt comfortable, he would send it to Dharamsala and his secretaries would go through it and get it approved [by His Holiness]. But what usually happens is that during his visit many people [not on the original schedule] request a time to meet him. Normally, His Holiness is someone who will say, "Yes, I'll do it." So his office finds it difficult to accommodate these people, and that's why these schedules become tight and he gets tired.

Annie Warner   He is very much active in the scheduling process. We try not to burden him with the small details, but he always looks over the complete schedule before he departs India and offers input. For example, if a day looks too hectic he may ask that some of the events be condensed. He is extremely particular and precise. We have an absolute minute-by-minute schedule from the time he lands in North America until the time he departs, which could be as long as thirty-five days, and he looks over each minute of that schedule before he leaves India. There are always last-minute additions to his audience schedule; there might be a teacher who has come from some distance whom His Holiness would like to see, or a family from Tibet returning home who would never again have a chance to see him. So we are sure to get them in.

Norbu Tsering   I didn't want to overschedule him [during the April 2004 visit to Toronto] because the teaching was from 7 A.M. to 4 or 5 P.M. We got a lot of requests—like from universities, organizations, and politicians—and we rejected them. We even rejected the premier of Ontario. There was no time and I did my best to avoid such over-scheduling. All events went according to the schedule, but there were a few private audiences, so there were some minor changes.

Patrick French   I've put it to Tenzin Geyche Tethong, his private secretary, for years and years, "Why do you make him do this kind of schedule?" and he said, "Because that's what he's chosen to do; he believes that that is what his destiny is. He thinks that the way that he can serve Tibetan Buddhism is by speaking to large numbers of people around the world." So I believe that it's a conscious choice that he's made. I suspect there's a side of him that really doesn't want to do it. But he knows how much effect it has, he knows how many people want him to do it, and that's what he has decided to do. It may be, now that he's approaching seventy, that there will come a point when he'll suddenly say something like: Right now I'm stopping. I'm not being the traveling, global Dalai Lama anymore. I'm going to go into retreat for a couple of years. That wouldn't surprise me at all.

Rinchen Dharlo   When he agrees to meet a person, he doesn't judge whether that person has something very important to discuss—whether the person comes from a very important institution or is a very simple, ordinary person. If he agrees to meet someone then he will make sure to keep this schedule. After he got the Nobel Peace Prize, he was not willing to cancel some of the appointments that he had. He said, "We agreed to meet these people a month and a half ago; how can I cancel these in order to have time to give interviews?"

In the past, he always tried to balance [his overseas visits]. I remember him saying, "Not too many visits to the United States—once a year—then I have to go to other places." In Europe there are so many countries, and then he also visits Japan, Australia, New Zealand, Russia, and Mongolia. For individual cities, it depends on how the invitations are accepted by his representative and by his secretaries. But for him, when he is asked for his formal approval, if he thinks that he's going to be able to make a difference for the people who are inviting him—if he thinks that he will make some contribution that would help them, then he accepts the invitation. But if he thinks his visit would not make any difference, then he won't accept, even if the invitation comes from a very prestigious university. First, he would see who is inviting him and what the purpose of the visit is. And if the visit is for teachings, he would ask the question, "Who would be attending the teachings?" And if he thinks his teachings would really be able to contribute, he would accept the invitation.

Security Concerns

Annie Warner   In the United States there are State Department officials who travel with His Holiness. In Canada [in April 2004] specific officers were assigned to His Holiness in each of the cities he visited but they did not accompany him during his travels. So the officers who were with us in Vancouver walked us onto the plane and then, as soon as we landed in Ottawa, the local officials were on hand to greet everyone.

Pema Chhinjor   In April 2004, when His Holiness was in Pasadena, I was amazed when I came to his teaching that all the security guards were

Chinese. When I tried to gain access to him, a couple of these security guards stopped me. I said to them, "This is very good. I also used to do this job." I waited outside and sent a message to a member of His Holiness's own security detail. Someone came out and told the Chinese guards, "He is one of the former security ministers." The guards said, "Sorry, sorry." But I told them that I appreciated the good job they were doing.

The Dalai Lama's Energy during Trips Abroad

Annie Warner   He usually rests during flights. On longer flights, he will usually eat a meal. He normally sits with his personal attendant in the first row of the business class section. He will often complete some of his morning prayers if he hasn't had a chance to say them before departing, or he will meditate for a portion of the flight. Usually, the flight attendants want to take a picture with him, and he always agrees to do that.

Rinchen Dharlo   It's quite surprising that despite his age he has so much energy. We get up only around six o'clock during his visits and by the time we go to bed we are so tired. Even during his travels he gets up at around three o'clock and he's in meditation, says his prayers, finishes all his meditation and prayers before six, and he takes his breakfast most times around six. And while he takes his breakfast, he also listens to the radio—mostly he listens to the BBC. After breakfast he takes time to read his paper and by 7:30 he's ready to meet people; sometimes we schedule some of the meetings as early as 7:30 or 8:00. He is so self-disciplined; he always eats on time, he only drinks tea and sometimes eats one or two cookies for dinner, and he keeps himself very strong. Formal receptions tire him a lot; he does not like to stand and receive people in line. Also, he prefers not to attend dinner receptions, which make him really very, very tired.

Lama Surya Das   He knows how to relax and that doesn't necessarily mean he's watching television. Maybe he's tinkering with watches or some mechanical thing or is in his garden. When I was in charge of the house we rented for him in Dordogne [in southwest France] in the late 1980s to teach at our center, some of my best memories of hanging out together with him were when he would be walking around at five or six in the morning, looking at flowers. I have been to the movies with him in Paris, to attend the premiere of [Bernardo] Bertolucci's *Little Buddha* film. He cried a few times, especially when the Buddha was sitting under the Bodhi Tree [under which Shakyamuni Buddha, c. 563–483 B.C., the Indian philosopher and founder of Buddhism, attained enlightenment] and being attacked. But going to the movies is not something he does—he's not a fan of Richard Gere's movies or of movies in general. Buddhist monks' vows are against going to theaters; strict Buddhist monks in Burma or Thailand would think he's not a good monk if he went to the movies.

Rinchen Dharlo   Actually, I suggested to his secretaries to have him stay a few days in cities or hill stations where not that many people would [likely] visit. Here in the States, we had several rounds of discussion that when he's basically going to be teaching it's better to be in a place like Tucson, Arizona, rather than in Washington, Toronto, New York City, or Los Angeles. We tried to do that, but I failed in trying to convince him to take two days of rest. He said, "What should I do with my resting here? It's boring. If I want to rest, it's always better to be where I stay in Dharamsala. I don't want to rest in other places; I don't get rest in these places."

Dr. Howard Cutler   He doesn't feel that he needs vacations. He doesn't separate out: this is my work time; this is my leisure time. He doesn't have an "off-duty" personality. If he does have free time, he would prefer to use it to study and meditate. A vacation to him is to go on a spiritual retreat, where he can engage in spiritual practices for hours on end. That recharges him.

Annie Warner   When he travels his motion is constant. If he is feeling good he may have audiences after his lunch and a rest. When he was in Toronto for a number of days [in April 2004], one of the monks who often cooks for His Holiness in Dharamsala prepared all of the meals, along with another Tibetan gentleman from Ottawa. During shorter stays, it is not uncommon for the hotel dining room to prepare his meals, which are then brought to him by room service.

Sister Mary Margaret Funk   When he didn't show up for us—he had a stomach ailment and he just really couldn't travel; it was a huge bowel blockage—he was in the hospital in southern India and then he recuperated back in Dharamsala. A Tibetan Buddhist monk told me he had been poisoned. That makes all kinds of sense because on the watch I've had him, we'd have his people with the food; he would be served separately. But then he'd want a piece of fruit cake and then he'd want his tea and there'd be no way you could possibly sterilize his food.

Professor Jonathan Mirsky   Like in all other émigré circles, there's a lot of very unpleasant gossip that swirls around the Dalai Lama and Tibetan exiles generally. There's been a kind of rivalry between the Dalai Lama and two other important lamas and at one point a rival camp. This has always included a certain amount of unpleasant accusations of murder and poi-sonings—all kinds of bad things like that. It's very hard to pin down how true any of that is.

The Dalai Lama's Promotion of
Western-Style Social Services

Dr. Alexander Berzin   One of the things that is very helpful in Christian-ity, for example, is that His Holiness is very delighted with their practice of service to others. For various social and geographic reasons, Tibet didn't really develop things like orphanages and old-age homes—all of these things were taken care of within the extended families—and so it is very interesting to see how Christianity does that and what could be learned.

Ven. Bhikshuni Tenzin Kacho   He's actively working on this; it's very, very exciting. In fact, there were a couple of Western monastics who wanted to start a monastery for Westerners studying in the Tibetan Bud-dhist tradition and they approached His Holiness for guidance and assis-tance. They proposed that they establish a community for twelve, and the Dalai Lama said, "No, no, let's establish it for two hundred!" And that is in progress right now: the land has already been appropriated near Sera Monastery in southern India, and His Holiness is engaged in their daily schedule—how that's going to be worked on, the prayers that they're going to be reciting daily. He's keenly interested in what's going on there. This is very current, and it's been growing with his understanding of the difficul-ties that many Westerners have faced in becoming monastics. A lot of them come with so much aspiration and interest, but once they're ordained, partly because the Tibetan community is in exile and struggling to sustain itself, there is very little support for the Westerners—in fact, we're asked to support *them*—so we've had to fend for ourselves a lot. But slowly it's turning around, realizing that we need to nurture the Western monastic community as well.

Sister Mary Margaret Funk   They're getting training now. And just within the last ten years, they're shifting into secular studies. They'd all been training just for enlightenment and learning their scriptures, so they really didn't know health care and social work. They've never been very secularly engaged because they've never thought it was worth it. I personally attempted to train Tibetan monks and nuns in social engagement. And, frankly, it failed.

The Status of Tibetan Women

Ven. Bhikshuni Tenzin Kacho   Among Asian societies, women have very important and dynamic roles in Tibetan society. At least part of this was in the traditional structure that was held in Tibet pre-1959; a huge percentage of the male population was in the monasteries, so women really ran a lot of things— stores and households, and other businesses. A few women get into the governmental and political arenas. I think it's really wonderful for women, and they tend to be quite strong and outspoken in the communities themselves.

Dr. Blu Greenberg   I asked a question [during the Dharamsala dialogue], "What about the women?" because he [the presenter] was talking about the advances made—the inroads in modern society.

Rabbi Irving Greenberg   It was very funny. Sitting behind him [the Dalai Lama] the whole time was this row of geshes who are a lot older than him. They are the chiefs of these academies and monasteries. They are overwhelmingly nonmodernized because they stay in the monasteries and academies and aren't exposed to this whole Western experience. Frankly, all of the geshes are old men, obviously in their seventies and eighties, and they seemed to doze off during the session.

Anyway, Blu asked this question [about women] and the Dalai Lama says, "We have to educate them; we've been pretty busy." And as he starts to talk about the improvement of women, these four or five geshes, wake up and one starts going "err err err" [mimicking the geshes' grunting sounds]. They are finding it quite upsetting and nudging each other. Halfway through his answer, their muttering got loud enough that the people in front, including us, were very aware of it, and it was obvious that the Dalai Lama also could hear. But he finished his answer, explaining to us all the different ways women can become more important in our leadership. And then, when he finishes, he whirls around and in Tibetan—we didn't understand a word—says, "err err err," and they say, "err err err." Then he turns around and says to us, "They agree with me." It was a perfect response. It made me feel again—I'm very envious—that it's a great way, if you want to bring changes, to speak as God and the geshes agree with you. But the whole thing was sort of cute, because it dramatized the different backgrounds and the extent to which he is, at least at some level, open to the West and to modernizing, compared to his inner core group.

Ven. Thubten Chodron   In 1993, there was a conference of some Western Buddhist teachers with His Holiness. There were maybe thirty of us from various Buddhist traditions, Tibetan and non-Tibetan. We met with His Holiness for five days and discussed different topics each day. On one of the days, we talked about the position of women; one woman did the presentation, but a few of us helped her plan it the night before. In Tibetan society they don't have this self-reflective ability to look at their own culture—they've never had the studies of anthropology, psychology, or sociology—so she went in there and gave her presentation to His Holiness. She said, "I'm going to lead you in a little visualization, so imagine, Your Holiness, that you come into a room, or you're invited to some teachings, and there is *Her* Holiness the Dalai Lama, the fourteenth in a line of women who have been consistently reincarnated as the spiritual and political leaders of Tibet. All around you are women lamas—everywhere—and you're a man and you wonder: what place do *I* have in this whole thing, because all the bodhisattvas in the paintings are women, all the important people on the stage next to Her Holiness are women? You wonder what you can do, so you ask one of the lamas and she tells you, "Well, if you practice very well, you can be reborn as a woman in your next life." You're not satisfied with that and so you go to another lama and ask, "What is the role of men in this tradition?" She tells you, "Everything is empty; there are no men and there are no women, so don't worry about it." And you're still not satisfied, so you go to another lama and she tells you, "Well, if you're very fortunate, you can serve all the nuns and create a lot of merit serving them."

By this time, all of the Westerners were really just cracking up, laughing so hard, because she had just reversed all the gender roles. But the Tibetans were sitting there with completely straight faces. They didn't understand; they just didn't get it. And then, when His Holiness began to speak, he started by saying, "All sentient beings, including animals and insects, have Buddha nature, and so all women need to be equal and have that brought out. They have full potential to be enlightened." So he has always affirmed women's spiritual ability, and I think he's becoming more aware that the women are treated differently and don't have the same opportunities.

Still, when I look around when there are these conferences—for example, the Mind Life Conferences—their private office does not invite any women; it's only men usually. I snuck in once or twice. So there's some growing that I would like to see happen in the Tibetan community in general. On the other hand, when I've been with His Holiness personally, like with this program, "Life as a Western Buddhist Nun," and also when I went to him, telling him I wanted to start a monastery, he's always emphasizing that women have equal opportunity and that they have equal responsibility. He said to me, personally, "You act and you do whatever you can and you make yourself educated. And if there are difficulties, then you come and tell us and we'll do what we can to help." But he's always very encouraging to just go ahead and act—don't let the system put you down, and don't just sit there and bellyache and complain and say there's prejudice and bias, and they won't let me do this, and poor me, I'm a woman. He doesn't like that kind of attitude. I've found that very, very helpful and encouraging advice.

Sister Mary Margaret Funk   They're Asian in culture and, frankly, they have a wonderful relationship with women. There aren't any stories that I have heard of women being mistreated, like being beaten by their husbands. The Tibetans, genetically, cannot drink so the Dalai Lama has really been trying to get them, even as they Westernize, to attend to their intolerance to alcohol—so I can't vouch today for all women not being abused by men. But a fascinating thing is that in the altiplano of Tibet, they practice polyandry and it's a very acceptable practice, which is the reverse of, say, the Muslim culture or the Latter Day Saints culture, where there is polygamy. Because of the altitude being so high and childbirth being so difficult, women have to have as many children as possible. Also, because the terrain is so severe and the men have to take their Yak butter all the way through the Silk Route and they're gone two and three months at a time, the brothers—there's a systematic order of who can have sex with the wife. Then, when the children are born, everybody is called "uncle" and there's never a question who their father is—the father isn't always the original mate of the mother. However, it's always known that it could have been an uncle. It doesn't really matter: life is precious. So, again, the women are treasured and honored and they become the head of the household, so it really is a more equal society than you would think. That being said, among the monks and nuns, a couple of monks were saying to me that they want to be apes because they don't want to come back as nuns, so being a monk is really a higher reincarnation than a nun.

The Status of the Female Clergy

While Dorje Phagmo, a Bodisattva whose name is commonly translated from the Tibetan language as "Thunderbolt Sow," did play a major role in eighteenth century monastic life as the head of a monastery, Samding, as opposed to being the abbot of a nunnery, most Tibetan female clergy have traditionally been relegated to a lesser status than their male counterparts.

Ven. Bhikshuni Tenzin Kacho As far as the monastic order is concerned, it appears that women did not have so much education in the monastic system unless they were specially connected, or unusual in their own wish to study. I have read and heard about women practitioners who were really quite inspired or driven to learn more about the teachings, so there's always that small percentage of practitioners. But, in general, the monastic system did not offer that much for the women. I believe that's slowly changing now, a lot because of the Dalai Lama's interest, a lot because of Western interest and inquiry—asking: why don't the women have the opportunities that the men have—so His Holiness has been very dynamic, really directly working and seeing that the opportunities for women were upgraded and offered and that they had access to better teachings and better conditions. It's all been fairly recent.

Dr. Alexander Berzin There certainly has been growing support for nuns. The nuns' situation, traditionally in Tibet—and traditionally around the Buddhist world—was not that great if we look at it objectively. And I think this is part of the general place of women in traditional Asian culture, although in Tibet, the women had a better position than in the other Asian countries. But still, the reality of the traditional societies was that women did not have an equal position to the men.

His Holiness has seen this as something that is very detrimental and unfair, and he's taken steps to try to change that situation, certainly in the exile community. And so there have been quite a number of nunneries that have been started. A lot of the impetus and finance for this has come from the West because Westerners are very sensitive to this type of issue. His Holiness has started an equal type of education system for the nuns—it wasn't as well developed traditionally in Tibet.

Ven. Thubten Chodron What I would really like to aim for is gender-irrelevant because when I think of the Buddhist intention, it was for all

sentient beings—male *and* female—to benefit and to attain enlightenment. And His Holiness has been very supportive of the Tibetan nuns.
When we started an education program called "Life as a Western Buddhist
Nun" in 1996, we had a program in India for three weeks. His Holiness
was very supportive of that, endorsed it, wrote a recommendation for us,
and gave us a group interview at the end of the program—there were
nearly a hundred women who attended that program.

Chapter Ten

CHINESE CALCULATIONS AND MISCALCULATIONS

The People's Republic of China has wrestled for more than five decades with the question of how to deal with the Dalai Lama. Having made the initial mistake of rendering it impossible for His Holiness to remain in Tibet, China has exacerbated the situation by refusing to seriously consider negotiating a settlement that would allow him to return with some measure of autonomy. At the same time, His Holiness, in pursuing a moderate approach as he travels the world, continues to focus attention on both the political and human rights aspects of the issue.

Why Did the Chinese Make It So Hard for His Holiness to Remain in Tibet? Wouldn't It Have Been Better to Have Made Some Accommodation with Him?

Tsering Shakya   There was a very important speech made in 1954 by Mao to Chinese commanders and soldiers who were going to Tibet. He analyzed this bad situation. It's really interesting. He was very perceptive; he knew that he needed the Dalai Lama to rule the country. The Chinese mistake has been not to really understand the historical cultural conditions of Tibet. They believed that somehow the revolution could be imposed on the people. The Chinese also had a very economic-determinant sort of

233

view. People's national identity is not a question of build them a road and they will automatically change their whole cultural and religious values. It doesn't occur like that.

Patrick French   Clearly Mao was not interested in dialogue; the Dalai Lama tried dialogue with Mao in the 1950s and he was betrayed. He was told at the time of the Seventeen Point Agreement in 1951 that Tibetan culture and identity would be preserved when, in fact, the Chinese Communist Party was interested in destroying it.

Tsering Shakya   This is a great paradox for China. They don't understand the West. They feel that what they are doing in China is exactly what happened in the West: We are modernizing; we are trying to be Western; religion is bad, religion is a terrible thing; we are a modern people. Yet you are concentrating on elevating this man who is a backward man; we are a more progressive element.

China is in some ways thinking about modernity. They are stuck in a 1930s and 1940s sort of mentality, where material progress and wealth are much more important than ideas and spiritual development and concerns like environment and ecology. In the West now it has cut across political lines; it's not between Left and Right; it's about human rights, poverty, a lot of spiritual concerns, genetic engineering. There's much more consensus in the West. So the Dalai Lama fits in very well with that sort of situation. And yet, China doesn't understand that the West has changed, the world has changed, but China hasn't changed. So China finds people like the Dalai Lama very puzzling because when you read Chinese intellectuals and writers, they have this sort of Darwinian evolutionary model of society's development: as your society progresses further and further, they believe that religion, and the religious, are redundant, that they are not important. And yet this is often not the case; in most postindustrial societies now they are more concerned with spiritual and social issues than they had been before. So that's why the Chinese find it very puzzling why the Dalai Lama has such stature in the West.

When Clinton met Jiang Zemin and they had this televised conversation, Clinton said that Jiang Zemin should meet the Dalai Lama, and he answered, "Yes, I understand that the Dalai Lama is very popular in the West. I need to study so I can understand. I must investigate."

Richard Blum   Jiang had been told by Clinton, Gore, Chirac, and my wife that he and the Dalai Lama should get together. It is my belief that just before Jiang stepped down as party secretary he was prepared to do this. You can recall the famous free-wheeling press briefing with President Clinton when Jiang shocked everyone by saying that some discussion could take place. But he evidently got shot down by the right wing.

Harry Wu They have to withdraw a few inches; they want to survive, but they are not going to change their minds. If today the communist leader in China was to say: give me some time; I will promote democracy, I would say: okay, give them up to a year. They will say, "No. We are communists." Their final goal is communism. They are not going to change their minds because reality forced them. It's too late. China lies. My father was a very wealthy banker. He said, "I'm going to stay." He refused advice from the British to leave, to go to Hong Kong. He said, "This is my motherland." My father died in 1986. He said, "It was my mistake." It was too late; his whole life was destroyed, his family destroyed. This is something that people learn from their blood, from their tears. And this is very powerful. The authorities say, "C'mon, we've changed, and we continue to do so." But they will not give up.

Professor Jonathan Mirsky You have to remember that the Chinese are phenomenally patient. World leaders in this part of the world [Europe] have policies that change or stay the same, but these democratic countries change governments a lot, and so there will be Blair and Blair will have been preceded by somebody else. One of the things you notice about the Chinese—I saw this when I lived in Hong Kong when I was representing the *Times* there—the Chinese always had the same officials, for years and years and years and years, who did the negotiating with the British about the future of Hong Kong after 1997. The British were forever changing their officials—people would get promoted; the person who had been doing the negotiations would now wish to have a more important job inside the Foreign Office and his place would be taken by somebody else—but the Chinese just always had the same line and they always had the same people doing it. And that's the way they are about Tibet: the same people attend to Tibet. It isn't as if the policy comes and goes; they have the same policy all the time. The guy who runs China right now, Wen Jiabao, was the party secretary in Tibet in 1988. I think I'm the only Western journalist who ever interviewed him when he was there in Tibet, and he hated the Tibetans; he hated being in Tibet; he was a very, very hard-line guy on Tibet. So now he's running China and I'm sure he feels the same way. That was a long time ago, and the Chinese don't change in these regards. The

Dalai Lama has changed and he's come to kind of feel around to see if there's some deal he can make with the Chinese. But nothing changes in that particular sphere.

Richard Blum   My own view is that, despite all the rhetoric, the Chinese will not allow His Holiness to come back. They defile him at every opportunity. They even claim that the reason photographs of the Dalai Lama are not up in Tibet is because the people don't want them. But if the Dalai Lama returned, the place would explode in joy; it would be the most momentous occasion in Tibet since he left in 1959. From their point of view, dealing with the cold, hard reality of it, they don't want to make a deal.

Orville Schell   There are not too many places in the world where the arrival of a leader, whether temporal or spiritual, would precipitate such a massive outpouring of goodwill and welcome. I can hardly imagine what it would be like. It is precisely that moment that China looks at almost with terror because it would be a moment when control would be beyond them and they would have to trust that His Holiness would do the right thing—that he would not hijack this moment for purposes of independence. I think he *wouldn't* do that. But the Chinese can't afford to take that risk. And it's a pity because, in my view, the risk of letting him go back is a risk well worth taking—to trust that His Holiness would fit in, in a cultural and religious sense, and would not covertly create independence for Tibet.

Richard Blum   The truth of the matter is that we had more leverage with China a dozen years ago, when their economy was just starting to develop. Today, China has more direct foreign investment than they know what to do with—it is the fastest growing major economy in the world.

You have to understand Chinese history; what their leaders want more than anything else is stability. You could argue about what price, but many of them lived through civil wars and the Cultural Revolution. At the end of the day—in twenty or fifty or a hundred years—the Chinese people will get what they want. The country will continue to move more toward being a democracy. On the other hand, the average person in the street is not that concerned with democracy. More than three hundred thousand Taiwanese have moved to Shanghai. Why would someone go from a democracy to this basically socialist dictatorship? The answer is that they see better opportunities for themselves and their families.

Dr. Tenzin Tethong   I don't think by doing something like that [making accommodations] that they could have really solved the problem, or made the problem less difficult to deal with in the future, because there's a fundamental flaw in this situation. Until it's attacked at its roots, just having the Dalai Lama back is not going to really solve it because as much as His Holiness is loved and revered—and he is the most powerful and most symbolic of the Tibetan people, Tibetan culture, and Tibetan politics— just having the Dalai Lama, shall we say, in a way satisfied is not going to satisfy all Tibetans. That's something His Holiness is aware of, which the Chinese are also aware of. So it still continues to be a very complicated problem.

If Deng Xiaoping [1904–97, Communist leader of the People's Republic of China, 1977–97] and Hu Yaobang's policies had been a little more successful and if His Holiness had possibly returned for a visit, and if some kind of arrangement had worked out in the following years, by the mid-80s, at least the situation could have had the potential to improve year by year. But it didn't happen and it's not primarily because the Tibetans and the Chinese couldn't get along; I think it was primarily driven by what was happening in China, By 1987, after the first Tibetan demonstrations, actually what was happening was that the first of the student demonstrations were taking place in China, so there was a serious issue about internal Chinese reform and when that took a more conservative trend, then the Tibetan initiative became secondary, just by default.

Deng Xiaoping's Misguided Gamble

Arjia Rinpoché   Deng Xiaoping of course had his ideas: China opened, and so the monasteries reopened, and the monks returned to the monasteries. Compared to before, everybody in Tibet was kind of grateful that we had some kind of freedom there—that we could build our monasteries; if you requested it, you could become a monk, even though there's lots of work. Compared to before, it was freer, better.

At the time the first delegation from His Holiness came to Kumbum, I was there with some other rinpochés, and we hosted the first delegation. The first time they came to our monastery, they influenced us—it was very good. After many years, people had some kind of fear—they couldn't talk to them [the delegation] directly. Then, after a year, the second delegation came to our monastery. Then, later, everybody was relaxed and the situation in Tibet was not so bad: it was getting better and better.

Pema Chhinjor   When I went back to Tibet in 1992, I saw that the people wanted to know about His Holiness and when he would be coming back. Although many of them are unaware of the political situation, they have the greatest hope and faith and devotion to His Holiness. When I met with His Holiness, I reported to him that *he* is the only hope for the Tibetan people.

Ven. Lama Thubten Zopa Rinpoché   One lama [during Ven. Lama Zopa's third visit to Tibet in 2002] especially invited me and he expressed so much concern that independence should happen very quickly. Otherwise, all the older people will die and there will be only the very young people, without much education. The people can't wait for His Holiness to return. They hope and they are longing, like a person who has no food, who is *starving*, that one day there will be freedom in Tibet.

Sun Wade   Regarding religion, the Chinese central government's policy toward the Dalai Lama is quite clear: as long as he really abandons his stand for Tibetan independence and stops activities in splitting China, and declares in public that he recognizes Tibet as an inalienable part of China, and also recognizes Taiwan as part of the Chinese territories, we can have contact and talk with him.

Tsering Shakya   Two things China is slowly learning; first, before, they just bulldozed any sort of traditional thing and rebuilt. But now Tibet is backed abroad; if you destroy a hamlet in Lhasa and build a glass house, it doesn't create a good image abroad. Second, tourists are coming who don't like that. They think: we don't want to see just another glass house; we want to see traditional houses and architecture. And another thing, it antagonizes the local Tibetan population. So for practical concerns of politics, and also from international pressure, they have to change their policy and protect some of the local environment and the traditional architecture of Lhasa to maintain the unique characteristics of Tibet.

And there are other things, like the big monasteries and the Potala. They have been given lots of money that they have realized from UNESCO, and they can renovate, do things without having to spend a penny, because they can go to UNESCO and they can go to the Ford Foundation, which is willing to fund it. So they are saying: we don't have to spend money; we can just go to these organizations and they will help us.

Dr. Tenzin Tethong   In 1980, while I was in New York, I was also asked to be a member of the second delegation of a group of Tibetan exiles to visit Tibet. I was nominally the head of the second group of Tibetan representatives from Switzerland, the United Kingdom, Japan, and India, and we visited Tibet in the summer of 1980 representing His Holiness and the exile government at the invitation—or with the consent of—the Chinese government. It was at the time Deng Xiaoping was trying to correct many of the big mistakes of the past and find a way to bring about some resolution of the Tibetan issue. A lot of this had been done under the then–general secretary of the Chinese Communist Party, Hu Yaobang. I visited Tibet with the delegation and we had a very good tour—first-hand knowledge of what was going on in Tibet, or what had gone on in recent years—and also connected with Tibetans all over the country.

We were directly able to communicate with Tibetans everywhere because, first of all, we spent most of our time in fairly remote parts of eastern Tibet, more than in Central Tibet, and each day, wherever we arrived, we immediately went out into the town or village and just met up with people. And, of course, wherever people knew that we were coming, large numbers were already waiting to meet us. Everywhere people came, and in many, many places people were immediately in tears because for the last twenty years or so most of the Tibetans in these areas had either experienced extreme violence or had been traumatized under fear of the police or the military. Tibetans had gone through cycles of violence, repression, manipulation, and fear, and they had nobody to turn to. And then, of course, in every town or village we knew there was a serious extent of destruction, so we said, "Where's the monastery? Where's the temple?" Almost everywhere there was nothing but ruins. Out of some sixty-five hundred monasteries and temples, only about a dozen have survived.

The only thing that didn't work out was toward the end, when we were in Lhasa. Tibetans by the thousands turned up everywhere we went, and it became so disruptive that the Chinese officials panicked and eventually kicked us out of the city before our scheduled stay was formally over. And they did it without any sort of proper discussion. They accused us of being responsible for "instigating" these large turnouts, and there were other, more vocal and obvious anti-Chinese sentiments expressed at that time.

Why Did the Chinese Allow the Delegation into Tibet?

Dr. Tenzin Tethong   Ever since the Chinese decided to go into Tibet, they knew it was a very complicated political problem that really needed serious attention. But, for whatever reasons, they were unable to do it, so when the Cultural Revolution came to an end, Deng Xiaoping and Hu Yaobang knew they had to change a lot of other things in China. In that state of mind, Tibet was obviously one of those issues they thought could be handled quite easily, so they were somewhat decisive in saying, "We're going to change it."

Around the time we went to Tibet, Hu Yaobang had actually made a secret visit to Tibet himself—he sent out his own personal staff, in fact, to do some minor investigation. After that he had said publicly, in Tibet, that in the last twenty years or so, the Chinese seemed to have done nothing much for Tibet—in fact, in some cases, they might have regressed. Hu Yaobang went so far as to say he wanted 80 or 90 percent of the Chinese cadres to leave Tibet in the next few years, and he apologized for all the wrong that had gone on in Tibet.

Now, on another level, throughout the sixties and seventies the whole of Chinese society was the victim of their own propaganda machine: in that propaganda environment they had always been told that the Tibetans had welcomed the liberation, that changes were taking place for the better every day in Tibet, in every sphere of life, and that Tibetans were now free of superstition and religion—becoming Marxists and socialists and modern and scientific—and that the Tibetans were ever grateful for the great social and political progress in changes that happened to Tibet. A lot of that was said generally by their propaganda machine and then, in particular instances, local Chinese officials would send this kind of report to more central authorities just to show that they were doing their job well.

When they decided to try and resolve the issue by saying okay, maybe the Dalai Lama's representative can come, some of the key people in Beijing thought: There's nothing to be embarrassed about letting them come in because we've probably changed the country for the better—where there were no roads before, there are roads; where there were no schools, there are schools; we have electricity; we have modernized—so they were very confident. One example that we use very often is that in the case of the first delegation—and also when we were visiting—in some of the northeastern parts of Tibet, local Tibetans were told by Chinese officials: an exile group is going to be visiting the area and they represent the Dalai Lama, but there's nothing to be upset about. In fact, we want you to greet them graciously and not do anything rash—no protests or stone-throwing or anything crude. The Chinese officials believed that the Tibetans would protest the Dalai Lama's representative.

In reality, it was not only just the opposite; it was the *extreme* opposite: everywhere, people came out and hugged and touched, certainly in the first group. One of the members of the first delegation was His Holiness's younger brother, and in our third group—the one that came right after us—His Holiness's younger sister was also in the group. In Lhasa, wherever we visited in the city, thousands of people turned up—early morning, late night—and it was getting a bit disruptive. And then when we visited the ruins of Kumbum Monastery on the third or fourth day, something like six thousand Tibetans turned up without Chinese permission; they had come in eighty trucks, which Tibetan truck drivers had just taken without official permission. So they immediately thought this was a sign of some kind of organization at work—and some kind of deliberately planned thing—and that made them very nervous.

Professor Jonathan Mirsky Including all the Tibetans I met [during a visit to Tibet in 1990] who were in the occupation government, the moment they would get away from a Chinese, these Tibetan cadres would all tell you that they thought the Dalai Lama was a great man and that they despised the Chinese. When I first went in 1981, it was absolutely illegal to have a photograph of the Dalai Lama, and almost every Tibetan one would meet, no matter how humble, had on his person, somewhere, a little photograph of the Dalai Lama. I made it a point to speak to as many Tibetans as possible—any Tibetan who could speak Chinese I spoke with, and I traveled around a bit—and I never met anybody who wasn't enthusiastic about the Dalai Lama, ever.

Pema Chhinjor [In 1992] I visited a school in my home town, in far eastern Tibet. One day when I was there, the children sang a song about His Holiness. I wrote the words down and gave them to him. More than a hundred people in the town gave me their names to present to His Holiness for his blessing. I told His Holiness that the Tibetans under Chinese rule are stronger than the Tibetans in exile. They have not lost their identity or culture. My impression is that the Chinese have not been able to win the hearts of the Tibetan people, with a few exceptions—those who work for the Chinese administration. The people I met in Tibet did not ask for presents; they only wanted pictures of the Dalai Lama.

Sister Mary Margaret Funk We went as tourists [to Tibet in 1995], not as monks and nuns, so we were treated normally. Tibet is a large mass—one-third of the United States—but it doesn't have the population. I would say, to China's credit, there's nobody starving there—they really do have a way of distributing food. They just expanded into that country.

We went to sixteen monasteries there. For the most part—maybe out of the sixteen, only three of them were really functioning as monasteries. The rest were just there for show—they had some monks there, but there was no real cycle of prayer and teachings. It was just being reconstructed, and they were even using Tibetans to reconstruct these places that they had torn down. But they were seeing these monasteries as tourist places, so they needed to get them back up into condition. We also found that the artifacts were plundered—the real things weren't there anymore, just cheap Buddhas, statues and whatever. Now, that being said, the nomads were the real thing, and they were still doing their pilgrimages and their circumambulations around the *stupas* [repositories for relics]; they had a light in their eyes that was so beautiful. But as for monks and nuns, we only went to three places that we think were authentic. There are many, many stories about how they suffered and how they were all trying to get out of there.

Ven. Lama Thubten Zopa Rinpoché   Tibet once had spiritual life. It was an incredible place, like a flower. But when I went back to Tibet—I went there three times after the Chinese communist government took it over, in 1986, 1987, and most recently in 2002—there was a huge change. I went to see some of the places where our Mahayana tradition was born. The third time, I spent two months there. I went to Amdo. I brought many books. They [the Chinese authorities] were very, very strict: you would come to the border and you had to go with a guide. I think that the bus drivers were also responsible to watch. The old people were chanting and they understood each other, but the young people were the guides and they were very strict—they were actually spying.

Pema Chhinjor   I saw many changes in Lhasa [in 1992]. You have to buy tickets to enter the Potala Palace. The Chinese have completely Sinoized everything, but they have failed to develop the country. In contrast, the British ruled Tibet for two hundred years and established universities, colleges, hospitals, and good roads.

Sister Mary Margaret Funk   When we were in Lhasa, out of every ten people, seven were Chinese. In Lhasa, they've kept the Tibetan quarter. That is pretty authentic, with a lot of open fruit markets, and the women wear their traditional Tibetan aprons and things. The rest of Lhasa is just a city. And the Potala is just another tourist area, with a Chinese restaurant on top. The Jokhang, which is the main temple in the main square of Lhasa, is still a place of pilgrimage. I suppose if there is one authentic place in the whole city, it's still the Jokhang Temple. But it's just a city now, and they have not done a good job with pollution. The altitude is so high, the cars don't have emission controls, and everybody is smoking—they had unlimited cigarettes and booze for anybody there. It was pretty sad. A lot of people were very ill, frankly, and they had a lot of problems with hygiene—I can't imagine how you can get plumbing to work at that altitude, either. It's the old culture living right alongside flushing toilets, so a lot of things weren't working very well. On the way into Lhasa , they've set up a kind of "Western Quarter," where there's a Holiday Inn. The Chinese put the most money into that little place—it's almost five miles out of town, really—and if you don't really know Lhasa, people think they are in Lhasa, and that looks real good. But it's not accessible by the people. There is much trouble, for example, with the educational system there. Every child has to learn Chinese, then they have to learn English, and the third language is Tibetan. So, frankly, it really is genocide of the culture.

Harry Wu   Today the government in Beijing has been training so many Tibetan-speaking people to become members of the party. Many of the people running the Laogai camps are Tibetan; they have replaced Chinese communists with Tibetan communists. But I found out that even these people, the communist members, when they hear "Dalai Lama" they will stop, even if they are communists; he's such a powerful figure there. That's why I tried to suggest a couple of years ago that he just go back there. He would change history.

    The situation has changed; religion is coming back. The people learned from their experience that communism fought God; the people don't trust them anymore. As human beings, they are seeking their faith. Millions of people—Christians, Buddhists, even Falun Gong are seeking the faith. They have to have something there to convert them. That's the current situation. If we don't support them, if we don't find this main courage, we've lost all of them.

Professor Jonathan Mirsky   The Chinese government has behaved really horribly in Tibet, and all of their reasons for doing this are lies. I have a long interest in Tibetan history that goes back to my academic period as a classical Chinese historian, so I'm completely on the side of the Tibetans, *completely.* I'm pretty pessimistic as to whether this is going to come off; I don't think it will. Even the author of *A Tibetan Revolutionary,* who says that he's a party member and thinks that Tibet should be a part of China, when he describes how the Chinese have behaved in Tibet, that really is it—they've behaved very, very badly. And they've had a lasting effect from which, I think, Tibet will never recover in any regard—culturally and physically. They're slowly corroding Tibetan civilization; they're turning Tibetans into people who have lost whatever kind of special somewhat spiritual quality they may have had and they're turning them into what they're turning their own people into: people who are interested in making a lot of money. If you go to Lhasa now, I understand that there are a lot of whores and a lot of bars.

I think that this is what animates the Dalai Lama; he knows that within another twenty-five years, the Tibetans will have been dissolved in a very huge Chinese presence, that whatever it was that has made Tibet distinctive will really become a minority phenomenon, and that the Chinese will have just swamped the place, as they to a certain extent already had when I was there.

Dr. Tenzin Tethong   I think that if His Holiness were able to return to Tibet in the near future, and if the circumstances of his return were very clear-cut and conditions really become quite stable and promising, there's a very good chance that a large number of Tibetan exiles would return to Tibet, because the possibility of having a more normal and less stressful life is going to be there. Most Tibetans who are in exile—primarily in India and Nepal—have not necessarily totally adapted to the larger Indian or Nepalese society. Most are still living within Tibetan communities, so there is a very good possibility that they would feel more comfortable back in Tibet. And, of course, almost all of the exiles still continue to have relations with family and hometowns in Tibet, which have been revived within the last ten or fifteen years, so there's a very good chance that large numbers in India and Nepal will return to Tibet.

Among the Tibetans in Europe and the United States, there's a good chance—maybe it's not as large as those in the Indian subcontinent—that a good, healthy percentage of Tibetans will return. But I don't think you can expect every Tibetan to return because many Tibetans have now discovered the larger world and will continue to live outside.

Have the Chinese Made a Mistake in Not Allowing the Dalai Lama to Return to Lhasa under Specific Conditions?

Robert Ford   Yes, of course; that is, in a sense, self-evident. But at the same time, the Chinese approach is quite different: there is this worldwide support for His Holiness—regrettably, not worldwide *government* support for him—in the sense that people are prepared to say: Look, these govern-ments don't seem to be prepared—even my own government, in Britain, doesn't seem to be prepared—to stand up and say this is wrong. All they seem to say is: "Well, you know, they base their complaints on human rights." But it's a much more profound problem: this is a people who have been denied everything—freedom of worship and so forth. They have been persecuted and maltreated. And, of course, they have lost a country. But the West, generally, doesn't seem to do very much of a concrete nature. I realize there are problems about this; I'm not suggesting that one should engage in military action—I wouldn't dream of that. But I would have thought that some form of pressure of one kind or another, entirely peace-ful—and this would accord with His Holiness's views—could have been brought to bear on the Chinese to get them to change their ways.

Sun Wade   Let me answer briefly about the future of the so-called Mid-dle Way. In the past, the Dalai Lama has put forward some so-called sug-gestions and proposals regarding the Tibetan issue. But the fact of those suggestions is that it's basically distorted. It's basic historic fact that Tibet has been an inseparable part of the Chinese territory since ancient times. Also, those proposals negated the system of regional ethnic autonomy, which has been in place in Tibet for many years. In September 1987, the Dalai Lama visited the United States, and in the congressional human rights commission he talked about the so-called Five Point Peace Plan, which is actually aimed at splitting the Chinese territory. And again, in June 1988, the Dalai Lama issued the so-called Seventeen Points proposal, in Strasbourg, France, at a meeting of the European Union. Those propos-als and suggestions constituted the so-called core content of the Middle Way. But the essence of those proposals and suggestions is to actually turn the realization of Tibetan independence into two steps. One step is to real-ize their so-called high degree of autonomy so as to resume the Dalai Lama's rule over Tibet; the second step is to realize independence for Tibet—they would say that they were realizing autonomy for independence.

Continuing Chinese Intransigence

When we called Sun Wade at the Washington, D.C., embassy of the Peo-ple's Republic of China seeking our interview, before agreeing to speak with us, he asked, "Why do you want to write about someone so unimpor-tant as the Dalai Lama?"

Sir Malcolm Rifkind   That's the official line: the Chinese position all along has had to be that the Dalai Lama is an insignificant, irrelevant individual who represents no one but himself, because if they were to cease to take that view and to actually give him the legitimacy of being a national leader, they have to then make some offer to him that is consistent with that status. So they have no choice. As long as they refuse to have any genuine autonomy for Tibet, they cannot acknowledge that Tibet's leader is indeed the spokesman of the Tibetan people. That is the box they have locked themselves into.

Sun Wade   There are people in the West who have actually been trying to criticize China in the name of religion and human rights. It's very simple. They use the Dalai Lama to criticize and defame China. This is a policy the Dalai Lama himself has decided. The policy of the central government toward him is quite clear, so the ball is in his court; he has to decide what he is going to do. We have our policy: we can have contact and talk with him about the future, but under certain conditions—that he has to abandon his stand for Tibetan independence and stop activities that threaten China.

It's certainly not helpful, actually, for those Western governments to invite the Dalai Lama to visit their countries. In the first place, we have on a number of occasions over the years lodged representations with the United States about the Dalai Lama's visits, because the United States has recognized Tibet is part of China and has been saying that they will not recognize Tibetan independence. So it's quite natural for us to ask them not to allow the Dalai Lama to engage in some of his activities in their territories.

Patrick French   With the benefit of hindsight, if the Dalai Lama had managed to cut a deal at the time when Deng Xiaoping had a personal interest in the Tibetan issue, in the early-to-mid-eighties, and if he'd been able to somehow negotiate his own return, that would have been to Tibet's benefit. But what I argue is that the well-meaning promotion of Tibet and the espousal of Tibet as a celebrity cause to some extent has pushed the Chinese government away from negotiations; it's made them increasingly nervous. They're actually trying to take on the matter of the political shape that would be needed to persuade the Dalai Lama in the present circumstances to return.

Wouldn't It Be a Great Public Relations Coup for the Chinese
to Simply Invite the Dalai Lama to Return to Tibet and Give
Him Whatever He Wants, Short of Independence?

Sir Malcolm Rifkind   Sure. Until 1997, it would have been inconceivable because China was a totalitarian system, and totalitarian systems do not share power and cannot conceive any independent autonomy within their framework. It would be rather like expecting Stalin to have allowed genuine autonomy within the Soviet Union, or Hitler in the Third Reich. What has potentially changed that position, although at the moment there is no obvious cause for optimism, is two systems in one country—that if Hong Kong can be part of China, with its different set of values and a different system, and if the Chinese are trying to tempt Taiwan back on a similar basis, then it is no longer inconceivable.

Why can China not allow Tibet genuine autonomy as long as the Tibetans are prepared to accept that they ultimately remain part of China? That may one day be an option, and if there is a solution to this problem, that's the way it'll go. It ought to be easier with Hong Kong as a precedent than it would have seemed possible ten or fifteen years ago. We just do not know what the future holds, and the Dalai Lama obviously takes the view that in the survival of his people, the only power he's got is the power of publicity; he knows that the Chinese hate the publicity that is constantly being provided by their regime in Tibet. And by maintaining that, which he is in a uniquely powerful position to do, he ensures that the issue cannot be just smothered away.

Tsering Shakya   Some Tibetans would argue that the Dalai Lama has actually failed because Tibet has become secondary to him—that Buddhism and spirituality has become the priority. So he does not engage in a very overt political campaign. That's not good for Tibet. Buddhism becomes central to his campaign, and although he doesn't say he's evangelizing, in a way, the spread of Buddhism is his main concern. So this is one of the internals of Tibetan political debate—that having a religious figure is your religion or your country's issue. Therefore, those people argue that we need a secular institution to say: put your country first and religion second. So this is problematic. Whereas the Dalai Lama will say, "Whatever is good for Buddhism is good for Tibet," some might say that is not the case.

Will China Eventually Demand of the West a Moment of Truth Regarding the Dalai Lama?

Sir Malcolm Rifkind   The Chinese, as with so many other issues, play a very, very long game. Nobody does seem to have any effective political control in Tibet, so the status quo from their point of view is livable. That will only change if political reform in China as a whole recommences in a fundamental way. Then, if you get real political liberalization in China at some stage, as part of that process Tibet could be a major beneficiary.

Father Laurence Freeman   He's got more authority being in exile. What I think is particularly painful for him is that he sees what's happening in Tibet; he meets with Tibetan nuns who have made that long trek across the Himalayas whose comment was that what kept them going as they walked through the snow was their love for the Dalai Lama. He meets with them and he just listens, and that probably does more to cure them than therapy or any amount of counseling could do. Their love and devotion for him and his pure attention to them, his compassion for them, is a powerful combination. That is a great cross for him to carry. But he said, "You know, I've learned a lot, I've seen a lot, and I've done a lot that I wouldn't have been able to do if I was in Tibet." He has expanded his intellectual and personal horizons. I think if he had a choice he would have stayed. But even with that kind of detachment, he could say that it's a tragedy. Yet out of that tragedy has come something quite remarkable in the last fifty years.

Dr. Chaim Peri   The Chinese will finally understand what they missed here because nobody is going to fight; nobody is going to take anything from them; they are just going to get an additional spiritual component that can attract the West to them. It has significance in terms of their economy, of how they are viewed in the world—now that the Olympics are coming, they're thinking of Beijing.

They should just get up one morning and say: We embrace you; you are our brothers and sisters. Come back; take your temple in Lhasa; have your autonomy; have your local government. Why are they being so stupid? If the world wants their inspiration, why shouldn't China? China is part of the world. That should be the message: embrace them; show the world they're part of you.

PART V

Looking Ahead

Chapter Eleven

DIALOGUES

In recent years, the Dalai Lama has engaged in religious dialogue with Christian, Jewish, and Muslim theologians and scholars, and he has participated in discussions with eminent Western scientists.

Rt. Rev. William E. Swing   His interest in interreligious dialogue starts at a pragmatic level. He is a man whose mission is to win to his cause, which is both secular and religious, the support of people worldwide. If he only appealed to Tibetan Buddhists, he wouldn't get anywhere. Initially, it was a matter of getting to know people of other religions. Now, I think, he feels genuine sympathy with people who say their prayers, wish to commune with God, or want to serve the poor, so this second layer would be finding kindred spirits. And a third layer is helping the world at a time when interfaith relations become a necessity. Thus, what the world is looking for, he is already doing. He has been catapulted into being a role model for interfaith relations.

Following an initial meeting among the Dalai Lama and Jewish scholars held in a Buddhist monastery in Washington, New Jersey, a delegation of eight Jewish religious personalities and academics arrived in Dharamsala in the late afternoon of October 23, 1990. The following morning began a memorable six-day dialogue with the Dalai Lama. The group, housed at Kashmir Cottage, a modest guest house with a memorable view from its porch of the Kanga Valley, consisted of: Paul Mendes-Flohr, a Brooklyn, New York–born Jew who had emigrated to Israel and now lives in Jerusalem, where he is a distinguished professor of modern Hebrew thought, who brought with him as a gift for His Holiness a Torah, a facsimile of the kind used by Sephardic Jews of Southern Europe, Asia, and the Middle East; Rabbi Joy Levitt, a Reconstructionist from New York; Dr. Blu and Rabbi Irving Greenberg, also New Yorkers and prominent members of the Orthodox community who were criticized in some Jewish circles for consorting with idol worshippers, or as a local Jewish publication put it, "Dillying with the Dalai"; Professor Nathan Katz of Florida; Rabbi Jonathan Ober-Man, an English-born resident of Los Angeles; the Polish-born Rabbi Zalman Schachter-Shalomi; and Dr. Moshe Waldoks, who had earned his doctorate in Jewish history but forsook academia and embarked on a new career as the coeditor of *The Big Book of Jewish Humor* and as a lecturer, storyteller, and humorist. Also present in Dharamsala, but not participants in the specific dialogue sessions, were several Jewish converts to Buddhism.

––––––––––

Dr. Blu Greenberg   The Cummings Foundation had arranged the trip. We were kind of concerned about kosher food, but we knew that we were going to work it out, even if it meant just bringing along our cans of tuna fish and boxes of matzos for the two-week period. But they were so accommodating that they actually koshered the kitchen before we got there.

Ven. Thubten Chodron   That was [done by] Rinchen Khandro [Choegyal, the proprietor of the cottage]. She has a staff there and is very concerned that their guests be treated properly. I don't know how much she understood the reasons for *kashrut*, but I'm sure that after they came she began to understand it. They were certainly willing to do whatever they could to make their guests comfortable. They realized that people have different dietary restrictions.

I think that some of the Jews were surprised at seeing the Buddha images and people bowing down to images. I spent some time with them, trying to explain that we're not bowing down to idols, so we're not breaking one of the Ten Commandments—that it's not a piece of glass we're expressing regard for; it symbolizes what the Buddha's qualities are, something that people from every religion and nationality can respect. Some of them relaxed a bit, even though at first glance it looked to them like we were worshipping idols.

A Dilemma for the Jews: Calling the Dalai Lama "Your Holiness"

Ven. Thubten Chodron   They had a whole big meeting about what to call him. The thing about "His Holiness" is that the translation of the Tibetan word by which the Tibetans address him is not "His Holiness." It's just an English term that somebody picked up. His Holiness didn't say, "People should call me Your Holiness," but, somehow, people got quite hung up with that and all the ramifications of the Pope being called "His Holiness" and what that does to Jews. They eventually decided on a Jewish term that was a term of respect for somebody from another religion. From His Holiness's side, he didn't care beans about what they called him; that is just not important to him.

Dr. Blu Greenberg   I was concerned over the phrase "His Holiness" and those who referred to him as "His Holiness."

They [monks of The Conference of All Buddhist Monks] all came in and prostrated themselves before him. But in his words at the conference, it was a human being talking, it wasn't God speaking. There was a wall there in a certain sense between the way they were treating him and the way he saw himself—not that he placed himself behind a wall but that he didn't let that obeisance penetrate to his existence, or consciousness; it was his laughter and his sense of humor and his glee and his cheerfulness [that came through]. Also he had a bit of a cold and his nose was dripping. Somehow it just made him so *human*. That would never happen with an august figure who thinks that he's God. And nobody was wiping his nose for him.

The Exchanges

Rabbi Irving Greenberg   One of the things that struck me—and struck us in the context of the aides and the assistants—was that he had a whole group, some of whom had undergone Westernization, some were well-trained, others less-trained, and they were the key aides because they knew

how to handle most of the Western issues such as correspondence, administration, and bureaucracy. As we talked about Jews and modernity, he realized that some of these people, who, like him, had gone through the
Westernization process, the modernization process, were becoming more
sophisticated, more aware. He still very much praises the whole tradition of
Buddhism, even though the West has influenced it. One example is this
God question. At one point in the process of an exchange, someone asked
him, "Do you think of yourself as God?" and he said, "I am not God; I'm a
monk, I'm a teacher." And the joke—I thought it was the funniest thing I
had heard, the answer of the week—was, "I went in twenty years from
being God to being human; I've grown a lot in the process." It is true; he
has grown enormously. Some of the others around him have grown also, but
clearly he is the top in terms of having absorbed a lot of that philosophy and
other things, of being much more sophisticated about religion, much more
able to articulate at higher levels.

The Dalai Lama's Favorite Exchange

Rabbi Irving Greenberg   The one that the Dalai Lama most enjoyed was
by Zalman Schachter because it was on angels. The two of them were into
angels and he [Schachter] overdosed on angels, but he [the Dalai Lama]
loved it because, as I came to see, Buddhist ideas begin to be at a higher
and higher level of being as you become more and more enlightened. So
angels played off that [the enlightenment] and he probably confused it in
his mind with that. Be that as it may, they *loved* angels.

Ven. Thubten Chodron   That got blown way, way out of proportion. Zalman Schachter brought up this thing about angels and His Holiness just
asked about it because in Buddhism there are certain beings who have
high spiritual attainment who can help practitioners, but they're not
angels. But there was that one little interchange and people just glommed
onto it and made this big deal about it and I don't think, personally speaking, that it was very important. It was like: okay, there are angels in
Judaism and Christianity and there are beings who help you in your practice, but that's not the real meaning of the religion.

Rabbi Irving Greenberg   The exchange that had the most impact on
them was Blu's presentation, which dealt with the home and family. Let's
face it, the leadership of the Tibetans is celibate monks; they never had a

clue as to a home or family being an important agency of religious teaching and socialization. They just didn't have it, from what I gathered. They were desperately looking for both ritual and theology that could help them—that was the Dalai Lama's concern. There's a whole area in which they have little or nothing to compare, so there was this idea: have Shabbat and they can learn. They were genuinely interested in the idea of developing some potential ritual, and that was the idea of encompassing what an orthodox Shabbat and family experience is. So they came. I think it really knocked their socks off, but in a good sense.

Ven. Thubten Chodron   The people I know in the Tibetan community were very, very happy with the dialogue and it gave them many ideas about maintaining their own culture. Of course, in the two religions, one being monastic-oriented, one being family-oriented, there are some big differences about maintaining the religious culture, but the Tibetans had a very positive experience.

My take on the six-day dialogue was that it was very beneficial for both sides. His Holiness was interested in the Jewish experience of living in exile and the applicability of some of what the Jews did to maintain their culture and their religion in exile—how to apply that to the Tibetan situation. And for the Jews, it was, perhaps, the first time they had met with people from another religion who had no prejudice against them and did not even know what a Jew was. In Jewish interreligious dialogue, there is such a history with Christians—the Holocaust and all of this business—that they always come in a little bit defensive. But the Tibetans had never even heard of the Jews and they were like: Who *are* you and what's your experience? What do you believe in? How do you run your culture, and how do you live with your families? It really took them all very much by surprise.

Subsequent Interfaith Dialogues

On November 11, 1998, Rabbi A. James Rudin, then director of the American Jewish Committee's Department of Interreligious Affairs, met the Dalai Lama when they both participated in an interfaith seminar under the aegis of Seton Hill, a Catholic women's college in Greensburg, Pennsylvania. The seminar took place before a capacity audience of 1,248 at the Palace Theater in downtown Greensburg, where there were welcoming banners and flags as well as a heavy police presence. The late Fred Rogers, a resident of Pittsburgh and an ordained Presbyterian minister, better

known as the lovable host of the PBS television program, *Mr. Rogers'*
Neighborhood, served as master of ceremonies. Dialogue participants, in
addition to Rabbi Rudin, were Bishop Anthony Bosco, a Roman Catholic,
and Imam Abdul Mawjoud, president of the Islamic Center of Pittsburgh.

In his address to the gathering, the Dalai Lama expressed his great
hope for the twenty-first century, displayed his self-deprecating humor in
referring to his "broken English," and preached his message of love and
compassion, warning that human activities "if isolated from human affection, become mechanized and can really bring disaster—even *religion*
becomes dirty."

Rabbi A. James Rudin   The Dalai Lama had a lot of security with him,
which surprised me in a small Pennsylvania town like Greensburg—
remember, this was before 2001—and it was just a typical interreligious
function. The Dalai Lama was told I was a rabbi. He was very excited
about meeting a rabbi—I wasn't the first one; he said he had met lots
of Jews—and he said all the right things. I was not too forthcoming. I
wasn't nasty, I just didn't gush over him. I said, "I'm very pleased to meet
you," but I didn't use any title; I just said "*you*." And then the fun really
began because one of the nuns from Seton Hill College [Sister Marlene
Mondalek, vice president, Sisters of Charity of Seton Hill] said, "Rabbi,
when you get up and walk to get to the lectern, you're going to cross in
front of the vision line of the Dalai Lama. You should turn, put your hands
together, and bow." And I said—I was very nice—"I can't do that; [as a
Jew] I can't bow because I don't bow to God." I don't think she quite
understood that. But the Imam was *thrilled*. He came over to me and
shook my hand and said, "I can't do that either, Rabbi. Thank you for
making it possible [not to bow]; my English is not so good, and you made
it easier for me." Sure enough, when it was my turn to speak, I just got up
and walked to the lectern as I always do and I read Psalm 107 [giving
thanks to the Lord for delivery of the exiled and downtrodden from their
oppressors], sat down, and that was the end of it. Then the Imam got up,
read a couple of lines from the Koran, and walked back to his seat. The
Dalai Lama never said anything and he didn't look hurt that the Imam and
I, a rabbi, walked by him; he didn't seem to care. The Catholic bishop did,
in fact, lift his hands in the "rooftop" position and nodded to the Dalai
Lama. I don't think anybody in the audience noticed anything one way or
the other because everybody's eyes were on Mr. Rogers—the students
were more excited about him than they were about the Dalai Lama; they

had grown up with Mr. Rogers. The nun's action was almost preemptive: she didn't want to offend a visitor; it was probably hospitality. I was thinking about it when I was on the plane coming home from Pittsburgh the next day. She was anticipating what he [the Dalai Lama] would want—that this is what we should be doing—or maybe she saw it being done in a movie.

The product that he was selling in Greensburg that day—that's the only time I've heard him and I suspect it's the same message over and over again to those kinds of audiences—was a very appealing message. It was not demanding. You didn't have to pray five times a day and face Mecca; you didn't have to face Jerusalem or keep kosher or be circumcised or segregate yourself from men or women, or learn another language—Arabic, Hebrew, Latin. It was just a sweet, kind, straightforward message. I was a little upset that some of the people there thought it was more profound than it really was. But some of the best preaching is simplicity. It was clear that it was *who* was preaching, not *what* was being preached. You don't have to proselytize and you don't have to be proselytized yourself—you don't have to go into the public schools like Franklin Graham [the son of and successor to the Rev. Billy Graham] and get converts for Christ—but had a local Buddhist monk from Pittsburgh come out to the campus with the same word-for-word message, there wouldn't have been a big crowd; there wouldn't have been police protection; there wouldn't have been flags. And, of course, America is a country *soaked* in celebrity worship and he's a celebrity, as was Mr. Rogers. The students were very attentive, and there was nothing in it that anybody could object to. If that was Buddhism, I can see its appeal because it's a nice, legitimate thought: do the nice things—treat people decently; be kind and compassionate; be good to yourself.

Dialogue with Christian Religious Groups

Rt. Rev. William E. Swing   He is familiar with Christian theology; he knows about Good Friday and the Cross, about resurrection and the coming of the Holy Spirit. He will make contact with values such as suffering and compassion, which Christians and Buddhists share. If you take out the specifics of the Christian story and just look at the headings, he would be very much at home with the same kinds of headings—compassion, suffering, oneness—that Christians talk about.

Preparing for the Dalai Lama's Participation

Sister Mary Margaret Funk   It's a nightmare—in *every* way. And the first time, we regretted terribly the fact that he didn't show up. Some participants said, "It's a blessing when the Dalai Lama comes and it's a blessing when he *doesn't* show." The free flow of dialogue was certainly much more active when he wasn't there because he is such an authority and you defer. Again, as you learn how to do it, you anticipate problems and you get ahead of them. Also, they [the Dalai Lama's staff] are better at it too—they now send out a packet to you that you wouldn't believe; it takes away any guesswork. They've had a big problem in the last eight years involving huckstering, people making the Dalai Lama a business enterprise, and that has really insulted him. You have to promise that you'll make no financial gain from the Dalai Lama's participation. But it's a nightmare peoplewise because everybody wants to see him despite the fact that he's been here many times. Also, his teachings have just gotten stronger and stronger and better and better. It's kind of a cumulative thing: if you've read many of his books, you see the depth of that man. And then you start listening to his teachings. He's probably still the very best teacher of our lifetime. So it's all worth it.

Father Laurence Freeman   The challenge that he offers, and I found very stimulating in my own dialogue [The Good Heart Seminar conducted in London in 1994], is to understand the real nature of dialogue, that if you go into dialogue with a view to conversion, then it's not dialogue; it *can't* be. If you go into dialogue just with a view to exchanging ideas, that's discussion, but it's not really dialogue. If you go into dialogue the way I think he can, which is to try to see reality from the perspective of the other person, have an exchange of viewpoints, that is where dialogue becomes very extraordinary and important for the future of the planet. That concept of dialogue doesn't apply only to religion, it applies to the Middle East crisis, the problem in Northern Ireland, and so on. That's why after Good Heart got the ball rolling, we then decided to work on this program called "Way of Peace, " a three-year program that followed up on something he said at the Good Heart seminar about the different forms of dialogue, pilgrimage, practice, retreating together, and working together for a better world. And so I said, "Why don't we do that—these different forms of dialogue?" He said, "Yes, let's do it," and we set the meeting in Dharamsala.

The first year, we did a pilgrimage. He invited Christian meditators—

about two hundred of us ended up going—and we ended up meditating together each morning with dialogue in the morning and afternoon. It was wonderful. At the beginning of that first session, after the meditation, I was in a car with him, going to the retreat center where we were having the dialogue. We were passing some of the old Tibetan stalls along the way and I saw the Tibetan thangkas [Tibetan paintings] hanging there, and so I said to him—we were talking about the Tibetan refugees and how they made their living—"I want to buy one of those thangkas to take back to our center in London." He looked at me a little strangely and we drove on. When we arrived, he made the presentation to me for our community of this big tube, for which I thanked him. Then he opened the tube and inside was a thangka beautifully wrapped in Tibetan cloth! As I unrolled it, he said, "Can you guess what it is?" I said, "A Buddha, or a wheel." It wasn't. It was the Nativity, the Christ, and it had been beautifully painted; it's the birth of Christ conceived and painted in the Tibetan form by Tibetan monks in Dharamsala—they were probably working from a Christmas card—so you have Tibetan angels and you have yaks instead of oxen. What it showed in terms of dialogue was seeing it through the symbols and through the eyes of the other.

Dialogue with Muslim Communities

Dr. Alexander Berzin   His Holiness met with Dr. [Tirmiziou] Diallo, the Sufi leader from Guinea, in West Africa, who was very interested in discussing with him the role of compassion in Sufism, and in Islam in general. His Holiness found this aspect very inspiring. His Holiness is basically concerned with general understanding, and so this type of contact enables him to forge these bridges: if people identify one or another religious group just in terms of their extremist fanatics, then this is a great injustice to that religion or that group of people. But what His Holiness always looks for is the common denominator among religions, or among different philosophies, and the common denominator with Islam is—as well as with any religion—working for the welfare of the world. And so he reaffirms that by not looking at Muslims in a paranoid way as some people might, especially these days—that openness and recognition that mainstream Islam is not at all the same as the small fundamentalist, fanatic branch of it. The same is true about Christianity or Islam or Judaism or Hinduism or any religion. So this is the main focus.

Scientific Dialogues

Adam Engle   His interest in science is an outgrowth of his teachings on compassion. Buddhism is a path of liberation, but, unlike other theologies, it is not based on the existence of a supernatural power. Rather, it is based on an understanding on the nature of reality, using that understanding to produce a knowledge base for liberation. In that sense, it is really a science; it is observation, testing, and empiricism, with a focus on reaching a state of enlightenment.

Dr. Thubten Jinpa Langri   Buddhism, like any other ancient philosophic and spiritual tradition, has its own worldview, including an understanding of the physical world. His Holiness on a number of occasions has stated that if certain aspects of the Buddhist understanding of the world turn out to be contrary to empirical evidence that we find in science, we need to change. In Buddhism, the approach is not so much the authority of scripture. Rather, reason and empirical evidence supersede scriptural authority.

Mind and Life Conferences

Adam Engle   I consult with him in person on a periodic basis, in Dharamsala. I will meet with him for about an hour, brief him on the institute's strategy, and receive his counsel. He is not really going to do a lot of preparatory reading, partly because the materials are not written in Tibetan. But he has accumulated knowledge through the years of dialogue. He has said privately to me that the work we are doing is too important to be dependent on any one person, including *himself*, that we should establish the work in a way that the dialogue and collaboration would go forward even when he was no longer able to participate.

Ven. Thubten Chodron   I've been to some of the Mind and Life conferences, where he interacts with Western scientists. I have observed his curiosity, open-mindedness, willingness to learn, and his nondogmatic attitude. His Holiness says, very openly, that if science can prove something that the Buddhists said was wrong, then, since we're looking for the truth—we're not just speaking to build an institution or substantiate some dogma—we have to follow what's true and change our position. So his spirit of inquiry with the scientists I found very, very nice.

Dr. Thubten Jinpa Langri   I have been with His Holiness at the Mind and Life meetings since they began in 1987. I don't know if people are intimidated by him, but although he is physically not a large man, his presence is *huge*. That is because when at a meeting he is totally absorbed, which is a rare quality, particularly in the modern world, where we tend to be involved in the so-called multitasking approach. It is rare to find a person who is fully focused and engaged at a given moment. This can be quite unnerving, particularly for those coming from a Western academic background. His Holiness will be following a scientific presentation and, all of a sudden, in the course of a description of an experiment, he will interrupt and say, "Why don't you do *this*?" And the scientists will be taken aback and say, "That is *exactly* the next step we took."

Adam Engle   At the Mind and Life meetings, there is what I would call a "first-time experience." Each scientist has the opportunity to make a presentation, providing background for the discussion. I heard one participant say, "I haven't been this nervous since I defended my dissertation." Some people tend to be overly cautious about tackling hard issues. When we had new people, there was a politeness—a reluctance for these people to roll up their sleeves and ask tough questions. As the meetings continued over the course of the week, these people generally relaxed and realized that the Dalai Lama is a colleague who is more than willing to be put on the spot. He is open and astute. There have been many occasions when scientists have described a line of research and His Holiness has interrupted to ask questions that jump several experiments ahead. Once a participant said, "Your Holiness, you would make an excellent scientist."

Scientists' View of the Dalai Lama as an Equal Partner in Dialogue

Dr. Piet Hut   The format of our meeting [in 1997, in Dharamsala] was that every morning one member of our group of five physicists and astrophysicists would give a summary of his own field. Then he [the Dalai Lama] would ask questions. In the afternoon, we had a more general dialogue. During the morning session it was clear that he was completely following every logical step very quickly. If we would leave out a step in the argument, he would immediately interject, "Oh, you mean like *this*!" Sometimes he would quickly guess, or understand, what the next step would be. So we all considered him to be an ideal student. He was completely engaged. His concentration was very unusual. That was quite an experience in itself. He is very easygoing. It is more the people around him who treat him in a very venerable way. But he, himself, behaves more like a colleague.

Ven. Thubten Chodron   It depends on the individual scientist: some are quite skeptical and some come in more open-minded. But what I have seen is a lot of transformation in the scientists who come. They may come in saying, "Who's this guy who wears red robes and shaves his head?" But then, when they're making presentations, His Holiness will often stop and ask questions. And the scientists have often remarked that he asks the very questions that they are in the middle of researching and investigating.

He will also talk about the subject they're investigating from a Buddhist viewpoint, and it's quite interesting to watch the scientists begin to take this in. It took us off in quite a different viewpoint because in Buddhism we talk about the growth—the extremely subtle level of mind that is not connected to the body, not dependent on the body.

Professor Paul Davies   We have to distinguish between religious authority and philosophical wisdom. I've also had occasion to meet the Pope and senior clergy in the Anglican Episcopal Church, and you get the impression that here is a very holy person with a very strong personality, exercising immense authority and moral leadership over his particular group. But you can't expect these people to be *au fait* with the forefront of scientific and philosophical reasoning. As far as I know, the Dalai Lama has not formally studied things like theoretical physics, for example, and seeing as how a lot of the issues that we discussed had to do with physics and cosmology—the nature of time, the nature of consciousness in Cartesian dualism, and so on—unless somebody had a Ph.D. in physics or the philosophy of science, it would be very hard for them, really, to be making a significant contribution. Of course, he is free to publish his work anywhere he likes: there's nothing to prevent him from writing a paper for a philosophy journal if he feels he wants to set out a point of view and has some new thinking. As a figurehead for Tibetan Buddhism and for expatriate Tibetans, and as somebody to further the cause of Tibetan injustice in a manner that is clearly Gandhi-like in his demeanor, there couldn't be a finer individual. But that doesn't immediately imply that he has insights into the nature of the physical universe that are likely to prove of value to Western scientists. They might, but they might not. At the end of the day, I think this issue about the scientific worldview and the Eastern worldview has probably been overhyped.

Chapter Twelve

THE FUTURE OF THE INSTITUTION
OF THE DALAI LAMA

What Impact Would the Death of the Fourteenth
Dalai Lama Have on the Institution?

Dr. Howard Cutler   I don't think there will be anyone in the sense of a
Dalai Lama. He grew up in the old system of thousands of years of tradition and was the culmination of all of that. Even though he has entered
into the modern world, the combination of his early training and his acces-
sibility to world leaders would be hard to replace.

Richard Gere   His Holiness has made the commitment; he will remain
as long as there are suffering beings. Of course he will reincarnate—
there's no question about it. How that will manifest, who knows? There
are myriad ways to help beings and there have been different types of
Dalai Lamas over the last fourteen incarnations who have achieved different things in different ways, some of them controversial, some of them
quite wrathful, some of them like His Holiness, who is so compassionate
and equipped in dealing with everything. It's certainly going to be interesting. And hopefully we'll be around to see this young Dalai Lama and see
what kind of personality and life force he has.

Professor Jonathan Mirsky   The next Dalai Lama is never found for a
couple of years, anyway, so let's suppose he dies in five or ten years. Then

263

there first will be a interregnum before another, authentic Dalai Lama appears. Then it could easily be twenty years before a Dalai Lama who is regarded as legitimate by most Tibetans grows up. It's a bad outlook. And, of course, in that same period, unless something amazing happens, the Chinese will have found their own Dalai Lama.

Geshe Tsultim Gyaltsen   I don't think the system will change. A long time ago, the BBC asked His Holiness, "After you pass away, will they have problems in Tibet?" And His Holiness said, "I will not bow down." That means that His Holiness will not bow under Chinese power. I believe that Tibet will be free before His Holiness dies. And His Holiness will have long life because, as he says, he needs to take care of the Tibetan people.

Rabbi A. James Rudin   He is celibate, he cannot marry, and he has no children, so when he shuffles off this mortal coil they will seek out the elders. You have the Lubavicher Rebbe, Billy Graham, and the Pope. The Dalai Lama's selection is a much more complicated process. You've had it in Judaism; it's called "the Exilarch"—a rabbi who is chosen to be the leader outside the Land of Israel, not *inside*. The Chinese will probably put their puppet inside Tibet, which would have its own authenticity because that lama would live in Lhasa, and then you would have the Exilarch outside, so it could be a real schism. The Dalai Lama, if he's smart, in the Moses model, could pick a Joshua while he's alive to succeed him and transfer—you can't transfer *charisma*—some of that power. The Jews, especially, should be able to understand that: for two thousand years we were out of our sovereignty in the seat where we belonged, which is Jerusalem, but we were able to sustain houses of learning and the clergy.

Patrick French   He has tried to make preparations in that they now have a prime minister of the exile government, and he's tried to transfer political power to some extent to those ministers. But, in practice, everybody is still more interested in the Dalai Lama than in the exiled prime minister; it's really what the Dalai Lama says that counts. Also, although to an extent the exile government has been democratized, it's him. People have tried all sorts of different ways to change that, but in the end it's *him*. Probably when he dies he will have left quite detailed instructions about what he wants to happen, because he'll obviously be worried that the Chinese will try to hijack the process that follows by finding a child they can install as a puppet Dalai Lama—and he's said previously that he won't reincarnate. But he has also given ambiguous answers and I suspect that there will be some document that after his death will be shown in which he will very clearly state what he wants to happen. And the exile government will try extremely hard to keep that cause alive and to rally everybody behind a single figure who will presumably be the prime minister in exile. That will be the ambition, but in practice it's very hard to see how that's going to work because the key to that movement depends so much on his charisma, on his travels around the world, on his ability to inspire large numbers of people. So I do feel quite pessimistic about what will happen.

Professor Jonathan Mirsky People don't want to think about this because it's so painful—this is not like: is Gordon Brown going to be the next prime minister here? This is a very fraught business. First of all, there have been fourteen Dalai Lamas. Most of them have not died in their beds; some of them have been very disreputable people indeed. This Dalai Lama is a remarkable person by any standard. If you read the accounts of Hugh Richardson when the Dalai Lama first appeared in Lhasa in the late thirties, Richardson, who was by no means a Buddhist but was a very acute British observer there, thought then that this was a remarkable child. Everybody said that about him—that there was something very knowing about him—and so he's a special man. He, of course, always says, "I'm just a monk. I'm just passing through; there will be another person to take my place, just as there is with everybody else." But most people don't like to think about that. I understand that. He's a very important and precious being and it's rather awful to think that everything about Tibet will be different when this particular Dalai Lama is no longer on the scene.

What is interesting is the struggle between the Chinese and the Tibetan exiles about the successor to the dead Tenth Panchen Lama. The Dalai Lama has said this to me but I'm not the only person he's said it to: the reason the Chinese kidnapped that little Panchen Lama and installed their own was to see what would happen, because the real problem for them is going to be, as the Dalai Lama has said, "When I die, the Chinese will want to appoint the next Dalai Lama." So that whole kidnapping was a kind of a rehearsal for this.

Dr. Tenzin Tethong It's a very strange situation: you have the Chinese Communist Party actually interfering and making decisions concerning the reincarnation of Tibetan lamas. The official Panchen Lama right now in Tibet is the one endorsed by the Communist Party, and the one selected and found by his people and confirmed by His Holiness is the one that's missing. The Chinese, in an almost unbelievably crude way, are intent on doing something like this, so I think they will try in the case of next Dalai Lama too. But there is an entire structure of the Tibetan Government-in-Exile, and it's very likely that the Tibetan exile community—the formal structure of the Government-in-Exile—will immediately begin the process of searching for the next Dalai Lama. There are probably going to be two processes running in the future, although we hope we won't come to a situation like that. Maybe the whole situation in Tibet can be resolved long before something like this happens.

Ven. Bhikshuni Tenzin Kacho   There would be a slowdown in some ways. But he's like a bodhisattva and a Buddha, and they keep returning for the benefit of others. He has suggested some really brilliant strategies of working with this transition, one of them being that he would personally like to go into retirement. A lot of people feel: oh no, you can't do that; we need you! But I was thinking that if in fact he did, then he'd still be with us and be available for consultation. However it unfolds, it will be difficult.

Tsering Shakya   The achievement of the Dalai Lama is the incredibly high international profile that he has managed to establish for Tibet and for the institution of the Dalai Lama and Tibetan Buddhism. There are other changes he has instituted in Tibetan society—emphasis on secular as well as spiritual education, reforms within the monasteries, and changing many religious practices. In those ways he has been able to influence so much change in the Tibetan community and in international situations.

Dr. Ronald B. Sobel   When the legions of Titus [Titus Flavius Vespasianus A.D. 39–81; Roman emperor, A.D. 79–81] were besieging Jerusalem, one of the greatest scholars, a man by the name of Yochanan ben Zakkai, was spirited out in the middle of the night in a coffinlike contraption, and he established a learning academy, a yeshiva, at Yavneh, outside of Jerusalem. Judaism was kept alive. In time, Yochanan ben Zakkai died. A disciple rose in his place and the disciple died, and a disciple rose in *his* place, and then a lot of disciples; there was always the leader to follow.

So it will happen—and it will happen in exile—that somehow, whatever the methodology employed, the tradition of a Dalai Lama is so strong that however the choice is made, it *will* be made, and there will be a continuity. The Dalai Lama and those who are closest and most devoted to Tibetan Buddhism do believe it, have to believe it and act on it, no matter how many years or decades or generations it takes.

Dr. Alexander Berzin   His Holiness doesn't want a situation similar to what had developed in Tibet with the institution of the Dalai Lamas, in which you have a regency before the new Dalai Lama is found through reincarnation and reaches maturity, and the whole government is under that guidance. He certainly has made very strong efforts for a more democratic, popular political structure to be in place, and he would very much like to step down from all types of involvement in that more political side; he's taking great steps to do that. But still, everybody looks to him for general advice and guidance, and as the person who symbolizes and represents Tibet around the world. But the position that the Fifteenth Dalai Lama will take depends very much on the conditions and situation. In these various reincarnate lamas, the way in which they develop depends very much on the way in which they are raised, their teachers and the social situation around them, so it's very hard to predict. I think that the Tibetan people certainly will have great hopes for him, for sure, and they'll have unbelievable respect for him that could easily be a situation similar to the Panchen Lama situation, in which the Chinese decide to recognize their own Dalai Lama, and that would be very unfortunate.

Pema Chhinjor   The Chinese leadership understands that the issue of Tibet revolves around the Dalai Lama, who is now [in 2004] sixty-nine. They believe that when he passes away, the issue will be finished.

Do the Exiles Hope to Return to Tibet?

Ven. Bhikshuni Tenzin Kacho   I believe that there's a sector of people who do; definitely His Holiness is in the forefront of that, with incredible optimism and the courage to continue to speak of how things are constantly shifting and changing, and that they will return one day. The incredible, radical changes that China has been going through in the last few decades is a sign that it could definitely happen: China is so much more open now to free enterprise and private enterprise, which was unavailable a few decades back, and they are definitely having to relate to the entire world now, as a world player. Also, within China itself, there have been fantastic Buddhist scholars, meditators, temples, history, lineage, holy places—it's just rich with Buddhist history, as well—and I believe that there are so many of the Chinese people who will come back to seeing that, especially as Westerners are seeing the limitations of material prosperity or the conditions of the mundane world, and that they will again turn toward this inquiry of Buddhism, of spiritual practice.

Tenzin Gephel   I would like to go back to Tibet and to see the improvement; I would like to preserve our own culture and religion in our own country. And I would like to see the freedom of Tibet—a complete, qualified autonomous region for the Tibetan people, and how we can make a contribution to the rest of the world in the field of peace and happiness, especially in neighboring countries, like China. Yes, I'd like to go back to Tibet; it's my *home*. I still hope; I always hope, since the situation can be changed. It might happen miraculously and it might happen because of the hard work of the Tibetan people, the hard work of the Dalai Lama, and his support from the rest of the world. The situation is changing all over the world, as well as in China itself. Because of that, I always hope to go back to Tibet during the time of the present Dalai Lama.

Geshe Tsultim Gyaltsen   The Chinese think that Tibet is part of China. That is a lie! We, the Tibetan people, say that the country of Tibet belongs to the Tibetan people. Truth is more important than anything else. It's much more powerful than chemical weapons; chemical weapons can just destroy lives, but truth cannot be destroyed. We have *truth* so, therefore, one day we should go back to our country. We cannot be refugees forever!

Does the Dalai Lama Believe He Will Ever Return to Lhasa?

Robert Ford   He lives in hope, of course. But one of the things that we in the West tend to forget—I've talked to him about this on a number of occasions and to Tibetans—their view and our view are quite different. As His Holiness said, "We are lucky because you Christians and other believers, you have to solve everything in your one lifetime; you then have to go on to your judgment, whereas with us, we can go on and on and on and we can be reborn and start a whole new life, and a whole new clean slate, and this dominates our philosophy." So here, again, you have to look at his view and the Western view of the future of Tibet. I sometimes used to—and still do—get very frustrated at the lack of meaningful support from the West for Tibet. I used to get very angry; I only get irritated now. Then I go back to the Tibetan point of view and say, "Well, it really doesn't matter because all our people suffer now, but it will all come right in the end." There is this little phrase from Buddhism that says: "Life is suffering and relief from suffering." Now, suffering can go on for one, two, three, four, five lives, many more, until you are released by attaining nirvana, and this is the way Tibetans generally look at things. They don't have this urgency that we have of wanting to get things done in our lifetimes, that we've got to change things, to do things. I'm not saying they don't want to do things; they do, but not in the same outlook, the same perspective, that we adopt.

Heinrich Harrer   It is my wish that one day we—all who support him and his country—will accompany His Holiness when Tibet is free. I will go around the world and collect pieces from all the museums, and then we will reclaim them and bring back what belongs to Tibet in a big procession to Lhasa with His Holiness—all the incredibly beautiful *thangkas* and images and bronzes. I brought things out, and later, when his family escaped, they brought more and more. His Holiness said, "We must be happy that you brought it because it's safe in the museum right here in Lichtenstein," where we have a museum. We also have a big museum in Zurich and one in my birthplace. His Holiness praises everybody who has collected things from Tibet. It proves to the world how incredibly intelligent and how incredibly good craftsmen they were.

Some people say that it's a hope against hope that he will go back. But every now and then something happens, like when the Germans reunited, or when the Russians gave up their communism. There might be a day coming when the Chinese will give up their communist ideas. But I'm very sad that the Olympic games have been given to the Chinese. This is a question of business—the world wants to make business with Asia—and the saddest thing that is going to happen is when the Chinese light the torch from Athens. When the Chinese take the torch from Athens to Lhasa—they will cross Tibet into China on the Tibetan border—the first thing they are going to show is the Potala. They say that the Potala is a Chinese building now, and the Chinese will use that propaganda for their country. The Dalai Lama is the only person who can do something for Tibet. And he's hoping against hope so we should never give up hope. He is, of course, very confident.

Tsering Shakya   He very much wants to return, but it will be very difficult for China to accept the Dalai Lama back. The main reason is that even if the Dalai Lama says, "I will not participate in politics; I'll just live in a cave," the fact is that his very presence will show that there is an alternative ruler, and people will always see him as the alternative. And that is something the Chinese Party and government cannot put up with. Both morally and in civil ways the Chinese have to be *the* governing power— unless China changes and becomes a more democratic society. The problem with China, like a lot of dictatorial regimes, is that they want to be the moral guardian of society; they want the political role—everything is determined by the party. Let's say the Chinese came and said, "Okay, we are only concerned with civil affairs; in spiritual and religious life, you can have your own leaders, you can have your own lamas, and you can build a palace; this is not the concern of the government." But totalitarian regimes don't do that. It's not just the Dalai Lama. The Chinese refuse to recognize Catholic bishops because the bishop appointed by Rome is not acceptable; the bishop must be appointed by the Communist Party. For Catholics this is unacceptable. So the Vatican and China have a very bad relationship. Whenever the Vatican appoints an official to China, the Chinese come and force him out, and Chinese Catholics don't accept a bishop appointed by the Communist Party. American presidents don't appoint bishops and they don't care who the rabbi is; it's not approved by Congress or the president. The Chinese fear that if there is a religious leader, he becomes an alternative to the Communist Party.

Professor Jonathan Mirsky His optimism is admirable but I don't, myself, share it. But I'm not the leader of Tibetans around the world and I don't know what the Dalai Lama feels in his heart; I'm sure that what he says is what he believes. In order for him to operate—he's in his late sixties now; he knows he's not going to last forever—he has to do what he can to get the best deal for Tibetans because the next Dalai Lama is going to be a child of three or four and, as he says, he's pretty sure that the next Dalai Lama is not going to be born in Tibet. So the Chinese will then find a Dalai Lama of their own—a child, like the Panchen Lama—and that will be that. The Dalai Lama, as he *is*, is the great hope for Tibetans, both in the diaspora and inside Tibet, and so it's very important that he expresses this hope, and the hope is that the Chinese will display human-heartedness. I've often said to him that I've had a lot more experience with the Chinese than he has and that I think the only hope for Tibet is if the party collapses and there is some kind of new style of government in China. But I'm not particularly hopeful of that either. And it's very, very rare to meet Chinese who think that Tibet should be independent.

Would the Dalai Lama's Return to Tibet Diminish His Huge Popularity around the World?

Rinchen Dharlo By being in exile he has been able to make a great deal of difference for the Tibetan people. Just as the Tibetan people look to him as the embodiment of the future Tibet and the embodiment of strength and hope in exile, the Tibetan refuges have been doing so well. Right now, over thirty thousand Tibetan children are studying in different schools and fifteen thousand monks and nuns are studying in monasteries. All this is because of *his* effort. And then the Tibetans are preserving their culture in exile—today one can find the essence of Tibetan culture only within the Tibetan refugee settlements in India and Nepal—and they are not only preserving the Tibetan language, culture and religion but also helping to strengthen this culture within the people of the Himalayan region, like the entire modern belt of India and Nepal inhabited by ethnic Tibetans.

Patrick French   The difficult thing is that if the Dalai Lama were to return now, which, obviously, for the moment looks unlikely, he'd probably be given some kind of symbolic position in Beijing and he would not really be able to have that daily interaction that would lead to the situation in Tibet's improving. It's a very hard call because the level and nature of the destruction means that for most of the period since he went into exile there was no possibility of dialogue of any kind.

When I was there in 1999 and I spoke to people from very different economic and political positions, the personal loyalty the Tibetans feel toward the Dalai Lama, the intense fascination with him as a religious entity—what he's doing, where he is, what his health is—is absolutely still there. I believe that if the Dalai Lama were to return to Lhasa, there would be an absolutely overwhelming surge of popular excitement and enthusiasm; there would be hundreds of thousands of people traveling immediately from all parts of Tibet to see him. And that's the great bind that the Chinese Communist Party is in: they've said that the Dalai Lama is a nonperson—you're not allowed to have pictures of him—and yet all those who have been in exile for forty-five years, every Tibetan, still sees him as the central figure in their own life.

Orville Schell   Nobody will ever be able to replace him because he represents continuity with that past—that last time when Tibet was separated, isolated, and culturally and religiously whole. The Chinese, in their practical, just-let's-win attitude, are right: when he goes, the whole terms of the game will change. I don't really know what the alternative to him is; I don't think there *is* one. It could be very bad for Tibet because if something happens there, there would be no one to calm it down.

INDEX